D0206174

IN DEFENSE OF PRISONS

Recent Titles in
Contributions in Criminology and Penology

IN DEFENSE OF PRISONS

Richard A. Wright

Contributions in Criminology and Penology,
Number 43

MARVIN WOLFGANG,
Series Adviser

GREENWOOD PRESS
Westport, Connecticut • London

HV
9466
.W85
1994

Library of Congress Cataloging-in-Publication Data

Wright, Richard A.
    In defense of prisons / Richard A. Wright.
       p. cm.—(Contributions in criminology and penology, ISSN
0732–4464 ; no. 43)
    Includes bibliographical references and index.
    ISBN 0–313–27926–8 (alk. paper)
    1. Prisons—United States.   2. Punishment—United States.
I. Title. II. Series.
HV9466.W85   1994
365′.973—dc20   93–15839

British Library Cataloguing in Publication Data is available.

Copyright © 1994 by Richard A. Wright

All rights reserved. No portion of this book may be
reproduced, by any process or technique, without the
express written consent of the publisher.

Library of Congress Catalog Card Number: 93–15839
ISBN: 0–313–27926–8
ISSN: 0732–4464

First published in 1994

Greenwood Press, 88 Post Road West, Westport, CT 06881
An imprint of Greenwood Publishing Group, Inc.

Printed in the United States of America

The paper used in this book complies with the
Permanent Paper Standard issued by the National
Information Standards Organization (Z39.48–1984).

10 9 8 7 6 5 4 3 2 1

Copyright Acknowledgments

The author and publisher gratefully acknowledge permission to quote from the following sources:

Richard A. Wright. "A Socially Sensitive Criminal Justice System," in *Open Institutions: The Hope for Democracy*, edited by John W. Murphy and Dennis L. Peck. Westport, CT: Praeger Publishers, an imprint of Greenwood Publishing Group, Inc., 1993, 141–160.

Richard A. Wright. "In Support of Prisons," in *Corrections: An Issues Approach*, edited by Lawrence F. Travis III, Martin D. Schwartz, and Todd R. Clear. Cincinnati, OH: Anderson Publishing Co., 1992, 99–114.

LONGWOOD COLLEGE LIBRARY
FARMVILLE, VIRGINIA 23901

For my father, E. Weldon Wright, who taught me to value thinking for myself and argumentation. (If he were still alive, I'm sure that he would claim that he didn't.)

LONGWOOD LIBRARY

1000248741

Contents

Acknowledgments

Writing is a hard, solitary task, best suited for stoics and recluses. Fortunately, I have a passion for this sort of masochism—one of my favorite ways to spend a day is to be shut off in my office, drinking my coffee, shoving together nouns and verbs with abandon. Most of what appears in the following pages emerged from an intense, intellectual confrontation with mounds of criminology/corrections books and photocopied articles. Making sense of this voluminous literature was a massive undertaking that gave me much pain, but even more pleasure. The final product is *my* hard-fought attempt to interpret the theories and research on punishment, so if you disagree with my arguments, blame me (and not my professors or my colleagues).

Still I owe an important debt of gratitude to numerous persons who assisted in the completion of this book. First and foremost, two student research assistants—Carolyn M. Ducaji and Amanda McIver—provided invaluable help with the library research and word processing for this project. These students cheerfully unburdened me of much of the drudgery associated with writing this manuscript. As we worked together, the two became my close friends, and I wholeheartedly wish them only the best in their lives.

I want to thank Lawrence F. Travis III, Todd R. Clear, and especially Martin D. Schwartz for inviting me three years ago to write a chapter that defended prisons for their book *Corrections: An Issues Approach*. As I wrote the chapter, I became convinced that the topic deserved a book-length treatment. Without their original invitation, this book surely would never have been written.

A similar thanks goes out to John W. Murphy and Dennis L. Peck for inviting me two years ago to write a chapter on criminal justice for their book *Open Institutions: The Hope for Democracy*. Writing this chapter greatly clarified my thinking about the operation of correctional departments and agencies. While working on this project, I hit upon the notion of conceptualizing the criminal justice system in general, and prisons in particular, as nonlinear institutions characterized by limited rationality. This idea became an important part of my book.

I also wish to acknowledge the help of my colleague in the Department of Sociology/Criminal Justice at the University of Scranton, David O. Friedrichs. Professor Friedrichs keeps files on everything from A to Z (Jack Henry Abbott to Franklin Zimring). His collection of newspaper articles on Abbott was especially useful in writing this book. I have benefited much from the fact that David is such a vociferous reader (and article clipper).

This manuscript owes its very existence to Marvin E. Wolfgang, who saw early promise in my initial book proposal to Greenwood Press. His behind-the-scenes endorsement of the proposal ensured that I received a contract to write this book. It takes great intellectual integrity and a magnanimous personality for a scholar of Professor Wolfgang's stature to lend his assistance to such a controversial book. I want him to know that I know that he possesses these virtues.

I'm certain that Professors Travis, Clear, Schwartz, Murphy, Peck, Friedrichs, and Wolfgang will disagree with some (indeed, perhaps many) of the arguments in this book. Although all helped in various ways with the completion of the manuscript, readers should know that my arguments on the nature of crime and punishment often are not the same as theirs.

A special thanks goes out to the editors of Greenwood Press for encouraging me to write this book, the second project that I've completed for Greenwood. I must say that I respect their careful assessment, and I can't thank them enough for not hassling me while I was struggling through the last few chapters of this book. I want the folks at Greenwood to know that I sing their praises whenever I get the chance.

Finally, my family—Sharon B. Wright, William E. Wright, Emerson T. Wright, and Austin C. Wright—deserve much credit for the timely completion of this project. Because I do most of my research and writing at home, my young sons sometimes must forgo some of their usual boisterousness when I am working. The boys especially merit kudos for turning off their Nintendo machine when I asked!

This book was funded by a University of Scranton Faculty Research Grant. I gratefully acknowledge the assistance that I received from this grant; the hardships involved in researching this book would have been much greater without these funds.

IN DEFENSE OF PRISONS

Chapter One

Confronting the Critics

Of all of the institutions in American society, prisons are among the most maligned and vilified. Imprisonment has many enemies and few friends. The critics of prisons come in all shapes, sizes, political persuasions, and walks of life. Criticisms have been raised by political radicals (Quinney 1974; Wright 1973), liberals (Currie 1985), and neoconservatives (von Hirsch 1976), and by attorneys (Stender 1973), journalists (Bagdikian 1972; Wicker 1975), novelists and playwrights (Shaw 1946; Wilde [1898] 1973), television scriptwriters (Bello 1982), psychologists (Sommer 1976), psychiatrists (Menninger 1968), sociologists (Goffman 1961; Lemert 1967; Schur 1973), religious groups (American Friends Service Committee 1971), ex-correctional officials (Fogel 1975; Murton and Hyams 1969; Nagel 1973), ex-convicts (Johnson 1970; Irwin 1980, 1985), current convicts (Abbott 1982; Jackson 1970, 1972), and criminologists far too numerous to list. The supporters of prisons include mostly current correctional officials (Pung 1983) and conservative politicians, who garner votes by exploiting the public's fear of street crime and by promising tough prison sentences for offenders. (Republican George Bush won the 1988 presidential election in part by depicting Democratic candidate Michael Dukakis as "soft" on crime and punishment—Monk 1991.) Only a handful of criminologists (see van den Haag 1975; Wilson 1985; Wright 1992) and a few conservative economists (see Reynolds 1990; Zedlewski 1987, 1989) strongly defend prisons.

The critics range from cautious reservations to virtual hysteria in their condemnation of prisons. An example of the former is Elliott Currie's

(1985, 52) moderate conclusion that "although imprisonment is all too often an unavoidable necessity, it is not an effective way to prevent crime." (One must wonder, though, why Currie considers prisons necessary if they are so ineffective.) Among the immoderates is Karl Menninger (1968, 79), who bluntly reviles prisons as "monuments to stupidity" in his book *The Crime of Punishment.* Menninger (1968, 89) continues: "[Prison] is a creaking, groaning monster through whose heartless jaws hundreds of American citizens grind daily, to be maimed and embittered so that they emerge [as] implacable enemies of the social order and confirmed in their 'criminality.' " As the title of his book suggests, Menninger views the offenses of criminals as relatively innocuous compared with the much more injurious social reaction of imprisonment.

While the critics vary in their stridency, there is much consistency in their indictments against prisons. On the microlevel of interpersonal relationships, the critics contend that prisons brutalize, stigmatize, and embitter inmates, driving them into criminalistic subcultures that reinforce their deviant attitudes and behaviors. It is also claimed that prisons are crime schools that teach inmates nefarious skills and beliefs. On a more macrolevel, the critics argue that prisons fail both to prevent crime in the community and to protect the citizenry from the paralyzing fear of crime victimization. Far from solving the problem of crime, many critics conclude that prisons create more crime than they deter.

I contend that the critics are wrong in these assessments. Recent empirical research shows that punishments work in preventing crime and that prisons are at least a modestly successful means of social control. Furthermore, much additional evidence suggests that the nonintervention alternative endorsed by many critics would be less effective than prisons in preventing crime.

The first three chapters in this book introduce readers to some of the basic concepts and theories involved in the debate over the effectiveness of prisons. Specifically, chapter 1 presents a brief overview of the criticisms of prisons and the "prison abolition movement" endorsed by some critics. A critical analogy is drawn between the purported ineffectiveness of prisons and the "failure" of law enforcement, and a satirical case is made for the abolition of the police. Chapter 2 examines in some detail the competing concepts and theories involved in the analysis of the social and individual objectives of imprisonment as a form of punishment. Chapter 3 reviews the empirical evidence showing the ineffectiveness of prisons as a means to promote rehabilitation, retribution, and social solidarity.

The next three chapters survey the recent empirical studies that offer both *positive support* and *negative support* for the continuation of the policy of imprisoning criminals. Chapters 4 and 5 examine the positive support for prisons by reviewing the empirical evidence that shows the effectiveness of prisons as instruments of specific deterrence and general deterrence (chapter 4) and incapacitation directed toward chronic offenders (chapter 5). Chapter 6 examines the negative support for prisons by reviewing the evidence regarding the failure and the risks associated with the implementation of "less punishment is better" policies of noninterventionism among offenders.

Finally, in the Epilogue, I offer my own policy recommendations for creating a more rational system of punishment that relies on imprisonment for the objectives of deterrence and incapacitation. The problems of implementing my policy recommendations in the politicized and pluralistic "real world" of criminal justice decision making are also considered.

A key assumption throughout this book is that imprisonment is more than a mere instrument of social control and crime prevention. Prisons also reflect the cultural sensibilities of the larger society in which they are located (Garland 1990). Imprisonment occupies an integral role both in the production and in the reproduction of social norms, values, attitudes, and beliefs. Modern systems of incarceration and punishment in the United States already reflect and reproduce the bounded rationality of the wider society. Perhaps more important, imprisonment serves the crucial purpose of *producing* a more rational set of cultural sensibilities. Commentators ranging from Fyodor Dostoevsky to Winston Churchill have concurred with U.S. Supreme Court justice Louis D. Brandeis's assessment that "the quality of a nation's civilization can be accurately measured by the methods it uses in the enforcement of its criminal law" (quoted in Bello 1982, 101). More to the point, the degree of a society's *rationality* can be measured by the quality of its systems of punishment. I believe that creating a more rational society should be the ultimate end of the social sciences and is an important goal for policymakers to pursue. Furthermore, creating a more rational system of punishments is an essential means for producing a more rational society. These are the ends and the means to which this book is dedicated.

ABOLISHING PRISONS . . .

Some of the more vociferous critics of prisons have endorsed the abolition of imprisonment as a form of punishment (for representative examples of these arguments, see Haan 1990; Mathiesen 1974, 1990; Nagel 1973; Pepinsky 1992; Sommer 1976). In the last twenty years, the prison abolition movement has evolved from small and widely scattered reform groups (comprised mostly of current and ex-convicts, the family members of prisoners, radical criminologists, and the members of pacifist Protestant denominations—e.g., the Mennonites, Church of the Brethren, and the American Society of Friends) to the recent organization of the International Conferences on Penal Abolition, convened in odd-numbered years in such far-flung locales as Amsterdam, Montreal, Warsaw, and Bloomington, Indiana.

Although the arguments of abolitionists differ somewhat in detail, all contend that the imprisonment of offenders is a bankrupt social policy. Dutch criminologist Thomas Mathiesen (1990, 19), for example, concludes that the prison "is a fiasco, and does not find a defense in the celebrated purposes espoused in penal theory" (i.e., rehabilitation, retribution, and deterrence). He distinguishes between traditional "positive" prison reforms, devoted to improving prison standards and the conditions of confinement for prisoners, and "negative" reforms, which seek to "remove greater or smaller parts" of prison systems (Mathiesen 1974, 202 [italics deleted]). Mathiesen rejects positive prison reforms as cosmetic changes that result in the more efficient operation of fundamentally corrupt, antiquated, and inhumane institutions and instead argues that the primary goal of the prison abolition movement must be negative reform.

Penal abolitionist Willem de Haan (1990, 9) dismisses crime as a "social construction" or "myth" that has no ontological dimension. He flatly asserts (1990, 9) that "there is no such thing as 'crime'. . . . This is not to deny that there are all sorts of *unfortunate events*, more or less serious troubles or conflicts which can result in suffering, harm, or damage to a greater or lesser degree. These troubles are to be taken seriously, of course, but not as *'crimes'* " (Haan 1990, 9 [italics added]). After using these semantic contortions to redefine murder, rape, and robbery as "noncrimes," Haan is free to recommend the abolition not only of prisons but also of the criminal law. He advocates the nonjudicial processing of "unfortunate events" in informal hearings (or "open-ended dialogues") that embrace the principle of the equality of all participants (both victims and offenders). The goal of these hearings is "redress," where conflict resolution and dispute settlement techniques are used to formulate an agreement whereby the offender makes amends to the victim. Haan's proposals for redress are modeled more on the discussions that occur in graduate seminars than on traditional courtroom procedures and practices.

Once we have abolished "criminal justice" and replaced it with some variation of "unfortunate events justice," the next step is to abolish prisons (rather than replacing them with "unfortunate events reformatories"). Abolitionists generally favor an immediate moratorium on all new prison construction (see Nagel 1973; Mathiesen 1974, 1990), followed by quick reductions in the number of prison inmates by certain fixed percentages. William Nagel (1973), for example, urges the rapid closing of all anti-quated maximum security "big house" penitentiaries and the decriminal-ization of various morals offenses (e.g., drug violations and prostitution) in order to reach a 30 to 40 percent reduction in the prison population. Robert Sommer (1976) more ambitiously calls for a 90 percent reduction in the number of prison inmates, to be achieved through a program of "amnesty," where the state chooses to "forget the acts" of those currently imprisoned for property and public order offenses. Sommer also recom-mends the imposition of flat, six-month prison sentences for all future convictees who pose a physical danger to themselves or others. (Prisoners who continue to present a physical threat to the community after serving these brief sentences would receive additional six-month sentences, im-posed one at a time through cumbersome jury trials.) Mathiesen (1990) endorses a two-thirds reduction of prison populations in Britain, Norway, and Sweden by the year 2000, followed by the full abolition of imprison-ment in these countries by the target date of 2010. To meet these goals, he recommends the implementation of policies of decriminalization and "depenalization" for most criminal offenses, the increased use of early releases for current prisoners, the imposition of much shorter maximum sentences on those still convicted and confined, and the gradual closing of entire prisons.

. . . AND DISBANDING THE POLICE

But why stop this spirit of political nihilism and intellectual anarchism with the abolition of only prisons and the criminal law? By selectively citing the research evidence, critics who wish to do so could make equally compelling cases for the end of law enforcement, criminal and civil courts, churches, schools, the state, and every other socially constructed and humanly flawed institution. To take one example, some research evidence demonstrates the "failure" of law enforcement. Studies show that:

—Increases in the size of police forces have little impact on urban crime rates (Greenberg, Kessler, and Loftin 1983; Loftin and McDowall 1982; Uchida and Goldberg 1986). David Greenberg, Ronald Kessler and Colin Loftin's (1983) study of the relationship between police employment rates and official mea-sures of crime in 521 U.S. cities and suburbs for the years 1960 and 1970 shows no evidence that hiring more officers reduced either violent or property crimes. A similar study of police force strength and crime rates for the city of Detroit for the years 1926 to 1977 also offers no evidence for a relationship between the two variables (Loftin and McDowall 1982).

—Variations in police patrol practices have little impact on the crime rates in urban neighborhoods (Criminal Justice Newsletter 1985; Kelling et al. 1974; Police Foundation 1981; Skolnick and Bayley 1986). Using a field experimental design in Kansas City, Missouri, George Kelling et al. (1974) divided fifteen independent, motorized police patrol districts in the city into three groups: one group retained normal police patrol techniques, another dramatically increased police patrol (to two to three times the normal rates), and the third abolished routine motorized patrols (so that the police responded only to specific citizen complaints). Subsequent analyses showed no relationship among the three variations in motorized patrols and crime rates in Kansas City neighborhoods. Additional research evidence suggests that (1) "two-person patrol cars are no more effective than one-person cars in reducing crime or catching criminals" (Skolnick and Bayley 1986, 4) and (2) the recent substitution of foot patrols for traditional motorized patrols in many large U.S. cities has had no impact on reducing urban crime rates (Criminal Justice Newsletter 1985; Police Foundation 1981).

—The sophisticated investigative techniques used by detective units seldom solve crimes (Eck 1984; Greenwood and Petersilia 1975; Skolnick and Bayley 1986; Willman and Snortum 1984). Suspects usually are identified at immediate crime scenes through the routine questioning of victims and witnesses by patrol officers, before detectives are assigned to cases. In their analysis of 153 detective bureaus, Peter Greenwood and Joan Petersilia (1975) conclude that detective investigations are of little help in solving crimes; they estimate that 50 percent of all detectives could be dismissed without negatively affecting arrest clearance rates (defined as the ratio of the number of offenses solved through an arrest by the number of offenses known to the police). Furthermore, a Police Executive Research Forum study indicates that 75 percent of all cases filed with detective bureaus are routinely dropped after only one day of investigation (Eck 1984).

—"Sting" operations—where elaborate procurement services are staged by the police to apprehend offenders—have no apparent long-term effect on the rates of targeted offenses (Langworthy 1989; Raub 1984). Robert Langworthy's (1989) study of a storefront police sting operation that fenced stolen cars in Birmingham, Alabama, shows that while the reported rates of auto theft increased significantly during the sting operation, car theft rates were unchanged before and after the sting intervention. He concludes that sting operations actually may *increase* crime rates by providing offenders with more opportunities to sell their illegal goods and services.

—The speed with which the police respond to citizen emergency calls has little effect on their chances for apprehending offenders (Skolnick and Bayley 1986; Wilson 1985). Summarizing the research on police response rates, Skolnick and Bayley (1986, 5) conclude that "the chances of making an arrest on the spot drop below 10 percent if one minute elapses from the time the crime is committed. Only instantaneous [police reaction] would be effective in catching criminals."

—Improvements in the technologies used by the police appear to have little impact on crime rates (Kelling 1978). Kelling (1978) contends that heavy funding for the development of new crime control technologies has produced few tangible benefits. He concludes that with the possible exceptions of police radios and bulletproof vests, "there is no evidence that any technological devices have significantly improved the effectiveness of police service" (Kelling 1978, 182–183).

—The arrest/clearance rates for police departments have no consistent effect on community crime rates (Greenberg, Kessler, and Logan 1979; Greenberg and Kessler 1982). For example, Greenberg and Kessler's (1982) lag regression study of police data from ninety-eight cities in the United States for the years 1964 to 1970 shows that arrest clearance rates had no predictable impact on the rates of property and violent crimes, when various socioeconomic variables (e.g., population density and percent of the labor force unemployed) were controlled. Greenberg and Kessler (1982, 784) conclude that there is "no consistent evidence for the proposition that higher arrest rates result in substantially lower index crime rates."

—Cities affected by police strikes experience no increase in their crime rates (Pfuhl 1983). Erdwin Pfuhl (1983) examined the crime rates in eleven U.S. cities that withstood major police strikes (lasting from two to thirty days) during the 1970s. He analyzed the crime rates in each city for two-month prestrike, strike, and poststrike time spans. The strikes had little effect on crime rates, even when Pfuhl controlled for the city's population size and the length of the strike.

—Different models of police administration appear to have little impact on the crime rates in large cities (Skolnick and Bayley 1986). Today there are two competing styles of law enforcement administration: the "professional model" versus "community policing" (Broderick 1990; Skolnick and Bayley 1986; Wright 1993). Police agencies that rely on the professional model emphasize rigid bureaucratization, police efficiency, a crime-fighting orientation, and the latest "high-tech gadgetry" (Broderick 1990); officers in these departments adopt a detached, aloof, and authoritarian demeanor, reminiscent of Sergeant Joe Friday in the old "Dragnet" television series (Wright 1993). Community policing emphasizes community participation (where the police and private citizens closely cooperate in various law enforcement programs), crime prevention, decentralization of command (or the reassignment of patrol officers from isolated precinct houses to smaller "storefront" ministations), and "civilianization" (or the hiring of numerous intercity and minority paraprofessionals to assist in public service programs); officers in these departments are community activists who have more in common with social workers than with traditional authoritarian cops (Broderick 1990; Skolnick and Bayley 1986;

Wright 1993). Jerome Skolnick and David Bayley's (1986) observational study of six major metropolitan police departments that pursued variations of these two models (from the Denver, Colorado, department, which typifies traditional police professionalism, to Santa Ana, California, where the department wholeheartedly embraces community policing) offers no evidence that *either* approach is conspicuously effective in reducing urban crime rates.

Some variations in police practices and law enforcement administration result in measurable benefits in reducing the public's fear of crime and in enhancing public attitudes of respect and support for their local police. Specifically, the implementation of foot patrols (Criminal Justice Newsletter 1985; Police Foundation 1981), high-visibility sting operations (Langworthy 1989), policies dedicated to quick responses to emergency calls (Wilson 1985), and the community policing model (Skolnick and Bayley 1986) appear to improve community attitudes toward the police. Still, there is some empirical evidence to indicate that variations in police (1) practices, (2) administration, (3) community visibility, and (4) efficiency have little impact on reducing the actual rate of crime.

Because priests and social workers undoubtedly are better able than cops to promote good community relations, why not disband the police? Following the logic of the penal abolitionists, investigative units dealing with public order and property offenses could be terminated first (after the decriminalization of drug possession and sales, prostitution, larceny, burglary, and arson); the homicide squad would be the last to go. As the police are pink-slipped, legions of social workers could be trained and hired to engage robbers and rapists—along with their victims—in conflict resolution and dispute settlement dialogues. As we gradually beat our "Police Special," .38-caliber, double-action service revolvers into plowshares, one can anticipate seeing ex-offenders and their victims strolling hand-in-hand through the transformed streets of Eden.

Many readers probably have some serious reservations about this scenario. Indeed, you should: Jack Gibbs's (1986) and Lawrence Sherman's (1990) extensive reviews of the crime prevention literature show that although some studies find that law enforcement practices have little impact on offending patterns, *most* find an *inverse* relationship between stricter law enforcement practices and crime rates (see chapters 4 and 6). For now, one important historical precedent illustrates the folly of disbanding the police: Johannes Andenaes (1952, 1974) reports that Nazi occupation forces toward the end of World War II arrested and detained the entire municipal police department of Copenhagen, Denmark, for seven months. During this period, policing duties were performed by an unarmed and ineffectual civilian "watch corps." The result was a dramatic and immediate tenfold increase in the rate of robberies and thefts. As I have argued elsewhere (Wright 1992, 100 [italics added]):

While the crime problem . . . may not improve dramatically by increasing the number of police officers or by altering their duties, crime rates certainly would worsen if police strength were cut (and if the few remaining officers were ordered to ignore "harmless" nonviolent property and public morality offenders). *Much the same reasoning can be used to justify maintaining current incarceration levels.*

Like the police, prisons are a necessary part of civilized societies. While we might sometimes question the methods that these organizations employ, it is no cliché to conclude that law-abiding citizens can sleep better at night knowing that the police and correctional officers are on their respective tours of duty.

Chapter Two

The Objectives of Punishment:
Concepts and Theories

Viewed at a distance, the policies found within the contemporary American criminal justice system (comprised of law enforcement, the courts, and correctional agencies and institutions) "appear to be going in a dozen different directions at once" (Wright 1993, 157). The objectives pursued by the criminal justice system in general—and prisons in particular—vary dramatically across time and place (Hagan 1989; Wright 1993). The punishment philosophies and programs enthusiastically endorsed by a state correctional department in one decade may be completely abandoned or reformulated ten years later; furthermore, the policies implemented by correctional officials in one prison within one state often differ considerably from those found in other prisons in other states and sometimes even within other prisons located within the *same* state. Chapter 2 tries to make some sense of this apparent chaos by examining the various social and individual objectives and outcomes of punishment and by proposing a "nonlinear" theoretical model to interpret the operations of American criminal justice.

State-administered punishment refers to the deliberate infliction of sanctions—or pains—by appropriate legal authorities to persons who have violated the law (see Armstrong 1971; Hart 1968; Mundle 1971; van den Haag 1975). The forms of state-administered punishment have changed widely over time and place, from gruesome methods of capital punishment (e.g., the practices of sawing offenders in half lengthwise in ancient China and impaling offenders on iron poles, tearing them in half using teams of oxen or horses, or burning them at the stake in medieval Europe) to banishment (e.g., the forced placement of offenders in such penal colonies as Norfolk Island and Tasmania by the British, Devil's Island by the French, or Siberia by the Soviets), corporal punishments (ranging from the amputation of the hands of thieves, the branding of prostitutes and adulterers, and the use of thumbscrews, racks, pillories, and stocks for assorted offenders in medieval Europe), jailing and imprisonment (originally used for debtors, alcoholics, lunatics, prostitutes, and petty thieves in medieval Europe), and fines (Barnes 1930; Bowker 1982; Ives [1914] 1970; Newman 1978; Sellin 1976). Most recently, punishments have been administered by correctional agencies and have assumed the forms of noninstitutional, community placement (e.g., probation and parole), institutional confinement in jails or prisons, fines, and occasionally executions (mostly reserved for particularly heinous murderers). Imprisonment, however, has emerged as the archetypical form of punishment for most serious property and violent offenders in modern industrial societies.

When considering the objectives of punishment, one can distinguish between two types of punishment outcomes (here defined as either the desired or undesired consequences or results associated with punishment): *social outcomes* and *individual outcomes*. The social outcomes are the consequences of punishment that primarily involve and affect not only the individual offender but also groups of persons other than the offender (including crime victims and their families and friends, the state, and society at large). In contrast, the individual outcomes are the consequences of punishment that primarily involve and affect the individual offender and only secondarily involve and affect other persons. The social outcomes are essentially explanations of what punishments do *for society*, while the individual outcomes are mostly explanations of what punishments do *to the offender*.

THE SOCIAL OUTCOMES OF PUNISHMENT

A comparison of the various social outcomes attributed to punishment reveals two distinct categories of justifications used for inflicting pain on offenders: the *recompense model* versus the *utilitarian model*. The recompense model emphasizes foremost that punishments should involve the repayment by the offender for his or her wrongs; the utilitarian model stresses that punishments should have certain positive social benefits in the form of the prevention of crime and the reduction of the overall crime rate. Numerous writers have noted that the recompense model advocates punishment for the purposes of atoning for the *past wrongs* committed by offenders; in contrast, utilitarians see punishment as a way to improve the *future* by reducing the predilections of offenders and others in society to commit crimes following the punishment (see Bedau 1977; Hart 1968; Hospers 1977a, b; Kaufmann 1977; van den Haag 1975; von Hirsch 1976, 1985). In addition, the proponents of recompense view punishment as a desirable social outcome (or end) in itself: punishment is justly deserved by offenders as a consequence of the wrongfulness of their criminal acts (Armstrong 1971; Hospers 1977a, b; Kant [1787] 1933, [1797] 1964, [1797] 1965; Lewis [1948] 1971; Rawls 1971; von Hirsch 1976, 1985). For utilitarians, however, punishment is envisioned as a means to accomplish other desirable social outcomes (or ends) beyond the act of punishment, such as the reform of offenders or the general prevention of crime in the larger society (Armstrong 1971; Hart 1968; Hospers 1977a, b; von Hirsch 1976, 1985).

In the history of punishment, recompense has taken three different forms: *revenge, retribution*, and *restitution*. Revenge is the oldest type of recompense and involves the efforts by individual victims and/or their family members to inflict pain and pursue personal amends at the expense of individual offenders and/or their family members (Armstrong 1971; Barnett 1977; Barnett and Hagel 1977; van den Haag 1975). Throughout antiquity, the "subjective craving for revenge" (van den Haag 1975, 11) sometimes escalated into "the uncontrollable violence of blood feuds" (Barnett and Hagel 1977, 9) between crime victims and offenders, and their respective families, clans, and tribes. Gradually, though, state authority emerged as a decisive mediating force that placed important limitations on the amounts and types of repayments that crime offenders owed to victims and to society.

Retribution and restitution emerged as the two styles of state-administered recompense. Underlying both is the idea of proportionality or commensurate deserts, which means that the degree of recompense should be calibrated carefully to fit the seriousness of the criminal offense (Armstrong 1971; Barnett 1977; Barnett and Hagel 1977; Bedau 1977; Golding 1977; Hart 1968; Hegel [1821] 1967; Hospers 1977a, b; Kant [1787] 1933, [1797] 1964, [1797] 1965; Kaufmann 1977; Lewis [1948] 1971; Mabbott 1971; Mundle 1971; van den Haag 1975; von Hirsch 1976, 1985). The essential difference between retribution and restitution as forms of recompense is that with the former, criminal offenders are punished proportionately to the seriousness of their offenses, while with the latter, crime victims are repaid proportionately to the extent of the losses incurred from offenses (Barnett 1977; Barnett and Hagel 1977; Hospers 1977a, b; Kaufmann 1977). As Lee Bowker (1982, 40) observes: "In retribution, the punishment is designed to lower the well-being of the offender by an amount equivalent to the amount of suffering caused by the crime. In contrast, the goal of restitution is to raise the well-being of the victim back up to the level that existed prior to the commission of the crime."

Retribution is based on the notion that justice (or equity and fairness) demands that criminal offenders be subjected to proportional punishments (Armstrong 1971; Bedau 1977; Fogel 1975; Golding 1977; Hart 1968; Hegel [1821] 1967; Hospers 1977a, b; Kant [1787] 1933, [1797] 1964, [1797] 1965; Kaufmann 1977; Kleinig 1973; Lewis [1948] 1971; Mabbott 1971; Mundle 1971; van den Haag 1975; von Hirsch 1976, 1985). The earliest formulations of retribution were based on the ancient concept of *lex talionis*, or an eye for an eye and a tooth for a tooth—a principle that recognized that punishments should be identical to, or at least closely resemble, the nature of the offense. While modern retributivists acknowledge the impracticality of *lex talionis*, they nonetheless insist that just deserts requires that punishments should be tailored to fit the "harmfulness" of offenses and the moral "blameworthiness" or "culpability" of offenders (Armstrong 1971; Bedau 1977; Golding 1977; Hart 1968; Hospers 1977a, b; Kaufmann 1977; Mundle 1971; von Hirsch 1976, 1985). Retributivists have tried to devise various sentencing systems and guidelines where the severity of various punishments is directly matched with the seriousness of various crimes (Hospers 1977a, b; Kleinig 1973; von Hirsch 1976, 1985).

Restitution was first developed as a means to curb blood revenge by King Ur-Nammu in the Sumerian city of Ur in 2100 B.C. (Bowker 1982; Menninger 1968). The original purpose of restitution was for the offender to reimburse the victim proportionately for all crime-related losses (Barnett 1977; Barnett and Hagel 1977; Bowker 1982; Hospers 1977a, b; Kaufmann 1977; Rothbard 1977; Sommer 1976). In recent criminal justice practice, however, restitution is often made by the offender directly to the state (as the party that is symbolically harmed by criminal conduct) through various forms of community service (e.g., the slumlord found guilty of building code infractions may be required to spend 400 hours tutoring disadvantaged schoolchildren—Bowker 1982; Sommer 1976). Restitution is frequently an additional form of recompense that is ordered by judges in conjunction with fines, probationary sentences, or prison terms.

Among the three types of recompense, only retribution can theoretically be accomplished through the punishment of imprisonment. Revenge is a personal form of recompense that occurs mostly outside the gamut of state-administered punishments. Those who claim that incarceration accomplishes the larger social outcome of revenge confuse the retributive purposes of punishment with individual vengeance and vendetta (Hospers 1977a, b). Regarding restitution, prisons do little to improve the well-being of the victims of crime, beyond placating their personal thirst for vengeance (Rothbard 1977). Also, given that inmates who work in prison industries usually earn only a few dimes per hour, they hardly can be expected, while serving time, to make a meaningful monetary repayment to their victims.

According to the logic of recompense, the effectiveness of prisons as instruments of retribution must be measured not by the social utility of incarceration in reducing the crime rate but rather by the success of prison sentencing systems and guidelines in proportionately matching the severity of incarceration as a punishment to the seriousness of different types of criminal offenses. Solomon Kobrin (1980) refers to this as the "fairness" or "justice" criterion for evaluating the effectiveness of imprisonment. Chapter 3 disputes the effectiveness of using prison sentences as proportional punishments. Importantly, though, if retributivists cannot neatly fit the severity of punishments for criminal offenders to the seriousness of offenses, then neither can restitution proponents neatly fit the degree of repayment to crime victims to the seriousness of offenses. (E.g., how can such offenders as rapists or murderers proportionately repay their victims?)

Again, the proponents of the utilitarian model see punishment as a means (or instrument) to accomplish certain desirable social ends (or benefits) in the future. Utilitarians in general argue that imprisonment potentially results in five beneficial social outcomes: *rehabilitation, social solidarity, general deterrence, specific deterrence*, and *incapacitation.*

Rehabilitation refers to the use of various treatment strategies and programs to reform individual offenders and to prevent future crime (Allen 1959, 1981; Barnett and Hagel 1977; Cullen and Gilbert 1982; Hospers 1977a; Menninger 1968; Weihofen 1971). Treatment programs in prisons include educational and vocational training, prison industries, recreational programs, and individual and group counseling and therapies. These programs are intended to teach inmates law-abiding personal and social skills and habits and to promote better insight among inmates into their attitudes and motivations (Weihofen 1971). Imprisonment for the purpose of rehabilitation is focused around meeting the treatment needs of individual offenders rather than the retributive goal of fitting punishment to the nature of the criminal offense (Allen 1981).

Rehabilitation emerged as the dominant purpose of imprisonment in the United States around the midpoint of the twentieth century and directly reflected the development of "psychiatry and scientific criminology [as] established fields of inquiry" (Weihofen 1971, 255). In his classic articulation of the assumptions underlying this scientific "rehabilitative ideal," Francis Allen (1959, 226) observes:

It is assumed, first, that human behavior is the product of antecedent causes. These causes can be identified as part of the physical universe, and it is the obligation of the scientist to discover and to describe them with all possible exactitude. Knowledge of the antecedents of human behavior makes possible an approach to the scientific control of human behavior. Finally . . . it is assumed that the measures employed to treat the convicted offender should serve a therapeutic function, [and] that such measures should be designed to effect changes in the behavior of the convicted person in the interests of his [sic] own happiness, health, and satisfactions and in the interest of social defense.

Another beneficial outcome sometimes attributed to crime and punishment is the enhancement of the bonds of social solidarity among the law-abiding segments of society (Conklin 1975; Durkheim [1893] 1964, [1895] 1982; Erikson 1966; Garland 1990). The proponents of this position argue that "strong bonds of moral solidarity are the conditions which cause punishments to come about, and, in their turn, punishments result in the affirmation and strengthening of these same social bonds" (Garland 1990, 28). In summarizing this view, David Garland (1990, 33) notes that because crime enrages public morality, its punishment "serves as an occasion for the collective expression of shared moral passions, and this collective expression serves to strengthen these same passions through mutual reinforcement and reassurance." Punishing the criminal minority upholds and revitalizes the integrity and propriety of the norms, values, beliefs, and conduct of the law-abiding majority. Because the criminal act threatens to rend the social fabric into normative remnants, the punishment response brings us together in a spirit of collective indignation to mend the cloak of our shared morality.

Deterrence is the use of threatened or actual punishments to convince persons not to commit future crimes (Andenaes 1952, 1966, 1971b, 1974; Barnett and Hagel 1977; Beccaria [1764] 1963; Bentham [1789] 1970, [1802] 1931, [1811] 1930, [1843] 1962; Geis 1972; Gibbs 1975; Golding 1977; Hart 1968; Hawkins 1971; Hospers 1977a, b; Monachesi 1972; Sykes 1958; Tittle 1980b; Wilson 1985; Wilson and Herrnstein 1985; Wright 1992; Zimring and Hawkins 1973). The proponents of deterrence as a utilitarian outcome of punishment assume that humans are rational actors (or creatures whose behavior is oriented toward maximizing pleasure and minimizing pain) who possess free will. Humans will choose to commit criminal offenses if they believe that criminal conduct is more likely than law-abiding conduct to lead to the maximization of pleasure (i.e., offenders commit crimes because they believe that "crime pays" more than lawful behavior). The objective of punishment is to prevent crime by persuading potential offenders that crime will result in more pain than pleasure.

Punishment theorists have long recognized that deterrence can take two forms—general deterrence and specific (or special) deterrence (Beccaria [1764] 1963; Bentham [1789] 1970, [1802] 1931, [1811] 1930, [1843] 1962; Gibbs 1975; Hart 1968; Wright 1992). General deterrence is the use of the threat of punishment to convince those who are not being punished not to commit crimes. By witnessing the punishment of Peter, Paul is persuaded that crime does not pay (Sykes 1958). Specific deterrence is the use of punishment to convince those who actually are being punished not to commit future crimes—in other words, Peter is punished to deter him from persisting in a life of crime (Sykes 1958). As Beccaria [1764] 1963, 42) observes in his early discussion of deterrence, punishments should be chosen that "make the strongest and most lasting impression on the minds of men [sic]" for the purposes of preventing "the criminal from inflicting new injuries on its [the nation's] citizens and to deter others from similar acts."

More recently, deterrence advocates have noted that punishment has an additional extralegal, informal function by inculcating law-abiding habits and stigmatizing those who commit crime (Andenaes 1952, 1966, 1971b, 1974; Hawkins 1971; Williams and Hawkins 1986; Zimring and Hawkins 1971, 1973). Johannes Andenaes (1952, 179–180 [italics deleted]) argues that "punishment as a concrete expression of society's disapproval of an act" helps to create "conscious and unconscious inhibitions against committing crime"—or, stated positively, "habitual law-abiding conduct." Gordon Hawkins (1971, 168) adds that the "ritualistic aspect of punishment" achieves certain extralegal benefits through the "dramatization of evil" and the "stigmatization" (or social condemnation) of offenders. Once the fear of stigmatization and law-abiding habits are firmly internalized, most persons continue to obey the law even in those occasional situations where an immediate rational calculation of self-interest would suggest that crime may in fact pay (Andenaes 1952, 1966, 1971b, 1974; Hawkins 1971).

The final utilitarian social outcome associated with punishment is incapacitation, defined as the prevention of crime in society at large through the use of punishment to remove criminals from circulation in free society (Barnett and Hagel 1977; Forst 1984; Greenwood 1982; Hospers 1977a, b; von Hirsch 1985; Wilson 1985; Wright 1992). Although capital punishment can be considered a drastic and permanent method to achieve incapacitation for particularly notorious offenders, most proponents view imprisonment as a more practical and less controversial modern instrument of incapacitation (Greenwood 1982; Forst 1984; Wilson 1985; Wright 1992). Recent public concerns over "chronic" or "habitual" offenders—or a small number of criminals who commit a large number of crimes—have fueled greater interest in the use of long prison terms to isolate these offenders and protect society from their crimes. A key to the effective use of imprisonment for the purpose of incapacitation is the creation of valid and reliable risk assessment instruments to identify chronic offenders (Greenwood 1982; Forst 1984; von Hirsch 1985; Wilson 1985; Wright 1992).

According to both Cesare Beccaria ([1764] 1963) and Jeremy Bentham [1789] 1970), the effectiveness of imprisonment as a utilitarian outcome of punishment—along with the effectiveness of all other social policies—can be judged on the basis of one principle: does it bring the greatest happiness at the lowest cost to the greatest number of people? Although this "principle of utility" certainly has some merit in the formulation of broad social policies, applying it specifically to the modern empirical study of crime and punishment is no easy task. How does the researcher operationally define happiness? Can one put a dollar value on the cost of the human suffering of crime victims? How do we choose our samples to reflect the preferences of the "greatest number of people"? While economists have had some limited success in quantifying cost-benefit factors relating to crime (see Becker 1968; Cohen 1988; Phillips 1980), Leslie Wilkins (1969) and Kobrin (1980) note that most criminologists opt for a simpler measure to evaluate the effectiveness of the utilitarian outcomes of punishment: is crime prevented? Chapters 3 to 5 examine in detail the empirical evidence relating to the success of the five utilitarian approaches in achieving the social outcomes of reducing recidivism rates (or the proportion of offenders who persist in committing crime once released from prison) and lowering the overall crime rate.

THE INDIVIDUAL OUTCOMES OF PUNISHMENT

So far we have been concerned mostly about the effect of punishments on the wider society in which they are practiced. Another important issue is the effect of punishments on the individual offender. What are the social psychological dynamics involved in the punishment of criminals? Is it possible—as numerous criminologists and social commentators have argued—that prisons are "crime schools" that make individual offenders worse rather than better?

Certainly the proponents of both recompense and utilitarianism are not entirely blind to the effects of punishment on individual offenders. For retribution to enhance a sense of recompense and justice in society at large, individual offenders must be prosecuted fairly and punished proportionately. For rehabilitation and general deterrence to reduce the overall rate of crime in society, individual offenders must be treated and cured, and individual citizens must be personally convinced that crime does not pay. Nonetheless, those who embrace recompense and utilitarianism as the goals of punishment tend to make sweeping and abstract generalizations about the nature of crime and punishment in their discussions of proportionality, social justice, crime prevention, and recidivism rates. Often the individual mugger, drug dealer, prostitute, or embezzler appears to be lost in the shuffle—or, more accurately, buried in the aggregate data file—in the consideration of the social outcomes of punishment. Two theoretical traditions in criminology, however, are primarily concerned about the impact of punishments on individual offenders—*labeling theory* and *rational choice* arguments. In general, labeling theorists argue that punishments tend to make individual offenders *more* deviant, while rational choice theorists claim that punishments *reduce* individual criminal propensities.

Reflecting a profound public distrust and cynicism about the purposes and operations of major social institutions, labeling theory emerged as an influential criminological perspective in the late 1960s and early 1970s (see Becker 1963; Lemert 1951, 1967; Schur 1965, 1971, 1973, 1979; Wilkins 1964). Labeling theorists argue that the negative social reactions to deviance and crime stigmatize offenders, isolating them from interaction with conformist and law-abiding segments of society. Once stigmatized and cut off from conventional society, those who are labeled develop deviant/criminal self-identities and roles and negative self-concepts. To assuage their damaged self-esteem, labeled offenders often turn to deviant/criminal subcultures for social support and sustenance. In the process, their deviant/criminal life-styles become more firmly entrenched, and their behavior further deteriorates. In effect, negative social reactions and deviant labels become "self-fulfilling prophecies": the attribution of deviance and criminality to the individual offender is an initially false belief that becomes true due to the overwhelming forces of social intolerance and stigmatization (Becker 1963).

Perhaps needless to say, labeling theorists have nothing kind to say about the outcome of imprisonment on individual offenders (Lemert 1967;

Schur 1973). Labeling theorists view prisons and juvenile reformatories as the ultimate symbols of social repressiveness, intolerance, isolation, and stigmatization. Incarceration completely severs the ties of the offender to law-abiding society and supposedly exposes the inmate to a deprived and degraded criminal subculture. Criminal motivations and skills purportedly are initially learned and then reaffirmed and fine-tuned within prison walls. The crime school image of imprisonment perpetuated by labeling theorists suggests that most offenders will leave prison far more committed to criminal life-styles and behaviors than when they entered. To avoid this unhappy scenario, labeling theorists urge the practice of nonintervention-ism—where policymakers decriminalize and ignore the deviance/crimi-nality of most offenders (Schur 1965, 1973).

Rational choice theory as it relates to crime and punishment is a modern, social psychological variation of deterrence arguments (as a result, general and specific deterrence can be conceptualized as both social and individual outcomes of punishment—see chapter 4, and also Becker 1968; Clarke and Cornish 1985; Cook 1980; Cornish and Clarke 1986, 1987; Nettler 1984; Wilson and Herrnstein 1985). The proponents of rational choice theory contend that prospective criminals are decision makers who weigh the likely benefits and costs—or rewards and punishments—of their behavior before engaging in action. This decision-making process is based on a fairly simple calculation: "The larger the ratio of the rewards (material and nonmaterial) of noncrime to the rewards (material and nonmaterial) of crime, the weaker the tendency to commit crimes" (Wilson and Herrn-stein 1985, 61). Rational choice theorists assume that (1) human behavior is largely rational (i.e., individuals reflect on the consequences of their actions and choose those behaviors that optimize rewards and minimize punishments) and (2) the motivations to commit crime are distributed fairly evenly across the population (i.e., there is larceny in everyone's heart; the choice not to commit crime is based primarily on the calculation of self-interest, regardless of considerations of morality and habit). Con-temporary rational choice theorists recognize that human decision making involves a "bounded rationality" (i.e., social and biological factors place certain limitations on one's ability to weigh the consequences of one's actions). Among the social factors that limit human rationality, Derek Cornish and Ronald Clarke (1986, 1987) note constraints on the decision maker's time, cognitive abilities, and the availability of relevant informa-tion. James Q. Wilson and Richard Herrnstein (1985) add three constitu-tional/genetic factors that further bound human rationality—inherited predispositions for impulsiveness, aggressiveness, and low intelligence. Considering these social and biological limitations, one would predict that the decisions of unintelligent, impulsive, and aggressive people who have little time to make choices and little information about the consequences of their actions would be less rational that the decisions of more favored citizens.

Rational choice theorists all concur that one way to reduce the likelihood that individuals will commit crime is to increase the costs or risks associated with criminal behavior. In an early statement of the rational choice model, economist Gary Becker (1968) argued that the number of offenses committed by a particular criminal is a function of two risk factors—the probability of conviction for each offense and the severity of the expected punishment for each offense. Clearly, criminal justice sanctions are an important element in the calculation of risks by prospective offenders; as Wilson and Herrnstein (1985, 507) conclude: "The punishments of the legal system are an essential part of the story of why criminal behavior may or may not take place. Avoiding punishment provides a major incentive for noncrime." Cornish and Clarke (1986, 1987) add, however, that calculations of the effectiveness of punishments by policymakers must be "crime specific," because different clusters of motives, opportunities, rewards, and costs exist for different types of offenses and offenders. In other words, research might reveal that bank robbers are more prone to weigh potential costs and benefits than murderers. As a result, increasing the probability of convictions and the severity of punishments would have a greater deterrent effect on individual bank robbers than murderers.

Again, it is important to note that labeling and rational choice theorists make diametrically opposed predictions about the effectiveness of punishments in general and imprisonment in particular for individual offenders (Gibbs 1975). Labeling theorists believe that imprisonment paradoxically contributes to the crime problem by stigmatizing and isolating offenders and by breeding criminal self-identities and subcultures. In contrast, rational choice theorists contend that imprisonment is an important risk factor that often deters individual criminality. Chapters 4 and 6 review the recent empirical evidence pertaining to these two competing arguments about the individual outcomes of punishment.

NONLINEAR CRIMINAL JUSTICE

As noted at the beginning of chapter 2, there are considerable disarray and debate in criminal justice policy-making in contemporary American society (Allen 1981; Bartollas 1990; Sommer 1976; Wilson 1977; Wright 1993). Much of this confusion and disorganization centers around arguments over the appropriate social and individual outcomes of punishment.

According to Robert Sommer (1976, 17): "Our penal system is afflicted with . . . a model muddle. Corrections employees, judges, police, legislators, and inmates all have diverse, vague, and often conflicting ideas of what prisons are supposed to accomplish."

Elsewhere I have proposed a "nonlinear model" of the criminal justice system to try to explain this policy-making disarray (see Wright 1993). This interpretation borrows the concepts of the "garbage can" theory (Cohen, March, and Olsen 1972; Perrow 1986) and "loose coupling" (Hagan 1989; Perrow 1986) from the sociology of organizations. The garbage can model depicts organizations in complex, democratic societies as decision-making "receptacles," into which heterogeneous members and interest groups "toss" highly variegated problems, agendas, and solutions. The complex bargaining, shifting coalitions, and multiple agendas that "fill" the garbage can result in the emergence of often random, accidental, temporary, unintended, and unexpected decisions and goals. Charles Perrow (1986, 137) notes that the garbage can model interprets organizational decision-making as the product of "incomplete information, [a] lack of knowledge of cause-and-effect relationships, and shifting goals and priorities."

Loosely coupled organizations and systems are characterized by decentralized decision making, multiple and inconsistent goals, slow communications, inefficiency and waste, and autonomous, largely disconnected subsystems (Perrow 1986). While their operations often appear virtually random and chaotic, loosely coupled organizations have the virtues of great flexibility and adaptability; these organizations/systems can absorb tremendous conflict and change within their social environments, while essentially remaining stable.

The criminal justice system in the United States often works like a garbage can. Politicians, the mass media, the public, various interest groups (e.g., the National Rifle Association), outside experts (e.g., criminologists), inside professionals and staff, and criminal offenders and crime victims toss their particular problems, agendas, and proposed solutions into the criminal justice system in an attempt to influence policy. Policies gradually emerge through a complex process of negotiation, bargaining, and compromise. Implemented policies seldom resemble the initial proposals of particular interest groups; rather, goals and solutions are twisted, amended, watered down, combined, and distorted, so that while most parties are appeased, few are fully satisfied. Emerging policies *in toto* defy simple classification into rational, predictable, linear categories—some policies will seem to support retribution while others support rehabilitation, deterrence, or incapacitation; some laws will appear to reflect broad consensus while others reflect the interests of powerful groups; and most important, sometimes social order will emerge, but at other times, social disorder and near chaos.

Not only does the criminal justice system correspond to the garbage can model, but its subsystems are loosely coupled across time and space (see Hagan 1989). Decision making within the criminal justice system is decentralized within each subsystem (police, courts, and corrections), and the lines of communication among the subsystems are tenuous over time (Hagan 1989). Decision making is also regionally decentralized into municipal, county, state, and federal governmental offices and agencies, further contributing to loose coupling. Temporal decentralization means that the policies adopted by one subsystem at one time may be only partially implemented, ignored, or even subverted by the other subsystems at other times (Hagan 1989). Regional decentralization means that even within subsystems, policies may be only partially implemented, ignored, or even subverted from one level of government to the next and from one community to the next. Because of loose coupling, environmental factors (ranging from changes in political administrations to the number of young, unemployed males in a community) that affect one subsystem in one region seldom have a systemwide influence. Ironically, while retribution may be flourishing as the practiced social outcome of punishment in one part of the criminal justice system, rehabilitation, deterrence, or incapacitation may flourish elsewhere.

The agendas being tossed into nonlinear criminal justice systems reflect the bounded rationality of various political interest groups seeking to maximize their influence over criminal justice decision making. For example, political conservatives (e.g., van den Haag 1975; Wilson 1985; Wilson and Herrnstein 1985), liberals (e.g., American Friends Service Committee 1971; Cullen and Gilbert 1982; Currie 1985; Fogel 1975; Gendreau and Ross 1979, 1987; Irwin 1980), and radicals (e.g., Haan 1990; Mathiesen 1974, 1990; Pepinsky 1992; Wright 1973) offer very different policy recommendations for improving the operation of criminal justice systems. Conservatives generally support retribution, deterrence, incapacitation, and rational choice arguments as the social and individual outcomes of punishment and favor a stable social order over the protection of due process and the other rights of offenders. Liberals emphasize the importance of the due process rights of individual offenders over the protection of social order but are divided on their recommendations for the appropriate outcomes of punishment. (E.g., some liberals—e.g., Cullen and Gilbert 1982; Currie 1985; Gendreau and Ross 1979, 1987— retain a strong faith in the rehabilitation of offenders, while others—e.g.,

American Friends Service Committee 1971; Fogel 1975; Irwin 1980—
contend that retribution is the only fair and just purpose of punishment.)
Radicals argue that the American criminal justice system unfairly protects
an exploitative class system and contend that greater class equality is an
absolute prerequisite before a fair criminal justice system can be created.
While radicals agree about the necessity for transforming capitalism and
creating a socialist system of economic equality, they differ about the
proper outcomes of punishment under socialism: Erik Olin Wright (1973)
recommends the retention of strong retribution, deterrence, and incapacitation policies (in order to punish the bourgeois "enemies of equality"); in
contrast, Willem de Haan (1990), Thomas Mathiesen (1974, 1990), and
Harold Pepinsky (1992) support the abolition of punishment under socialism, in favor of a criminal justice system that emphasizes restitution and
the mediated settlement of disputes. The complex and negotiated criminal
justice policies that emerge at various times and places in modern democ-
racies represent an effort to appease and to forge a compromise among
these diverse and often conflicting interests.

What follows is a comprehensive summary of what modern criminological research shows about the effectiveness of the various social and
individual outcomes of imprisonment. In general, my summary indicates
that prisons are mostly ineffective as instruments for promoting the social
outcomes of rehabilitation, retribution, and social solidarity but are moderately effective in promoting general deterrence, specific deterrence, and
incapacitation. Furthermore, the empirical evidence favors rational choice
over labeling arguments regarding the individual outcomes of imprisonment. I conclude that rational correctional decision making should largely
embrace the conservative recommendations for the continued use of
imprisonment for the purposes of deterring and incapacitating offenders.
Certainly, though, in the hurly-burly real world of politicalization, negotiation, compromise, trade-offs, appeasement, and temporal and regional
decentralization within the nonlinear American criminal justice "system,"
implementing absolutely rational and effective punishment policies will
always remain an elusive goal. My more modest objective is to foster a
more rational correctional system in the service of a more rational society.

Chapter Three

The Failure of Prisons: Rehabilitation, Retribution, and Social Solidarity

The critics of prisons often depict them as absolute failures or, as William Nagel (1973, 177) contends, institutions that are "grossly ineffective [and] grossly dehumanizing." While Nagel's assessment itself is grossly exaggerated, empirical evidence clearly indicates that prisons do not effectively accomplish all of the objectives of punishment reviewed in chapter 2. Specifically, criminological research in the last twenty-five years has cast considerable doubt on the ability of prisons to achieve rehabilitation, retribution, and social solidarity. Chapter 3 examines these three failures of prisons.

THE DEMISE OF REHABILITATION: LAST RITES FOR THE MEDICAL MODEL

The belief that various treatments can be used to rehabilitate prisoners has long been a seductive chimera in corrections. David Rothman (1971, 1980) chronicles the emergence of periodic rehabilitative cycles in the history of American corrections. The Quakers, who established the first penitentiaries in the United States (the Walnut Street Jail in Philadelphia in 1790; the Western Penitentiary in Pittsburgh in 1826; and the Eastern Penitentiary in Cherry Hill, Pennsylvania, in 1830), sought to promote penance (the root word of penitentiary) among inmates through solitary confinement, an absolute rule of silence, Bible readings, and self-reflection on one's misdeeds. Because few inmates appeared to be rehabilitated by these measures, interest in treatment dissipated in the United States until the emergence of the reformatory movement in the 1870s and the establishment of the first reformatory at Elmira, New York, in 1876. The major proponents of the reformatory movement—Enoch and Frederick Wines and Elmira superintendent Zebulon Brockway—emphasized the importance of individualized treatment for young male offenders. Reformatories relied on educational and vocational programs, mark systems (to reward good behavior and to punish troublemaking), and indeterminate sentences (where the length of one's incarceration depended on the successful completion of treatment programs and the accumulation of good marks) as the major instruments of treatment. Enthusiasm for treatment again waned toward the end of the nineteenth century when charges of brutality were leveled against reformatories. (E.g., Superintendent Brockway frequently resorted to beating his young male charges. A hearing conducted in 1894 on the cruel and excessive punishments practiced in Elmira Reformatory revealed that Brockway's subordinates routinely whipped inmates twice a week and that 30 percent of the inmates had been beaten at least once during their "treatment"—Rothman 1980.)

Reflecting a renewed spirit of optimism and a strong faith in the ability of the social sciences and political institutions to solve basic social problems (see Allen 1981)—along with a certain degree of historical amnesia—still another wave of interest in rehabilitation emerged among criminologists, correctional officials, and policymakers in the United States immediately following World War II until the mid-1970s. The numerous evaluation studies of the treatment programs established in prisons during this era, however, fairly conclusively demonstrate that prisons simply cannot effectively achieve the rehabilitation of inmates as a utilitarian social outcome.

Behind the rhetoric of the most recent wave of rehabilitation programs was a strong commitment to the so-called medical model of corrections (see Allen 1959, 1981; Cullen and Gilbert 1982; Ferri [1901] 1971; Menninger 1968; Sechrest, White, and Brown 1979). In this model, crime is viewed as a "disease," which requires some form of rehabilitation as a "cure." Offenders are assumed to be "sick," "abnormal," or "psychologically defective"—their cure involves exposure to various treatment programs, including psychotherapy, individual and/or group counseling, vocational training, and/or basic education. Because rehabilitative thinking assumes that the individual offender is personally defective, it denies the rationality and competence of the criminal. Commenting on the medical model, C. S. Lewis ([1948] 1971, 306) contends: "To be 'cured' against one's will and cured of states which we may not regard as [a] disease is to be put on a level with those who have not yet reached the age of reason or those who never will; to be classed with infants [and] imbeciles."

Rehabilitation involves a "planned intervention that reduces an offender's criminal activity" (Sechrest, White, and Brown 1979, 4 [italics deleted]) by "transforming individuals into less undesirable, more complete and adequate, [and] better-functioning social beings" (Hartjen 1974, 130). Although both are utilitarian outcomes of imprisonment and both strive to inculcate law-abiding habits among offenders, rehabilitation differs from specific deterrence because the latter assumes that most offenders are rational and achieves its beneficial effects through the use of fear and intimidation to convince offenders that crime does not pay, rather than treatment programs to improve the offender's personal and social skills (Sechrest, White, and Brown 1979). Furthermore, rehabilitation can be distinguished from retribution not only on the basis of utilitarian justifications but also because the former assumes that treatments should be calculated to fit the *needs of the criminal*, while the latter prefers the assignment of punishments to fit the *seriousness of the crime*.

Criminal justice systems that endorse rehabilitation as the foremost purpose of incarceration possess certain unique characteristics (see American Friends Service Committee 1971; Cullen and Gilbert 1982; Fogel 1975; Irwin 1980). The emphasis on individualized treatments tailored to meet the needs of the offender results in the extensive use of (1) indeterminate sentences, (2) behavior modification programs involving token economies and graded systems of classification (where offenders are granted greater privileges based on good behavior), and (3) parole (the ultimate reward for good behavior). In general, judicial and correctional officials exercise considerable discretion in rehabilitative systems—two offenders convicted of similar offenses may serve substantially different prison sentences, based on the assessment of their different personal needs.

Most correctional systems in the United States embraced rehabilitation as an important purpose of incarceration during the 1950s and 1960s. These were the halcyon days of the so-called correctional institution (see Irwin 1980): traditional prisons were transformed into rehabilitation centers, where social workers, psychologists, and educators organized programs in behavior modification, individual and group counseling, vocational training, and GED (general equivalency diploma) certification for the benefit of inmates (now euphemistically called "residents"). The assumption was that once cured of the disease of crime, ex-offenders could be returned to society as productive and law-abiding citizens. Slowly, though, dissatisfaction with rehabilitation programs surfaced in the late 1960s and early 1970s (Cullen and Gilbert 1982; Irwin 1980). A rapid rise in the rates of street crime during these years contributed to criticisms of correctional treatment from politicians and social commentators on both the right and the left. Conservatives—long suspicious of correctional institutions for "coddling" criminals—called for the abolition of rehabilitation in preference to "get-tough" sentencing policies that highlighted the rights of society to be protected from criminals, rather than the treatment needs of the offender. A post-Vietnam and post-Watergate sense of pessimism in the effectiveness of the state in implementing meaningful reform programs likewise caused many liberals to abandon the rehabilitative regimen of indeterminate sentencing, treatment, and parole, in favor of retributive forms of sentencing and correctional systems that placed greater importance on protecting the rights of offenders rather than curing their perceived defects (Allen 1981; Cullen and Gilbert 1982; Fogel 1975; von Hirsch 1976). Numerous strikes and riots among prison inmates in the late 1960s and early 1970s—culminating in the horrifying slaughter of thirty-nine prisoners and guards during the suppression of the prisoner insurrection at the Attica Correctional Facility on 13 September 1971— also shattered political support for rehabilitation programs (see Cullen and Gilbert 1982; Irwin 1980).

These political controversies and grotesque media events overshadowed the preliminary attempts by researchers to measure the success of correctional institutions in rehabilitating their "residents." Two important early studies, however, hardly offered any reassurance to the proponents of rehabilitation (see Bailey 1966; Kassebaum, Ward, and Wilner 1971). In a meticulous seven-year study of the group counseling techniques implemented at the California Men's Colony—East (a medium-security correctional facility), Gene Kassebaum, David Ward, and Daniel Wilner (1971) found no evidence supporting the success of rehabilitation programs. With the cooperation of correctional officials, the researchers in 1961 and 1962 randomly assigned 825 inmates to various forms of group counseling treatments and another 600 inmates to a control group receiving no treatment. The counseling therapy involved the formation of groups of ten to twelve inmates who met weekly with correctional counselors to discuss their personal needs and problems. The outcome measures used to evaluate the effectiveness of the treatment included comparisons of (1) the attitudes of inmates toward prison staff, (2) the number of disciplinary infractions incurred by inmates, and (3) a thirty-six–month follow-up analysis (ending in June 1967) of the recidivism rates among inmates who were fortunate enough to be paroled. Importantly, Kassebaum, Ward, and Wilner (1971) found *no significant differences* among those inmates who participated in group counseling programs versus those in the control group, for *any* of the three outcome measures.

Walter Bailey's (1966) analysis is an early effort to judge the effectiveness of correctional treatment programs using a technique now known as "metaevaluation." Metaevaluations summarize the findings of the social impacts of a group of individual evaluation studies that analyze one type of policy implementation (e.g., correctional rehabilitation programs—see Rossi and Freeman 1985). Supporters of metaevaluations claim that they offer "more definitive evidence of the effectiveness or ineffectiveness of social programs than can be obtained by undertaking an additional" single program evaluation (Rossi and Freeman 1985, 219). Bailey (1966) examined 100 studies of correctional treatment programs implemented in the United States from 1940 to 1960. Although he uncovered a number of studies that attributed positive results to rehabilitation programs, virtually all of these studies employed faulty research designs (e.g., extremely small samples, no control groups, and/or nonrandom assignment of subjects to experimental and control groups). Bailey (1966) concluded that the benefits of then-current treatment programs in prisons were minimal and of questionable generalizability to other prisoners in other prisons.

The Kassebaum, Ward, and Wilner (1971) and Bailey (1966) studies anticipated an avalanche of subsequent research that disputed the effectiveness of rehabilitation programs, both inside and outside prisons. Metaevaluation studies in particular have had a devastating impact among criminologists on the perceived effectiveness of rehabilitation. The pivotal study in this genre is Douglas Lipton, Robert Martinson, and Judith Wilks's *The Effectiveness of Correctional Treatment* (1975), a 735-page encyclopedic review of the failure of criminal justice treatment programs. Fortunately, for those who prefer brevity, Martinson summarized the findings of the larger study in his short article "What Works?—Questions and Answers About Prison Reform" (1974). Martinson's (1974, 25—[italics deleted]) frequently cited conclusion was that "with few and isolated exceptions, the rehabilitative efforts that have been reported so far have had no appreciable effect on recidivism," or, to answer tersely the specific question posed in the title of his article, "Nothing works."

The so-called Martinson Report findings were based on an assiduous analysis of 231 evaluation studies of criminal justice treatment programs implemented in the United States and Europe between 1945 and 1967. Numerous types of treatment programs were examined, including educational and vocational training for both juvenile and adult offenders, individual counseling (including psychotherapy), group counseling, milieu therapy (which tries to reform inmates by transforming their entire institutional environment), medical treatments (including psychosurgery and drug therapies), deinstitutionalization (where offenders are diverted from traditional institutional settings—see chapter 6), and probation and parole as alternatives to incarceration. The program outcome measures used to assess the effectiveness of treatment programs included the personality and attitude changes of offenders, educational achievements, vocational success upon release from prison, adjustment to prison life, and (especially) recidivism rates. No discernible trends are apparent in the effectiveness of *any* of the treatments on recidivism rates, although a few faint glimmers of hope occasionally appear when considering the other outcome measures. For the skeptical reader, Lipton, Martinson, and Wilks (1975) include lengthy annotations reviewing all 231 evaluation studies. Readers who are masochistic enough to wade through these annotations are literally overwhelmed with a sense of the futility of treatment programs.

It is somewhat of an understatement to say that the Martinson Report sent shock waves throughout the entire correctional treatment community. Unfortunately, though, the bad news was only beginning. Two additional metaevaluations that were directly inspired by the Martinson Report were Lee Sechrest, Susan White, and Elizabeth Brown (1979) and David Greenberg (1977). Sechrest, White, and Brown (1979) reanalyzed a random sample of the 231 evaluation studies originally examined by Lipton, Martinson, and Wilks (1975). In addition, they reviewed an unspecified number of more recent treatment program studies published between 1968 and 1977, in order to bring the Lipton, Martinson, and Wilks findings up to date. From this analysis, Sechrest, White, and Brown (1979, 3) concluded that the Martinson Report findings were substantially correct; considering recidivism rates as their primary outcome measure, they contend: "The entire body of [treatment] research appears to justify only the conclusion that we do not know of any program or method of rehabilitation that could be guaranteed to reduce the criminal activity of released offenders."

Like Sechrest, White, and Brown (1979), Greenberg (1977) examined more recent evaluation studies (most published between 1967 and 1975) in an attempt to determine if more current treatment programs were any more effective than those examined in the earlier Martinson Report. He analyzed 115 treatment programs, ranging from individual and group counseling approaches to educational and vocational training, conjugal visitation, work and home furloughs, and behavior modification programs. Importantly for my purposes, forty-one of the studies surveyed by Greenberg specifically dealt with treatment programs implemented in traditional correctional settings. Differences in recidivism rates between experimental and control groups were the primary outcome measures considered by Greenberg. Again, Greenberg (1977, 140–141) concluded that the Martinson Report findings were essentially accurate; he noted that while a handful of studies report favorable outcomes, "most of these results are modest and are obtained through evaluations seriously lacking in rigor. The blanket assertion that 'nothing works' is an exaggeration, but not by very much."

An impressive array of additional metaevaluation studies corroborates the ineffectiveness of rehabilitation (see Fishman 1977; Lab and Whitehead 1988; Robison and Smith 1971; Ward 1973; Whitehead and Lab 1989; Wright and Dixon 1977). For example, Robert Fishman's (1977) longitudinal analysis of eighteen different treatment programs implemented for offenders in New York City between 1971 and 1975 shows that the 2,860 men who participated in these programs had similar arrest rates in the year immediately following program participation as in the twelve to twenty-four–month time period immediately before participation. Fishman (1977, 297, 299 [italics deleted]) concludes that no one type of treatment was found to be "better than another" and that, in general, "rehabilitation by the [programs] was considered to be a failure."

William Wright and Michael Dixon (1977) and Steven Lab and John Whitehead (1988) and Whitehead and Lab (1989) specifically examined the effectiveness of rehabilitation programs that service juvenile offenders. Wright and Dixon (1977) analyzed ninety-six studies published between 1965 and 1974; Lab and Whitehead (1988) and Whitehead and Lab (1989) reviewed an additional fifty studies appearing between 1975 and 1984. Each metaevaluation study looked at a variety of different treatment programs (ranging from individual and group counseling to educational and vocational training, juvenile gang worker outreach programs, and so on); each used recidivism rates as an outcome measure; and each concludes that treatment programs have little impact on recidivism rates. Importantly, the Lab and Whitehead (1988) and Whitehead and Lab (1989) studies also show that (1) no one type of treatment was more effective than any other in reducing recidivism, (2) more recent treatment programs (evaluated since 1980) were no more effective than earlier treatment programs, (3) the findings of treatment ineffectiveness persisted even when the variables of offender gender and offense history (e.g., seriousness of offenses, number of arrests, and so forth) were controlled, and (4) the seventeen studies employing more rigorous research designs (i.e., the random assignment of offenders to experimental and control groups) were *less* likely to report success than less rigorous studies.

James Robison and Gerald Smith (1971) and Ward (1973) independently examined unspecified numbers of evaluation studies on the treatment programs implemented by the California Department of Corrections during the 1960s. These researchers chose to focus on California's rehabilitation programs because the correctional officials in this state were widely recognized to be the most progressive in the nation and the most sophisticated in implementing treatment programs. Still, Robison and Smith (1971, 74 [italics deleted]) conclude that no treatment techniques "have unequivocally demonstrated themselves capable of reducing recidivism," and Ward (1973, 1986) more cynically adds that inmates seem to come "back to prison whether they participated in treatment or not."

Despite this overwhelming evidence, a small but stalwart minority of criminologists continues to argue that the treatment of offenders is effective and rehabilitation should be retained as a primary goal of correctional institutions (see Andrews et al. 1990a, b; Cullen and Gilbert 1982; Garrett 1985; Gendreau and Ross 1979, 1987). Four metaevaluation studies report positive evidence supporting the effectiveness of offender treatment programs (see Andrews et al. 1990a; Garrett 1985; Gendreau and Ross 1979, 1987). Carol Garrett (1985) reviews 111 studies published between 1960 and 1983 of juvenile offender treatment programs implemented in both correctional and community settings and concludes that life skills treatment programs (devoted to enhancing the everyday social and coping skills of delinquents) offer a variety of benefits to participants. However, to reach this optimistic conclusion, Garrett places great importance on studies that use outcome measures (e.g., vocational and educational achievements, personality and attitude changes, and institutional adjustments) *other* than recidivism rates. Among the thirty-four studies in her metaevaluation that relied on recidivism rates as an outcome measure, treatment programs were found to produce virtually no benefits.

Using recidivism rates as an outcome measure, D. A. Andrews et al. (1990a) examined eighty correctional treatment studies published from 1959 to 1989, including forty-five of the fifty juvenile treatment studies previously analyzed by Lab and Whitehead (1988) and Whitehead and Lab (1989). They divided their sample into programs that classify offenders according to their "amenability" to treatment and nonselective programs. Amenability generally refers to efforts "to match rehabilitative [programs] with the characteristics of individual [offenders]" (Sechrest, White, and Brown 1979, 22). Andrews et al. (1990a) specifically define amenability (which they refer to as "appropriateness") as the targeting of "higher levels" of treatment services to "higher risk" clients who have "greater needs." Although they report a statistically significant relationship between treatment programs that targeted appropriate offenders and reductions in aggregate recidivism rates, their categorization of programs appears to be biased: programs that were already found to work seem to be disproportionately classified as "appropriate." To avoid these classification dilemmas and to ensure the reliability of their data, Andrews et al. (1990a) should have hired independent coders to reclassify the appropriateness judgments of a random sample of their eighty studies and then calculated intercoder reliability correlation coefficients between their judgments and those of the independent coders. The authors, however, omit this crucial methodological step. As a result, Whitehead and Lab (1990, 412) correctly conclude that it "appears that [Andrews et al. (1990a)] make the[ir] determinations [of program appropriateness] more out of convenience for their argument than based on hard proof that the[ir] distinctions reflect 'objective' decisions."

Paul Gendreau and Robert Ross (1979, 1987) have been particularly vocal defenders of rehabilitation. In their reviews of unspecified numbers of studies published between 1973 and 1978 (1979) and 1981 and 1987 (1987), they describe numerous examples of treatment programs that appear to lower the recidivism rates among participants. When analyzing treatment programs involving many different styles of intervention (including diversion/deinstitutionalization, family intervention counseling, job training, probation and parole, and educational programs), Gendreau and Ross (1987, 395) flatly conclude that "it is downright ridiculous to say that 'Nothing works,' " and add that "offender rehabilitation has been, can be, and will be achieved." However, Gendreau and Ross tend to see success where many of the rest of us might see failure. Their articles get considerable mileage from discussing a handful of programs that appear to work, while casually dismissing the far more numerous programs that fail. Typical of their *modus operandi* is their recent assessment of diversion/deinstitutionalization programs (see Gendreau and Ross 1987, 354–358). Twelve evaluation studies of these programs are cited by the authors—ten (83 percent) show that these programs have no beneficial effects on recidivism rates, while two (17 percent) indicate statistically significant positive results. Gendreau and Ross (1987, 355–358) devote one three-sentence paragraph to reviewing the ten program failures but two pages of glowing discussion to the two program successes. They charitably conclude that "diversion can work if something of substance and integrity is provided to the young offender" (Gendreau and Ross 1987, 357). However, discerning readers may not see a 17 percent success rate as a cause for much celebration.

The proponents of rehabilitation (see Cullen and Gilbert 1982; Gendreau and Ross 1979, 1987) often make four arguments for the continued support of correctional treatment programs: (1) treatment programs should be evaluated by outcome measures (e.g., favorable personality and attitude changes among offenders) other than recidivism, (2) more experience with treatment program implementations will result in better interventions with greater "program integrity" (or quality), (3) polls among inmates show strong support for the provision of treatment program options in prisons, and (4) treatment programs may not make participants any better, but there is no compelling evidence that these programs make offenders any worse. Imagine how absurd these same rationalizations would look if offered by a first-year law student who was passing only 17 percent of his or her courses but who wished to continue to matriculate in the law school program:

—Since I've been enrolled in law school, my friends have noticed an improvement in my personality and my attitudes.
—If you improve the quality of the law school faculty and the content of the curriculum, by next year I should be able to pass 25 percent of my courses.
—I should be permitted to stay in law school because I like the courses a lot.
—At least I haven't forgotten more than I've learned about the law since I first entered law school.

Certainly few law school professors would be persuaded by the merits of these arguments; likewise, criminal justice policymakers should not be duped by the spurious reasoning of rehabilitation advocates.

Critics have noted four reasons for the failure of rehabilitation programs in correctional settings. First, treatment interventions are seldom based on sound and explicit theoretical assumptions (Greenberg 1977; Sechrest, White, and Brown 1979). Rehabilitation programs often echo the antiquated medical model notion that criminal behavior is a disease that requires treatment for a cure. Any program that assumes at the outset that its clients are personally defective and nonrational —or, to reiterate Lewis ([1948] 1971, 306), persons "to be classed with infants [and] imbeciles"— could hardly be expected to inspire much in the way of accountable and rational behavior among participants. Quite simply, prison officials must first grant that inmates are rational and responsible actors before they can expect inmates to behave in a rational and responsible fashion. Other rehabilitation programs appear to be almost entirely atheoretical—based on "conventional wisdoms" (Sechrest, White, and Brown 1979) similar to those offered by one's grandparents or "hit-or-miss efforts" (Greenberg

1977) that drift along aimlessly according to whatever treatment style is currently fashionable. As Greenberg (1977, 141) observes: "Where the theoretical assumptions of [treatment] programs are made explicit, they tend to border on the preposterous. More often they never are made explicit, [so] we should be little surprised [when these] efforts fail."

A number of critics have noted that inadequacies in the research designs of the evaluation studies conducted to assess the effectiveness of treatment programs contribute to the failure of rehabilitation (Greenberg 1977; Lipton, Martinson, and Wilks 1975; Martinson 1974; Sechrest, White, and Brown 1979; Wilkins 1969; Wright and Dixon 1977). Small sample sizes, the failure to use control groups (which permit comparisons between those who receive program treatments and nonparticipants), nonrandom assignment of subjects to experimental and control groups, the choice of noncomparable outcome measures (e.g., recidivism rates versus educational achievement), and the use of different follow-up time periods (e.g., six months, one year, two years, or longer) to judge program effectiveness are problems that plague much of the evaluation research on prison treatment programs. For example, nonrandom assignment of subjects to experimental and control groups usually means that better-risk offenders receive the experimental treatments (e.g., in comparisons of the effectiveness of the sentences of probation versus imprisonment, nonrandomization results in lower-risk offenders receiving probation, while tougher criminals are sent to prison). Such selectivity factors can seriously bias the findings of evaluation studies. Poor research designs cause treatments that really work to be judged ineffective and (more likely) treatments that really don't work to be judged effective, producing still more confusion and doubt in the rehabilitation literature.

Both the skeptics (Sechrest, White, and Brown 1979) and believers (Gendreau and Ross 1979, 1987; Quay 1977) in rehabilitation agree that one factor that undoubtedly leads to the failure of treatment programs is low program integrity. Administered treatments frequently are of poor quality—those charged with implementing programs are often inadequately trained, and the treatment interventions are sometimes insufficient in duration and intensity. Herbert Quay (1977) correctly notes, for example, that the group counseling treatment programs in the California Men's Colony—East correctional facility—evaluated by the Kassebaum, Ward, and Wilner study (1971)—lacked strong integrity: many of the group leaders had little or no training in counseling techniques, and counseling sessions typically lasted only for an hour or two each week. Although rehabilitation proponents often contend that programs with stronger integrity will produce more favorable results, they offer no empirical evidence to support these arguments.

Finally, it is possible that the amenability of offenders to different treatments may play some role in the effectiveness of rehabilitation programs (see Andrews et al. 1990a, b; Glaser 1975; Hood and Sparks 1970; Lerman 1975; Palmer 1975; Sechrest, White, and Brown 1979; Wilkins 1969). For treatment programs to succeed, Ted Palmer (1975, 150 [italics deleted]) contends that correctional officials must ask, "Which methods work best for which types of offenders and under what conditions or in what types of settings?" Treatment regimens (e.g., vocational training programs involving instruction in auto mechanics or furniture repair) that seem to show some promise when implemented among lower class street criminals will be ill-suited to well-educated, white-collar offenders. Similarly, one would predict that rehabilitation programs that work for juvenile offenders might fail miserably if implemented among adults.

Despite the claims of Andrews et al. (1990a, b), though, it appears that correctional officials to date have had little success in tailoring specific rehabilitation programs to meet the needs of particular types of offenders (see Hood and Sparks 1970; Lerman 1975). Moreover, it is doubtful that most prisons have sufficient resources to match treatment programs to the specific needs of most offenders. As Sechrest, White, and Brown (1979, 45–46 [italics deleted]) caution:

Even if it could be demonstrated that rehabilitation could work if amenable offenders were offered appropriate treatments by matched [correctional?] workers in environments conducive to producing maximal effects, is it likely that most correctional institutions or agencies would have the facilities to produce the desired results? The number of permutations could become so large and unwieldy that [the] planning and control of rehabilitative efforts would prove [to be] virtually impossible.

Although some prison critics conclude that rehabilitation can never succeed inside coercive prison settings because "treatment and punishment do not mix" (Fogel 1975, 57; see also American Friends Service Committee 1971; Nagel 1973), there simply is no compelling evidence to suggest that rehabilitation programs implemented either inside *or outside* correctional institutions show much promise for reducing the recidivism rates among criminal offenders. Policymakers should consider rehabilitation strategies and the medical model as dead on arrival.

THE RETURN OF RETRIBUTION: AN AYE FOR AN EYE?

Disillusionment with rehabilitation has brought renewed interest in the ancient concept of retribution. Retributivists endorse the idea that a punishment should be commensurate to the crime; in other words, an offender "should be punished in proportion to the penalty he [*sic*] deserves for the crime. The degree of punishment should depend on the degree of the offender's desert" (Hospers 1977a, 22 [italics deleted]). Proponents of "commensurate deserts" (see von Hirsch 1976, 1985) and the so-called justice model of corrections (see Fogel 1975) have recently endorsed retribution as the only ethical and fair goal for prisons. Unfortunately for retributivists, though, it is doubtful that prisons are suitable instruments for the meting out of strictly commensurate deserts.

Retribution as a philosophy for punishment is virtually as old as the law itself. Historians of the law usually cite the Code of Hammurabi (formulated in Babylonia in 1700 B.C.) as the first set of laws premised on retribution. Although some Babylonian laws strayed from the notion of strict proportionality (Kaufmann 1977), the Code of Hammurabi recognized that most punishments should be not only commensurate but, more definitively, *identical* to crimes (establishing the principle of *lex talionis*). Because the rabbis of the Old Testament embraced this view, retribution in this form became ensconced in the Judeo-Christian tradition.

While Enlightenment philosophers abandoned the impractical idea that punishments should be identical, "mirror images" (Hospers 1977a, b) of crimes (e.g., what is an identical punishment for the fifty-year-old found guilty of child molestation?), they persisted in the belief that a just punishment should "fit" the nature of the offense (see Beccaria [1764] 1963; Hegel [1821] 1967; Kant [1787] 1933, [1797] 1964, [1797] 1965). In his influential treatise *On Crimes and Punishments*, Cesare Beccaria ([1764] 1963) sharply condemned the cruel, excessive, and unequal punishments that prevailed throughout eighteenth-century Europe. He urged reform-minded lawmakers to calibrate punishments carefully to ensure that they were proportional to the gravity of the offense. Beccaria's consternation over disproportional punishments was shared by the founding figures of the United States—the Eighth Amendment to the Constitution prohibits excessive bail and fines, along with "cruel and unusual punishments." Similarly, in his first inaugural address, Thomas Jefferson advocated "equal and exact [but clearly not identical] justice to all men [*sic*]," which for him included such Draconian measures as castration for polygamists (quoted in Kaufmann 1977, 223).

One of the most influential proponents of retribution was philosopher Immanuel Kant ([1787] 1933, [1797] 1964, [1797] 1965; see also Bedau 1977; Hospers 1977a, b; Kaufmann 1977; Murphy 1970; von Hirsch 1976). Kant argued that the citizens of a just society are under a "reciprocal obligation to limit their behavior so as not to interfere with the freedom of others" (von Hirsch 1976, 47). Crimes violate this obligation by infringing on the rights of victims; the criminal selfishly attains an unfair advantage over others by failing to exercise forbearance. For Kant, the only just way to restore equilibrium to society (and to uphold the mutual obligation of forbearance) is through the imposition of "a counterbalancing disadvantage on the violator [so that he or she] ceases to be at [an] advantage over [others]" (von Hirsch 1976, 47). Only commensurate punishments can "annul" the harm of offenses (Bedau 1977).

Modern philosophers note that retribution possesses certain distinctive features that sharply set it apart from the utilitarian social outcomes of punishment (e.g., deterrence and incapacitation). First, retribution obstinately disregards the social benefits of punishment—criminals are punished not to lower the overall crime rate or to prevent recidivism but because the punishment is their just deserts (Bedau 1977). Punishments are just only if they are commensurate to crimes, regardless of whether they produce any "good effects" for society (Hospers 1977a).

A second and related point is that retributivists reject any punishment (notably, general deterrence) that treats the offender as a *means* to accomplish other desirable social ends or benefits. Echoing Kant's categorical imperative, punishments are considered to be ethical only if they treat offenders solely as ends (Hospers 1977a, b; Lewis [1948] 1971; Rawls 1971). As Lewis ([1948] 1971, 304–305) observes: "When you punish a man [sic] in terrorem, [and] make of him an 'example' to others, you are admittedly using him as a means to an end: someone else's end. This, in itself, [is] a very wicked thing to do."

Third, retribution is an abstract rationale for punishment, which for the most part ignores the specific characteristics and needs of individual offenders and victims (Bedau 1977). The social circumstances (e.g., income, education, gender, race, and age) of offenders and victims are of no importance in calculating just deserts: the gravity of punishments is based on the seriousness of crimes, not the needs of criminals (or victims). This clearly distinguishes retribution from both rehabilitation (which considers the needs of offenders in determining treatments) and restitution (which considers the needs of the victim in estimating recompense).

Fourth, unlike utilitarian punishments, which are focused on reshaping future events (through the rehabilitation or the specific deterrence of the offender), retribution is concerned solely with undoing past wrongs (Hart 1968; Hospers 1977a, b; Kaufmann 1977; von Hirsch 1976, 1985). Predictions about the future behavior of offenders are of no concern to retributivists; punishments should be based only on the nature of the past offense. The purpose of punishment is to cancel the advantages accrued to the offender from past crimes. Once the offender is punished in kind, the moral slate is supposedly wiped clean.

Finally, modern variations of retribution (see Bedau 1977; Hart 1968; Pincoffs 1977; von Hirsch 1985) place great importance on *mens rea* (literally, the guilty mind or the criminal intent of the offender). As Hugo Bedau (1977, 62) notes, "Not only harm to the innocent but harmful intention in the offender is necessary before a person deserves to be punished; . . . the absence of the harmful intention must negate the justice of any imposed punishment." As a consequence, the mental state of the offender at the time of the offense is of great importance in the assignment of a just punishment. Retributivists acknowledge that certain aberrant mental conditions—for example, duress or compulsion (where Person *A* commits a crime only because he or she has been threatened with serious physical harm by Person *B* for not committing the offense) and insanity— along with considerations of recklessness and negligence in behavior, must be recognized by the criminal law in assessments of criminal intent (Hart 1968; von Hirsch 1985).

In recent years, retributive philosophy has enjoyed a tremendous resurgence in popularity, largely due to the formulation of the "justice model" of corrections (see Fogel 1975) and the "commensurate deserts" (or "just deserts") model of sentencing (see von Hirsch 1976, 1985). Both models reject the rehabilitative medical model assumption that prisoners are defective patients who require treatment as a cure. David Fogel (1975) and Andrew von Hirsch (1976, 1985) are harshly critical of the individualization of treatments under rehabilitation, where prison sentences are meted out on the basis of the needs and characteristics of criminals rather than the seriousness of crimes. The inequities found in rehabilitative systems— for example, indeterminate sentences and judicial and correctional discretion—lead to widespread disparities and inconsistencies in sentencing, ultimately making a travesty of justice in the processing of offenders. Not only is rehabilitation unfair, but Fogel (1975, 119) recognizes that it is an abysmal failure: "In light of the available data, it is embarrassingly obvious that we have not been able to devise effective methods of rehabilitating inmates inside the [prison] walls."

Fogel's (1975, 184) justice model is guided by the "superordinate goal" of "justice-as-fairness." Specifically, this means that prison sentences should be "fair, just, and . . . offense-related and appropriate" (Fogel 1975, 193). This requires the elimination of criminal justice discretion in the areas of sentencing, parole, and correctional administration. To accomplish these ends, Fogel (1975) calls for the enactment of flat sentences (where the conviction for particular offenses automatically results in prison sentences of predetermined, fixed lengths) and the abolition of parole. The justice model also emphasizes that prison officials must be compelled to abide by the rule of law, granting prisoners the same constitutional due process rights and protections (including timely information of the nature of accusations, the right to cross-examine witnesses, the appropriate assistance of counsel, and the right to appeal hearing decisions) accorded to free citizens.

Retributive themes are even more evident in von Hirsch's (1976, 1985) commensurate deserts model. Von Hirsch contends that offenders should be punished primarily because they deserve it and only secondarily for the purposes of accomplishing various utilitarian social benefits. Just deserts are based on one principle: "Severity of punishment should be commensurate with the seriousness of the wrong" (von Hirsch 1976, 66 [italics deleted]). He (1985, 169) elaborates: "Punishment connotes censure. Penalties should comport with the seriousness of crimes, so that the reprobation visited on the offender through his [sic] penalty fairly reflects the blameworthiness of his [sic] conduct."

For von Hirsch (1976, 1985), the seriousness of a crime is determined by two components—the extent of harm to the victim (defined as injuries either caused or risked) and the degree of culpability of the offender (or the magnitude of the offender's blame or criminal intent). In adducing appropriate punishments, both the seriousness of the current crime and the offender's previous record should be considered. Commensurate deserts necessitate the grading and ranking of the seriousness of particular crimes and the severity of particular punishments, so that just punishments can be assigned proportionately to suitable crimes. Von Hirsch's (1976, 99) most important policy recommendation involves the enactment of presumptive sentencing, where "a specific penalty [is] based on the crime's characteristic seriousness. This would be the disposition for most offenders convicted of the crime. However, the judge should be authorized—within specific limits—to depart from the presumptive sentence if he [sic] finds aggravating or mitigating circumstances." In practical terms, presumptive sentencing results in judicial guidelines that match certain categories of offenses (that are similar in their degrees of seriousness) with certain categories of punishment (that are similar in their degrees of gravity—see von Hirsch 1985).

While the use of imprisonment for the purposes of retribution appears to be a possibility in the fairly abstract proposals of Fogel and von Hirsch, devising concrete and objective "real world" prison-sentencing guidelines that approximate proportionality is an elusive goal. Two hundred years ago, utilitarian philosopher Jeremy Bentham (quoted in Hart 1968, 161) argued that the concept of proportionality in retribution was " 'more oracular than instructive' "—a conclusion that is still appropriate today. The formulation of a "scientific" system of retribution for any given criminal justice jurisdiction requires a consensus on three complex issues (see Allen 1981; Bedau 1977; Erickson and Gibbs 1979; Hart 1968; Hospers 1977a, b; Kleinig 1973; Pincoffs 1977; von Hirsch 1976, 1985): (1) the rank ordering of the seriousness of a large number of criminal offenses, (2) the rank ordering of the severity of a large number of alternative punishments, and (3) the matching of the seriousness of crimes rankings with the severity of punishments rankings. Although an impressive array of criminological studies has been devoted to each issue, numerous lingering doubts remain about the possibility of accomplishing all three.

An especially rich literature exists on the topic of seriousness of crimes rankings. The landmark study in this area is Thorsten Sellin and Marvin Wolfgang's *The Measurement of Delinquency* (1964)—a path-breaking examination of the seriousness of 141 delinquent acts (ranging from obscene telephone calls to homicide). The authors devised an ingenious technique to "convert a generally assumed qualitative factor [the seriousness of delinquent acts] to a unidimensional [ratio-scaled] quantitative measurement" (Sellin and Wolfgang 1964, 288). Four groups of respondents were compared in the study—251 sociology students enrolled in two Philadelphia-area universities, 286 police officers, and thirty-eight juvenile court judges. Statistical analyses showed that respondents in all four sample subgroups ranked the seriousness of the 141 delinquent offenses "in a similar way, without significant differences" (Sellin and Wolfgang 1964, 268—[italics deleted]). The final scaled scores of the seriousness of offenses ranged from the score of one (for several offenses, such as simple thefts of under ten dollars) to twenty-six (for criminal homicide).

Numerous seriousness of crimes studies in the United States, using a variety of different samples, have produced results similar to those of Sellin and Wolfgang (see Cullen, Link, and Polanzi 1982; Figlio 1975; Rossi et al. 1974; Wolfgang et al. 1985). For example, in 1972 Peter Rossi et al. (1974) asked 200 Baltimore residents to rank the seriousness of 140 crimes. The correlations of the rankings between various subgroups—blacks and whites, males and females, and those of different educational attainments—were consistently high, ranging from .61 to .93. Although the authors found that less-educated black males rated crimes of violence less seriously than other respondents, they nevertheless conclude that a broad consensus exists in the way that people rank offenses. A replication of the Baltimore study conducted on 105 residents in Macomb, Illinois, in 1979 again revealed a high correlation (.92) between the Baltimore and Macomb respondents, although the latter rated white-collar offenses somewhat more seriously (Cullen, Link, and Polanzi 1982). Robert Figlio (1975) similarly found high correlations (from .86 to .95) in the seriousness of crimes rankings when he compared the responses of 193 prison inmates with 524 juvenile reformatory residents and 216 university students.

To date, the most ambitious study to employ the original Sellin-Wolfgang seriousness of crimes scale is *The National Survey of Crime Severity* (Wolfgang et al. 1985). This analysis was part of the January to June 1977 National Crime Survey and involved the responses of 51,623 respondents in 30,589 households nationwide. These data enabled the authors to devise a ratio scale for 204 offenses, ranging from a score of 0.25 (for the offense of a juvenile under sixteen skipping school) to 72.1 (for an offender who plants a bomb that explodes in a public building and kills twenty people). Once again, this study showed that respondents ranked the seriousness of offenses in a similar fashion, with a few notable exceptions relating to crimes of violence—southerners, nonwhites, persons from lower income, occupational, and educational groups, and nonvictims (i.e., respondents with no recent history of crime victimization) all rated these crimes less seriously than other respondents.

A number of additional studies examine respondent rankings of either the severity of punishments (see Blumstein and Cohen 1980; Erickson and Gibbs 1979) or the seriousness of crimes and the severity of punishments considered together (see Evans and Scott 1984; Scott and Al-Thakeb 1977; Thomas, Cage, and Foster, 1976). Among the former, Maynard Erickson and Jack Gibbs (1979) devised a ratio-scaled ranking of the severity of seventeen punishments (ranging from fines of $100 to a sentence of fifteen years in prison) similar to Sellin and Wolfgang's earlier seriousness of delinquency scale. Estimates of crime severity were collected from random samples of public and police respondents in four Arizona communities during 1974 and 1976. The authors conclude that the perceived severity of offenses can be ranked and that the differences between these ranks reflect real differences in the severity of punishments. For example, a .93 correlation was found between the perceived severity of various prison sentences and the actual length of these sentences. Furthermore, the severity of punishments rankings were similar among the subgroups in the study (i.e., among police officers versus civilians and rural versus urban residents).

Alfred Blumstein and Jacqueline Cohen (1980) asked a random sample of 603 respondents from the Pittsburgh area to list their recommendations for the appropriate prison sentences for twenty-three criminal offenses (respondents were not asked to rank the seriousness of these offenses). When comparing their severity of punishments data to both Sellin and Wolfgang's (1964) and Rossi et al.'s (1974) seriousness of crimes findings, Blumstein and Cohen (1980) found high correlations (between .73 and .97) between the ranked seriousness of crimes and the ranked severity of recommended punishments, suggesting the possibility that crime serious-ness and punishment severity can be proportionately matched. Still the authors discovered some significant differences among the subgroups in their sample—male, white, less-educated, and older respondents all as-signed harsher punishments than others. Blumstein and Cohen (1980, 259 [italics deleted]) also found (1) that subgroups "agreed on the relative severity of sentences to be imposed for different offenses, but disagreed over the absolute magnitude of the sentences" and (2) that considerable variation in the responses existed *within* subgroups (between those assign-ing shorter and longer sentences).

Perhaps the first study empirically to link subgroup perceptions of the seriousness of crimes to subgroup perceptions of the severity of punish-ments was Charles Thomas, Robin Cage, and Samuel Foster (1976). The authors distributed a questionnaire to a random sample of 3,334 persons in an unidentified, large metropolitan area. Respondents were asked to rank the seriousness of seventeen offenses and to assign six categories of punishments (from small fines to executions) for all offenses. When comparing the way that various subgroups in the sample ranked the seriousness of crimes and ranked assigned punishments, the authors (1980, 116) found "a remarkable level of consensus"—for example, the correla-tions of the seriousness of crimes rankings ranged from .92 (between blacks and whites) to .99 (between those in higher-versus lower-prestige occupations). Correlations were similarly high between subgroups in the ranked assignment of the severity of punishments and in comparisons of the rankings of the seriousness of crimes with the rankings of the severity of punishments.

Two subsequent studies that also related seriousness of crimes and severity of punishments rankings are Sandra Evans and Joseph Scott (1984) and Scott and Fahad Al-Thakeb (1977). These authors examined the additional dimension of cross-cultural differences in crime and punishment rankings, by comparing samples of Ohio State University under-graduates with students enrolled in Kuwait University and with availability samples of respondents chosen from six European nations (England, Finland, Sweden, Norway, Denmark, and the Netherlands). While correlations were uniformly high when comparing the severity of punishments rankings among American, Kuwaiti, and European respondents, Kuwaitis ranked the seriousness of crimes somewhat differently than other respondents. These latter differences largely reflected the fact that Kuwaiti respondents ranked morals offenses—for example, prostitution and adultery—as much more serious than respondents in America and Europe.

Despite the findings of these studies, numerous problems remain in creating a sentencing system where punishments in reality are commensurate to crimes. First, researchers to date have failed to devise valid measures of crime seriousness that incorporate the dichotomous meanings of retribution theorists. Recall that retributivists from Kant to von Hirsch identify two separate dimensions of crime seriousness—harm (or the degree of injury to the victim) and culpability (or the degree of the criminal intent of the offender). However, most seriousness of crimes surveys fail to define the term *seriousness* when asking respondents to rank offenses (Miethe 1982). As a result, it is unclear if respondents in these studies are interpreting the word *seriousness* to mean harm or culpability, or both, or even neither (Warr 1989). To examine these separate dimensions of crime seriousness, Mark Warr (1989) asked a random sample of 336 Dallas residents in a mail survey first to rank the seriousness of thirty-one offenses (ranging from petty vandalism to multiple homicides) and then to rate these offenses by both their harmfulness and their "moral wrongfulness" (or offender culpability). When comparing the seriousness of crimes rankings with the harmfulness and wrongfulness rankings, Warr (1989) discovered that for property crimes, wrongfulness—but not harmfulness—primarily determined the crime seriousness rankings of respondents, while for public order offenses (e.g., trespassing and disturbing the peace), harmfulness—but not wrongfulness—primarily determined these rankings. Warr (1989, 810) concludes that instead of simply "combining wrongfulness and harmfulness in some manner, [most] respondents appear to attend to the [one] dominant feature of the crime—either its wrongfulness or harmfulness—in judging seriousness." Until researchers do far more to separate, measure, and weigh these two dimensions of crime seriousness, no precise interpretation of seriousness of crimes survey findings is possible.

Those retributivists who attempt to weigh culpability in sentencing considerations often take into account the previous record of the offender (see von Hirsch 1976, 1985). Here the assumption is that a greater degree of criminal intent can be attributed to repeat offenders when compared with first-time convictees. Von Hirsch (1985, 85 and 83) contends that there should be "a partial and temporal tolerance for human frailty" for the first-time convictee, because the criminal "act was out of keeping with his [sic] previous behavior." However, the consideration of repeat offenses in sentencing decisions obviously leads to disproportional sentencing (Conklin 1989)—either first offenders receive lenient sentences and repeat offenders are proportionately punished (von Hirsch's scenario), or first offenders receive proportional sentences and repeat offenders are punished in *excess* of the seriousness of their current offense.

Retributive sentencing has also been criticized for ignoring the social contexts in which crimes and punishments occur (Cullen et al. 1985; Hospers 1977a, b; Kaufmann 1977). Francis Cullen et al. (1985, 112) note that seriousness of crimes rankings cannot account for the "aggravating and mitigating circumstances that inevitably surround illegal conduct in everyday life." As an example of mitigating circumstances, Wolfgang's (1958) analysis of Philadelphia police records shows that homicides are often victim-precipitated. In these cases, the murder victim "was the first [person] to show and use a deadly weapon, to strike a blow in an altercation—in short, the first to commence the interplay of resort to physical violence" (Wolfgang 1958, 252). The classic illustration here is the "battered woman syndrome," where chronically abused wives eventually respond by killing their husbands (see McNulty 1989). Simple eye-for-an-eye calculations of commensurate deserts in homicide cases may fail to consider such mitigating circumstances.

Not only does retribution ignore the social context of the crime, but it also underestimates the important social circumstances relating to the distribution of punishments. Variations in social class and demographic factors mean that two different offenders guilty of similar crimes may experience the severity of supposedly identical punishments in very dissimilar ways (Braithwaite and Pettit 1990; Kaufmann 1977). As Walter Kaufmann (1977, 229) argues:

The deceptive charm of fines and prison terms is that both permit neat quantification and measurement and thus go well with the old conceit that desert is calculable. Actually, of course, it is common knowledge among those who have reflected on these matters that a $20 fine is not the same for a rich man and a poor man, nor is the same prison sentence for two people necessarily the same punishment.

Certainly a sixty-five–year-old corporate executive would perceive a ten-year prison sentence much differently than a twenty-year-old unemployed construction worker. Retributivists claim to favor "justice," yet they ironically care little about how offenders actually perceive punishments.

Critics of retribution also note that calculations of commensurate deserts often vary from group to group, across time and place (Kaufmann 1977; Rose 1966). As Kaufmann (1977, 228) observes, "What one generation considers simple justice often strikes the next generation as simply outrageous." Although researchers studying seriousness of crimes and severity of punishments rankings have discovered that different subgroups in the United States rank crimes and punishments in fairly similar ways, some important differences still exist. Specifically, Wolfgang et al.'s (1985) study shows that persons from different regional, racial, and social class backgrounds vary in the seriousness that they attribute to crimes of violence. Other research suggests that post-Watergate concerns over white-collar crime contributed to an increase in the perceived severity of these offenses during the 1970s (Cullen, Link, and Polanzi 1982). Furthermore, severity of punishments research shows that gender, age, racial, and educational factors affect the harshness of the punishments that respondents believe should be assigned to particular crimes (Blumstein and Cohen 1980).

Perhaps the most devastating criticism of attempts by researchers to rank the seriousness of crimes and the severity of punishments is Terance Miethe's (1982) assertion that the purported consensus found among respondents on these rankings is a methodological artifact. Miethe (1982) correctly notes that the majority of these studies report high correlations in the rankings *between* subgroups (e.g., between blacks and whites or between men and women), while ignoring the variation in seriousness of crimes or severity of punishments rankings *within* subgroups, for particular crimes and punishments. Measures of dispersion—for example, analysis of variance—are seldom used by these researchers to examine the variations (or ranges) in the rankings among respondents. In seriousness of crimes research, Miethe contends that these ranges are particularly wide for less serious offenses, especially for morals crimes, like prostitution and drug offenses. The calculation of simple means and correlation coefficients on these data conceals the great diversity in seriousness of crimes rankings among respondents, producing the illusion of consensus on rankings where little really exists.

A study by Cullen et al. (1985) confirms the accuracy of Miethe's (1982) criticism. These authors reanalyzed the data from Cullen, Bruce Link, and

Craig Polanzi's (1982) study of the 105 respondents from Macomb, Illinois, who ranked the seriousness of 140 crimes. By relying on correlation coefficients calculated on comparisons of different subgroups within their study and comparisons of their aggregated data with earlier studies, Cullen, Link, and Polanzi (1982) originally concluded that widespread consensus exists in crime seriousness rankings. However, the reanalysis of these data using analysis of variance techniques (a statistical procedure that summarizes the dispersion of respondent scores) revealed *low agreement* on seriousness of crime rankings for many offenses, especially morals offenses and white-collar crimes. The reanalysis also indicated significant sociodemographic differences (between respondents from various educational and community-of-origin backgrounds) in the rankings of crime seriousness. Like Miethe, Cullen et al. (1985) argue that earlier studies exaggerate the consensus in seriousness of crimes rankings by concentrating on comparisons between various subgroups of respondents, to the exclusion of the analysis of the ranges of different rankings within subgroups for certain types of offenses.

Miethe's criticisms (1982) and Cullen et al.'s (1985) and Warr's (1989) empirical findings cast much doubt on the ability of researchers to rank order the seriousness of crimes and the severity of punishments and to match the two rankings into presumptive sentencing guidelines. Given the current state of empirical research on seriousness of crimes and severity of punishments rankings, Cullen et al. (1985, 112) reasonably conclude that it is "premature to use [these] data as a basis for policy decisions." The criticisms of retribution indicate that a "scientific" system of commensurate deserts—where the severity of punishments is neatly calculated to "fit" the seriousness of crimes—remains unattainable. For this reason, it is difficult to justify the use of imprisonment for the social outcome of retribution.

PUNISHMENTS AND SOCIAL SOLIDARITY: DOES CRIME BRING US TOGETHER OR TEAR US APART?

One of the more imaginative utilitarian outcomes that some sociologists relate to imprisonment is the idea that crimes and punishments promote social solidarity (see Garland 1990). This argument originated in two of Émile Durkheim's most celebrated works—*The Division of Labor in Society* ([1893] 1964) and *The Rules of Sociological Method* ([1895] 1982). Durkheim ([1893] 1964) contends that crime is an affront to the "collective conscience"—or the shared and fundamental morality—that binds societies together. By offending the sacred collective conscience, crimes draw together law-abiding citizens in a spirit of consensual outrage and indignation. As a result, crimes and punishments ironically benefit societies by reinforcing the bonds of social solidarity; crime "creates a climate in which the private sentiments of many separate persons are fused together into a common sense of morality" (Erikson 1966, 4).

In a frequently quoted passage from *The Division of Labor in Society*, Durkheim ([1893] 1964, 102) argues that "crime brings together upright consciences and concentrates them. We have only to notice what happens, particularly in a small town, when some moral scandal has been committed. [People] stop each other on the street, they visit each other, they seek to come together to talk of the event and to wax indignant in common." He goes on (([1893] 1964, 108) to characterize the rehabilitative and deterrent social outcomes of punishment as "doubtful"; in contrast, the "true function [of punishment] is to maintain social cohesion intact, while maintaining [the] vitality" of the collective conscience. Durkheim ([1895] 1982, 67) concludes that crime and punishment not only are inevitable but also are necessary, useful, and "integral part[s] of all healthy societies."

Numerous other important sociological theorists concur that social conflicts in general (Coser 1956; Wolff 1950) and deviant behavior and its punishment in particular (Erikson 1966; Garfinkel 1956) often contribute to solidarity by clearly demarcating the social boundaries between conformist in-groups and nonconformist out-groups. George Simmel (see Wolff 1950) and Lewis Coser (1956) contend that conflict with out-groups helps both to clarify group norms and to strengthen social bonds within in-groups. Harold Garfinkel (1956) specifically depicts criminal trials as "degradation ceremonies" or "secular" forms of "communion" that reinforce group solidarity through the stigmatization of convicted offenders. Building on these views, Kai Erikson (1966) argues that deviance and punishment produce benefits for society by sharpening the normative boundaries between the conformist "we" and the nonconformist "they." By defining which norms, values, and behaviors are "outside the margins of the group," Erikson (1966, 11) contends that deviant "theys" assist in guarding "the cultural integrity of the [larger] community." The continual conflict between deviants who test normative boundaries and the rest of us who defend these boundaries assists in the socialization process by training new generations "about the contours of the [social] world [that] they are inheriting" (Erikson, 1966, 13). Erikson (1966, 13) concludes that "deviant forms of behavior, by marking the outer edges of group life, give the inner structure its special character and thus supply the framework within which the people of the group develop an orderly sense of their own cultural identity."

In an attempt to test these arguments empirically, Erikson (1966) examines three "crime waves"—the Antinomian controversy of 1636 to 1638, the Quaker invasion of 1656 to 1665, and the Salem witch trials of 1692—that emerged among the Puritans in the Massachusetts Bay Colony in the seventeenth century. He asserts that all three heresies set into motion normative "boundary threats" and "crises" that helped to reaffirm the unique religious spirit of the Puritan community. By confronting each heresy, the Puritans redefined and rediscovered their own distinctive beliefs and traditions.

Some prominent sociologists dispute these views. For example, the so-called Chicago school of criminology—promulgated by such University of Chicago sociologists as Clifford Shaw, Henry McKay, Frederick Zorbaugh, and Leonard Cottrell in the 1920s through the 1940s—depicts crime and punishment as products of social disorganization that contribute little to the solidarity of the larger society. Those in the Chicago school (see Shaw et al. 1929; Shaw and McKay 1942) argued that high rates of urbanization, industrialization, immigration, and migration in modern societies lead to impersonality, anonymity, the dissolution of stable patterns of norms and values, and the breakdown of informal social controls (exercised by families, churches, and neighborhoods). Social disorganization results in higher rates of crime and delinquency and the creation of delinquent and criminal norms and values that replace the now ineffective traditional normative system. Far from promoting social solidarity among law-abiding in-groups, the cultural transmission of delinquent/criminal norms and values becomes an additional cause of social disorganization in modern societies.

Several contemporary authors largely concur with the interpretations of Chicago school criminologists (see Bartollas 1990; Bartollas and Dinitz 1989; Conklin 1975; Lewis and Salem 1986; Tittle 1980b). For example, Clemens Bartollas and Simon Dinitz (1989) see crime as a symptom of the breakdown in social order that occurs when societies undergo modernization. They (1989, 185) distinguish between orderly "folk" societies, which are characterized by homogeneity, tradition, strong kinship relations, teamwork, and high morale, versus "industrialized and urbanized societies, [which] have almost completely the opposite characteristics." Far from promoting social solidarity, Bartollas and Dinitz (1989, 187) contend that there "is no doubt that hard-core [street] criminals are destroying the quality of life and disrupting urban communities." They add that the preferred method for processing these offenders in the United

States today is to remove them from society through incapacitation—an "out of sight, out of mind" form of punishment that can hardly be expected to strengthen and to revitalize the collective conscience.

Recent studies appear to favor the argument that crimes and punishments tear us apart more than they bring us together (see Conklin 1975; Lewis and Salem 1986; Tittle 1980b). In an important analysis of the impact of crime on society, John Conklin (1975) argues that crimes seldom promote social solidarity. Instead, he (1975, 99) contends that the fear of crime contributes to social disorder by promoting interpersonal suspicion, "insecurity, distrust, and a negative view of the community." Conklin uses a variety of empirical indicators—ranging from an examination of journalistic sources to his own study of the fear of crime among the residents of two Boston neighborhoods—to reach this conclusion.

One of the more interesting journalistic cases that Conklin (1975) discusses is Truman Capote's famous account in *In Cold Blood* (1965) of the effect of the Clutter family killings on the citizens of the small farming town of Holcomb, Kansas. Four members of the Clutter family were savagely murdered (in execution style by shotgun blasts to their heads) in their remote farmhouse outside Holcomb early on the morning of 15 November 1959. The killers—two drifters who were strangers to the Clutters and the townspeople—remained unknown and at large for almost two months.

As Conklin (1975) notes, the residents of Holcomb and the surrounding area did not "come together" to "wax indignant" in the face of these killings (as Durkheim would predict). Instead, the murders produced strong feelings of dismay, personal fear, and interpersonal suspicion. Holcomb residents rushed to hardware stores in nearby Garden City, Kansas, to purchase guns and new locks and bolts for their doors. Capote reports that for weeks, many townspeople left all their houselights turned on overnight, slept with their clothes on, and sometimes sat up all night in fear that the killers would kill again.

The killings also turned neighbor against neighbor as rumors spread implicating various townspeople. Capote (1965, 88) writes that "this hitherto peaceful congregation of neighbors and old friends had suddenly to endure the unique experience of distrusting each other." The local police in particular became the targets for the fear and anger of Holcomb's residents: in the cafés and on the sidewalks, the police were often confronted by outraged citizens, incensed over their inability to solve the crimes. Several longtime residents even decided to move away from Holcomb in response to the terror and panic created by the killings.

Even after the killers were finally arrested, fear still gripped the community; Capote (1965, 261) reports that the townspeople continued to keep "their doors locked and their guns ready." Rumors persisted linking local residents as purported accomplices to the crime. As the pathetic backgrounds (e.g., alcoholic parents and abusive treatment in orphanages) of the accused killers came to light during their trial, the townspeople hotly debated the fairness of the eventual sentences of execution by hanging.

Based on the accounts of Capote and others, Conklin (1975, 68) reasonably hypothesizes that "crime often drives people apart by creating distrust and suspicion, even in small homogeneous communities with little history of crime." In support of this view, Charles Tittle's (1980b) 1972 self-report study of the rates of nine deviant acts (ranging in seriousness from illegal gambling to assault) committed by a random sample of 1,993 persons (age fifteen and over) in three states (Iowa, New Jersey, and Oregon) revealed an inverse relationship between the self-reported rates of past offenses and the degree of cohesion and "spirit" in the communities where respondents lived, controlling for the size of communities. Conklin's (1975) own analysis of the impact of crime on the residents of two Boston neighborhoods confirms this finding. He refers to the neighborhoods by the pseudonyms "Belleville" and "Port City"—the former is a suburban community with a low crime rate; the latter, an urban locale with considerably more crime. Conklin conducted extensive interviews, using a random sample of 266 families from the two communities. Controlling for various socioeconomic and demographic factors, he (1975, 93) discovered that a higher rate of "fear-producing [street] crimes" generated greater "feelings of insecurity, distrust of others, and dislike for one's community" in Port City than in Belleville.

In general, Conklin (1975) argues that people are more likely to respond to the fear of crime by employing "avoidance techniques" (e.g., staying home at night, avoiding answering the doorbell, and avoiding strangers on the streets) and "individual mobilizations" (e.g., purchasing deadbolt locks, guns, burglar alarms, and watchdogs and taking self-defense courses) than by pursuing "collective mobilizations" (e.g., forming neighborhood crime-watch groups or joining civilian police patrols). Conklin (1975, 185) flatly concludes that "collective response[s] to crime [are] relatively uncommon. People rarely mobilize for action to prevent crime, even when there is little cost or risk involved."

Surveys conducted by public opinion pollsters support this view: avoidance techniques are the most common coping mechanism that people use to adapt to crime (85 percent of a random sample of Americans report that they lock their doors at night), followed by individual mobilizations (20 percent of Americans claim that they own watchdogs, and 16 percent report that they own guns) and, finally, collective mobilizations (only 5 percent of Americans belong to neighborhood crime-watch groups—see Friedberg 1980; Gallup 1981; Lotz, Poole, and Regoli 1985). Conklin (1975, 105) argues that the predominance of avoidance techniques and individual mobilization *reduces* social solidarity because these coping mechanisms "harm the community at the same time that they may protect specific individuals. They erect barriers between neighbors and they generate distrust."

Dan Lewis and Greta Salem's (1986) study of the fear of crime in ten neighborhoods in three large cities (Chicago, Philadelphia, and San Francisco) also supports the argument that crime contributes more to social disorganization than to social solidarity. Using extensive fieldwork data collected from the ten communities, along with a telephone survey conducted on a random sample of 6,820 residents during the years 1976 and 1977, Lewis and Salem (1986) found that the fear of crime among respondents was inversely related to the degree of social solidarity in the neighborhoods. Specifically, the three neighborhoods where residents were the most fearful of crime also had the highest crime rates and the greatest awareness of crime victimization and scored high on numerous indicators of social disorganization (measured by a composite variable that the authors refer to as "incivility," operationally defined by the conspicuous presence of youth gangs hanging out on street corners, abandoned and/or burned-out buildings, vandalism, and public drug transactions). Lewis and Salem (1986) conclude that high crime rates, widespread fear of crime, and social disorganization coincide in certain urban neighborhoods, again supporting the argument that crime undermines social solidarity.

As the previous discussion implies, sociologists have written much more extensively on the impact of crime than the impact of punishment on social solidarity. One can reasonably assume that on occasion, the disruption to the social order caused by crime is partially restored by the act of punishment. There is no evidence to suggest, however, that punishments on balance restore *more* social solidarity than crimes initially disrupt. Although offenders certainly were being apprehended and imprisoned in the high-crime neighborhoods studied by Conklin (1975) and Lewis and Salem (1986), these punishments obviously were ineffective in eliminating the fear of crime, interpersonal distrust and suspicion, and general social disorganization caused by widespread street crime. In this regard, Capote (1965) notes that even after the Clutter family killers were convicted and executed, the residents of Holcomb, Kansas, still expressed considerable fear in living in isolated farmhouses. Despite the arguments of Durkheim ([1893] 1964, [1895] 1982) and Erikson (1966), the cumulative effect of crime and punishment apparently tears us apart more than it brings us together.

CONCLUSIONS

While it is misleading to suggest that prisons are complete failures, it would be equally misleading to imply that they are complete successes. Like all social institutions, prisons are human creations that reflect the foibles, peculiar beliefs, and deficiencies of their creators. Idealists and romantics who demand absolute perfection in social institutions certainly will find much to complain about by stepping inside the walls of modern prisons, but it is doubtful that they would find fewer problems inside America's schools, factories, or churches or even in many of their own marriages and families.

Although social institutions as human creations are inevitably imperfect, humans as a species also possess the special genius to recognize failure and to act in more rational ways to pursue success. The preponderance of empirical evidence quite simply indicates that prisons are ineffective in achieving the social outcomes of rehabilitation, retribution, and social solidarity. For correctional officials and policymakers to continue to strive toward these goals flies in the face of both research and reason.

Abandoning any large-scale social commitment to these three failed prison objectives is the first step toward implementing a rational correctional policy in the United States. But what about the effectiveness of the remaining social outcomes of punishment —general deterrence, specific deterrence, and incapacitation? If these three objectives show promise, they must reasonably become the cornerstones for the creation of sensible correctional policy. Chapters 4 and 5 turn to the consideration of the effectiveness of the remaining utilitarian outcomes of punishment.

Chapter Four

Positive Support for Prisons, I: Deterrence

Perhaps no topic in criminology during the last two decades has been more hotly debated than deterrence. The criminology literature virtually is awash in claims and counterclaims about the effectiveness of formal, state-sponsored sanctions in eliciting sufficient fear in citizens to convince them not to commit crimes. These debates have appeared in a series of "waves"—one group of scholars embracing certain theoretical assumptions and employing particular research methodologies will initially claim that deterrence works (or doesn't), only to be followed by another group of scholars (embracing different assumptions and employing different methodologies) that generates contradictory evidence. The interpretations of these waves of literature largely depend on when and where one is standing on the beach—for example, most criminologists in the 1950s probably concurred with Harry Barnes and Negley Teeters's (1951, 337) reference to the "futile contention that punishment deters from crime." The authors conclude that the deterrence doctrine "is belied by both history and logic," and add that deterrence is "simply a derived rationalization" for revenge and "a disguised living out of their own aggressive hostile impulses" for "the popular masses" (Barnes and Teeters 1951, 337-338). By the 1970s, however, many criminologists probably had shifted their opinions to conform with Charles Tittle and Alan Rowe's (1974, 461) assessment that although deterrence is not "the touchstone for explaining all human behavior," it nonetheless is an explanatory variable with "great" potential in the analysis of criminal behavior. Some criminologists have published papers on *both* sides of the debate; for example, Theodore

Chiricos and Gordon Waldo first wrote two articles critical of deterrence arguments (see Chiricos and Waldo 1970; Waldo and Chiricos 1972), then found evidence supporting the deterrence doctrine (see Anderson, Chiricos, and Waldo 1977), but most recently have returned to their earlier critical position (see Paternoster et al. 1983; Saltzman et al. 1982). Using the same data set, Donna Bishop in the same year published two articles supporting deterrence arguments (Bishop 1984a, b) and another article sharply critical of the perspective (Thomas and Bishop 1984). If Ralph Waldo Emerson (quoted in Henry 1965, 45) is correct in his remark that "a foolish consistency is the hobgoblin of little minds," then some criminologists indeed have very large minds.

Formal academic training affects where one stands on the beach as the waves of deterrence arguments crest and subsequently break. Economists—who see humans as rational actors who weigh costs and benefits, acting to minimize the former while maximizing the latter—naturally are sympathetic to the idea that legal/formal sanctions can be used to increase the costs of crime so that crime doesn't pay (see Becker 1968; Cook, 1980; Tullock 1974). In contrast, many sociologists appear to share Émile Durkheim's ([1893] 1964, 108) bias that punishment "does not serve, or else only serves quite secondarily, in correcting the culpable or in intimidating [his or her] possible followers. From this point of view its efficacy is justly doubtful and, in any case, mediocre." The consensus among sociologists seems to be that informal sanctions—rooted in the beliefs and opinions of one's family members and friends—are far more effective in achieving social control than the formal sanctions administered within the criminal justice system (see Gibbs 1975; Tittle 1980b; Tittle and Logan 1973). Finally, legal scholars concerned about the effectiveness of deterrence often adopt a more interdisciplinary approach by recognizing that both formal and informal sanctions can prevent crime (see Andenaes 1952, 1966, 1971b, 1974; Zimring and Hawkins 1971, 1973).

Despite the ebb and flow of theoretical arguments and research evidence for and against the effectiveness of punishments as deterrents, some critics of prisons have had no trouble in decisively and flatly concluding that punishments cannot deter crime (see Biles 1979; Brodt and Smith 1988; Currie 1985; Nagel 1973; Sommer 1976). On the issue of general deterrence—or the use of the threat of punishment "to convince those who are not being punished not to commit crimes" (Wright 1992, 101)—prison critics often note that different rates of imprisonment (compared across time and place) appear to have little effect on overall crime rates (Biles 1979; Brodt and Smith 1988; Currie 1985). Critics argue, for example, that throughout U.S. history, increases in imprisonment rates are often associated with increases in crime rates. In addition, critics observe that when compared with other countries, the United States not only has one of the highest rates of imprisonment (defined as the number of incarcerated persons per 100,000 population) in the world but also has the highest crime rate. Elliott Currie (1985, 58) concludes that this evidence constitutes "a substantial prima facie case that if indeed imprisonment" works as a general deterrent "in some marginal sense," it doesn't "work very well."

As I show later in this chapter, Currie, Stephen Brodt and J. Steven Smith, and other prison critics disregard much general deterrence research using aggregate data that indicate that there is a significant *inverse* relationship between imprisonment rates and crime rates (Gibbs 1986; Gibbs and Firebaugh 1990). For now, though, it is sufficient to note that one can make superficially strong cases either for or against the effectiveness of criminal justice sanctions on crime rates, using bivariate and largely anecdotal data. As evidence favoring general deterrence, for example:

The United States faced a dramatically escalating rate of bank robbery in the 1930s. The FBI chose to attack this problem by pursuing a well-publicized get-tough policy where particularly notorious bank robbers (e.g., John Dillinger, and Bonnie [Parker] and Clyde Barrow) summarily were ambushed and shot to death. The result was a *drop* in bank robbery rates from a high of 609 in 1932 to 129 in 1937 (Wright 1992, 102; see also MacDonald 1975).

On the other hand, in response to a similar dramatic increase in skyjacking incidents in the late 1960s and early 1970s, President Richard Nixon ordered a team of "skymarshals" to fly on domestic airlines, with widely publicized authorization to "shoot to kill" attempted skyjackers (Chauncey 1975). Robert Chauncey's (1975) data show that this policy, implemented late in 1970, had *no* effect on the number of domestic skyjackings—more airplanes were skyjacked after Nixon's skymarshal order (twenty-seven in 1971) than before (twenty-five in 1970). (Notably, though, the evidence suggests that other policy changes implemented both earlier and later—especially the screening with metal detectors of all passengers, luggage, and carry-on items—apparently did deter skyjacking—see Chauncey 1975.) In the final analysis, simple attempts to link punishment responses to crime rates may tell us less about the overall effectiveness of general deterrence than they tell us about the need (1) to exercise caution when drawing conclusions from bivariate studies that don't control for exogenous variables (e.g., the percent of the population in a crime-prone age group or the percent of the population that is unemployed) and (2) to consider the possibility that one punishment response that deters one type of potential offender at one time and at one place may have different effects on other types of potential offenders at other times and at other places (Wright 1992).

On the topic of specific deterrence—or the use of actual punishments "to convince those who are being punished not to commit future crimes" (Wright 1992, 101)—prison critics are equally prone to ignore complex research findings to arrive at straightforward (and erroneous) conclusions. Here the preferred tactic is to cite simple recidivism rates as evidence that offenders don't respond favorably to punishment (see Currie 1985; Nagel 1973; Sommer 1976). For example, Currie (1985) offers what he contends are "astonishing" data that show that approximately one-third to two-thirds of all inmates eventually return to prison. Robert Sommer (1976, 21) speculates that the recidivism rate is somewhere between 33 percent and 90 percent but, in a spirit of exactitude, concludes that "a recidivism rate of 50 percent seems a reasonable if not a conservative estimate." Both Currie and Sommer concur with William Nagel's (1973, 181) assessment that "obviously prisons don't deter criminals, some of whom have been in our jails a score or more times."

Simple calculations of the return rates of inmates to prison, however, tell us virtually nothing about the effectiveness of punishments as specific deterrents. For example, despite high simple recidivism rates, prisons may still exert an important "suppression effect" on crime by convincing offenders to commit *fewer* crimes after than before imprisonment (Cook 1980; Farrington 1987; Murray and Cox 1979; Wright 1992). More importantly, "simple recidivism rates offer no comparisons of offenders who are arrested and incarcerated with those who avoid apprehension" (Wright 1992, 103). As Herbert Packer (1968) observes, although it is clear that many of those who are arrested and incarcerated persist in a life of crime, it is probable that those who avoid arrest are even more likely to continue committing crimes.

Judging the effectiveness of punishments as deterrents is a complex issue about which it is difficult to reach definitive conclusions. Again, one's appraisal of the waves of deterrence literature depends in part on where one is standing on the beach at what time. I contend that there is sufficient empirical evidence, however, to conclude that criminal sanctions are moderately effective deterrents for some persons (both potential and actual offenders) at some places at some times. As others have concluded, it is clear that legal/formal "sanctions apparently have some deterrent effect under some circumstances" (Tittle and Logan 1973, 385) or that in "some situations some individuals are deterred from some crimes by some punishments" (Gibbs 1975, 11). Part of the purpose of chapter 4 is to specify under what circumstances deterrence appears to work. Later in chapter 6, I show that there is virtually *no* evidence to suggest that punishments routinely "backfire" as specific deterrents by making some offenders worse.

DETERRENCE: COMPLEX CONCEPTUALIZATIONS AND METHODOLOGICAL COMPLICATIONS

Modern interest in deterrence as a utilitarian social outcome of punishment can be traced historically to the works of Cesare Beccaria ([1764] 1963) and Jeremy Bentham ([1789] 1970, [1802] 1931, [1811] 1930, [1843] 1962). Both scholars believed that humans are by nature essentially "self-seeking" (Beccaria) or "hedonistic" (Bentham); as a result, human actions are for the most part rational or oriented around the desire to maximize pleasure and minimize pain. Beccaria and Bentham thought that much pleasure can be derived from criminal behavior, so that state-administered formal sanctions are necessary to convince humans that crime is on balance more painful than pleasurable. In Bentham's ([1843] 1962, 399) words: "The profit of the crime is the force which urges a man [*sic*] to delinquency; the pain of punishment is the force employed to restrain him [*sic*] from it. If the first of these forces be the greater the crime will be committed; if the second, the crime will not be committed." In general, Beccaria and Bentham argued that laws and punishments deter crime by instilling "fear," "intimidation," and/or "terror" in humans.

In their writings, Beccaria and Bentham anticipated some of the pivotal concepts that inform modern research and debate on deterrence. Both recognized that punishments serve as specific and general deterrents; Beccaria ([1764] 1963, 42), for example, remarks that the purpose of punishment "can only be to prevent the criminal from inflicting new injuries on its [the nation's] citizens and to deter others from similar acts." Furthermore, both argued that the effectiveness of punishments as deterrents depends on three properties: *celerity* (the promptness of the application of punishments), *certainty* (the probability that an offender will be apprehended and punished), and *severity* (the painfulness of the punishment to the offender). As Jack Gibbs (1975, 15) notes, the central axiom of deterrence theory can be traced to Beccaria and Bentham: "The greater the celerity, certainty, and severity of punishment for a type of crime, the more are individuals deterred from that type of crime."

Both Beccaria and Bentham also speculated about the relative importance of the celerity, certainty, and severity of punishments on the effectiveness of deterrence, another favorite pastime of modern deterrence theorists. For example, Beccaria ([1764] 1963, 58) reasoned that the certainty of punishments has a more lasting impression on actual and potential offenders than punishment severity, because "even the least evils, when they are certain, always terrify men's [sic] minds." Although he also in principle favored certain over severe punishments, Bentham ([1811] 1930) believed that certainty and severity complement each other; that is, less certain punishments must be more severe to achieve the goal of deterrence.

Several features relating to the celerity, certainty, and severity of punishments are of interest to modern deterrence theorists. First, contemporary theorists concur that Beccaria and Bentham drastically overestimated the importance of the celerity of punishments in deterring crime (Gibbs 1975; Zimring and Hawkins 1973). There simply is no plausible reason punishments must be prompt to achieve general deterrent benefits (Gibbs 1975; Zimring and Hawkins 1973). As Gibbs (1975, 9) asks, "If someone reads an account of an execution, why would he or she be deterred more if the crime took place six weeks rather than one [or even ten] year[s] previously?" Celerity also probably plays little role in the effectiveness of punishments as specific deterrents. While aversive conditioning studies in psychology show that prompt punishments are more effective in extinguishing undesirable behaviors than postponed punishments (see Bartol 1991), these findings relate to punishment delays of seconds and minutes, not weeks, months, and years (Gibbs 1975). For most criminals, once several days have elapsed after they commit their offenses, whatever specific deterrence benefits could be attained through "prompt" punishments are already lost. Unless some means can be devised to follow offenses with instantaneous arrests, trials, convictions, and punishments— a clear impossibility in criminal justice systems that strive to protect due process and the rights of offenders—celerity probably is of little concern to those who wish to deter future offending. Thus, although there are virtually no studies of the impact of the celerity of punishments on the effectiveness of deterrence (Selke 1983), this is not a serious omission in the research literature.

On the topics of the certainty and the severity of punishments, some contemporary theorists claim that "threshold effects" may exist that influence the effectiveness of punishments as deterrents. For the certainty of punishments, it is possible that particular levels of arrest probability (say, 20, 30, or 40 percent) must be achieved in the community for deterrence to be effective (Tittle 1980b; Tittle and Rowe 1974). For the severity of punishments, threshold effects exist if more severe types of punishment (e.g., imprisonment) deter crimes that cannot be deterred by less severe types of punishment (e.g., probation—Cook 1980).

Finally, the nature of the relationship between the certainty and the severity of punishments and deterrence has generated much interest among modern theorists and researchers (Bailey and Lott 1976; Tittle 1969a, 1980b). Two models depicting this relationship have been suggested by deterrence theorists: an "independent effects" model:

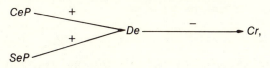

and an "interactive effects" model:

$$CeP \xleftarrow{\quad + \quad (-) \quad} SeP \xrightarrow{\quad + \quad} De \xrightarrow{\quad - \quad} Cr,$$

where *CeP* is the certainty of punishments, *SeP* is the severity of punishments, *De* refers to deterrence, *Cr* is the symbol for the criminal acts of individuals or the crime rates of groups, "+" denotes a direct relationship, and "−" denotes an inverse relationship. The independent effects model recognizes that the certainty of punishments may deter crime, even if the severity of punishments has no deterrent effect (or vice versa). The interactive effects model predicts that changes in the certainty of punishments will often result in changes in the severity of punishments (or vice versa), which will in turn alter the effectiveness of deterrence. An example of a direct interactive effect is the argument that the severity of punishments may be inversely related to crime rates only when arrest probabilities are high (Bailey and Lott 1976; Tittle 1980b). An example of an inverse interactive effect is the observation that legislation providing for extremely severe punishments for particular offenses may ironically reduce the certainty of arrest and punishment, because police, prosecutors, and juries become reluctant to apprehend, prosecute, and convict offenders who are likely to receive excessively harsh sentences (Andenaes 1974; Zimring and Hawkins 1971, 1973).

Numerous other issues in deterrence less anticipated by Beccaria and Bentham interest modern criminologists. Chief among these is the relationship between state-administered *legal/formal sanctions* (e.g., arrest, fines, and imprisonment) and various *informal sanctions/extralegal factors* (ranging from the strength of one's moral commitment to the law to the condemnation of one's own family members and friends for committing deviance) in deterring crime (see Andenaes 1952, 1966, 1971b, 1974; Gibbs 1975; Grasmick and Bursik 1990; Hawkins 1971; Tittle 1980b; Williams and Hawkins 1986; Zimring and Hawkins 1971, 1973). Again, independent effects and interactive effects models have been proposed by deterrence theorists to describe these relationships. For the independent effects model,

for the interactive effects model,

$$L/Fos \xrightarrow{\quad + \quad} InS/ExF \xrightarrow{\quad + \quad} De \xrightarrow{\quad - \quad} Cr,$$

where L/FoS refers to the influence of legal/formal sanctions, and Ins/ExF denotes the effects of informal sanctions/extralegal factors (the other symbols remain the same as in the certainty/severity of punishments models).

One example of the interactive effects among legal/formal sanctions, extralegal factors, and deterrence is the phenomenon known as "habituation" (see Andenaes 1952, 1966, 1971b, 1974; Gibbs 1975; Hawkins 1971; Zimring and Hawkins 1973). Andenaes (1952, 1966, 1971b, 1974) argues that the fear of legal/formal sanctions over time can lead to the inculcation of both conscious and unconscious moral inhibitions, so that law-abiding behavior becomes a matter of habit (as an extralegal factor). For example, a teenage driver who obeys speed limits because of the fear of traffic citations and the loss of a license often matures into a middle-age driver who obeys speed limits because of habit. Franklin Zimring and Gordon Hawkins (1973, 85-86) conclude that "the habituative effect of the law is a major factor in legal social control. . . . Repeated observation of a rule which may initially be conscious and deliberate can induce an habitual disposition and ultimately automatic compliance."

While most sociologists seem to favor the independent effects model in the analysis of the impact of legal/formal sanctions and informal sanctions/extralegal factors on deterrence (see Gibbs 1975; Grasmick and Bursik 1990; Tittle 1980b), Kirk Williams and Richard Hawkins (1986) have recently drawn on the earlier contributions of legal scholars (e.g., Andenaes 1952, 1966, 1971b, 1974; Zimring and Hawkins 1971, 1973) to make a strong theoretical case for the interactive effects model. Williams and Hawkins (1986) argue that the threat of legal/formal sanctions *conditions* informal sanctions/extralegal factors by increasing one's moral commitment to the law (an extralegal factor) and by triggering the social condemnation of family and friends following an arrest and imprisonment (an informal sanction). They specifically identify three extralegal/informal "costs" that they contend are largely an *outcome* of legal/formal sanctions:

(1) *stigmatization costs* (arrest and imprisonment result in the social degradation of the offender and the loss of community and interpersonal respect), (2) *attachment costs* (relationships with one's family and friends may be strained or severed by an arrest and imprisonment), and (3) *commitment costs* (one's past accomplishments and future goals relating to education, employment, and marriage are threatened by arrest and imprisonment—Williams and Hawkins 1986). Because they conceptually misspecify stigmatization, attachment, and commitment costs as *independent* of legal/formal sanctions, Williams and Hawkins (1986) contend that many deterrence theorists (including Gibbs 1975; Tittle 1980b) underestimate the effectiveness of arrest and imprisonment as deterrents.

Theorists who largely assume the independent effects of legal/formal sanctions and informal sanctions/extralegal factors on deterrence often prematurely devalue the importance of arrest and punishment in preventing crime (see Gibbs 1975; Tittle 1980b). Although recognizing that arrest can sometimes cause stigmatization, Gibbs (1975, 85) nonetheless argues that the "fear of stigmatization is analytically distinct from and in addition to whatever fear one may have of legal punishment." He concludes that the effects of legal/formal sanctions on stigmatization (and ultimately deterrence) are "problematical." Tittle (1980b, 9-10) flatly asserts that "sanctions threatened by friends, relatives, or a personally relevant collectivity are likely to be more effective than those that are imposed by a court of law," without adequately recognizing that the former are often an outcome of the latter. Future research on deterrence will need to specify more clearly the causal relationships between legal/formal sanctions and informal sanctions/extralegal factors.

Another crucial conceptual distinction made by modern deterrence theorists and researchers centers around the difference between *actual* (or *objective*) deterrence effects versus *perceptual* (or *subjective*) deterrence effects (Chiricos and Waldo 1970; Geerken and Gove 1975; Gibbs 1975; Jensen 1969; Tittle 1980b; Waldo and Chiricos 1972; Zimring and Hawkins 1971, 1973). Actual deterrence is an outcome of one's *real* probabilities of experiencing prompt, certain, and/or severe punishments at the hands of criminal justice officials; perceptual deterrence refers to one's *subjective estimation* of the likelihood of experiencing prompt, certain, and/or severe punishments. Those concerned about the distinction between actual and perceptual deterrence have written mostly about the certainty of punishments. Actual certainty effects are determined by the real probabilities of arrest and imprisonment, measured by either police clearance rates or statewide imprisonment rates. Perceptual certainty refers to one's subjective estimations of the likelihood of arrest and/or imprisonment for committing various offenses. The consensus among most criminologists who write on deterrence is that the perceptual certainty effects of arrest and punishment (1) often exercise independent effects on deterrence, apart from the effects of actual certainty (Geerken and Gove 1975; Jensen 1969; Tittle 1980b; Zimring and Hawkins 1973), and (2) may be more important in deterring crime than actual certainty effects (Chiricos and Waldo 1970; Geerken and Gove 1975; Gibbs 1975; Tittle 1980b; Waldo and Chiricos 1972; Zimring and Hawkins 1971, 1973). Given the low objective likelihood that most reported crimes (excluding murder, rape, and assault) will be cleared through an arrest, it probably is fortunate that most people are more deterred by perceptual than actual certainty.

The theoretical distinction between actual and perceptual deterrence also necessitates the use of different research methods and analytical techniques to measure the effectiveness of deterrence on crime (Chiricos and Waldo 1970; Gibbs 1975; Tittle 1980b; Waldo and Chiricos 1972). Researchers concerned with actual deterrence effects (see Gibbs 1968; Tittle 1969a) use official, aggregate data, measuring punishment effects (as the independent variable) through police clearance rates or regional imprisonment rates, and crime rates (as the dependent variable) primarily through an analysis of FBI *Uniform Crime Reports* index crimes. In contrast, researchers concerned with perceptual deterrence effects (see Bailey and Lott 1976; Waldo and Chiricos 1972) typically administer self-report surveys to respondents to discern individual estimations of the likelihood of arrest and punishment (as the independent variable) and information about one's past deviant behavior (as the dependent variable). Until recently, aggregate-level studies of actual deterrent effects have used large geographical areas (typically states) as the unit of analysis. Consequently, actual deterrence studies offer less insight into the particular types of offenders and offenses that may be susceptible to deterrent effects than perceptual deterrence studies, where the unit of analysis is the individual.

Still another conceptual distinction of some importance in contemporary discussions of deterrence is the difference between *absolute deterrence* and *marginal deterrence* (Cook 1980; Gibbs 1975; Tittle 1980b; Tittle and Logan 1973; Zimring and Hawkins 1973). Absolute deterrence refers to the crime reduction benefits achieved through the administration of a particular type of punishment when compared with the use of no punishment; marginal deterrence refers to the variable effects on crime rates of the use of punishments of different severities. As Gibbs (1975) notes, researchers who study absolute versus marginal deterrence ask very different questions about the effectiveness of punishments. For absolute deterrence, the research question is, How much does a given punishment deter crime compared with no punishment whatsoever? For marginal deterrence, one asks, How much more does punishment *A* (a more severe punishment) deter crime than punishment *B* (a less severe punishment)? Confusion about the difference between absolute and marginal deterrence marred much early research on the effectiveness of punishments.

Deterrence theorists and researchers also distinguish between *total* (also called *absolute*) deterrence effects and *partial* (or *restrictive*) deterrence effects (Cook 1980; Gibbs 1975; Tittle 1980b; Zimring and Hawkins 1973). Total deterrence occurs when the threat of punishments persuades an individual to forgo committing an offense entirely; partial deterrence occurs when punishments convince offenders to curtail the frequency or seriousness of their offenses. For example, total deterrence is achieved for drunk driving if the threat of punishments (e.g., loss of one's license or jail) convinces the prospective offender *never* to drink and drive; partial deterrence would mean that the threat of punishments persuades the offender to drink and drive less often and/or to consume less alcohol before driving. As noted at the outset of this chapter, although punishments sometimes may fail to achieve total deterrence, they can still prevent much crime (through partial deterrence) by suppressing the frequency and seriousness of offenses (Cook 1980; Farrington 1987; Murray and Cox 1979).

Three relatively new concepts in the deterrence literature that are important in evaluating the effectiveness of changes in criminal justice policies and procedures are *initial deterrence, residual deterrence,* and *deterrence decay* (Sherman 1990). Initial deterrence refers to the short-term effects on the crime rate of some "crackdown" or "get-tough" policy on crime pursued by criminal justice officials; often, initial deterrence effects are measured while the crackdown is still in progress. Residual deterrence refers to the long-term effects of crackdowns on crime rates, usually measured after the crackdown policies have been terminated. Deterrence decay is the gradual decline in the immediate effectiveness of some get-tough policy on the crime rate after the policy has been enforced for some time.

Finally, deterrence theorists and researchers express considerable interest in the *contingent* (or variable) *effects* of punishments on different types of offenses and offenders (see Andenaes 1966, 1971a, 1974; Chambliss 1967; Clarke and Cornish 1985; Cook 1980; Cornish and Clarke 1986, 1987; Geerken and Gove 1975; Gibbs 1975; Richards and Tittle 1981, 1982; Tittle 1980b; Zimring and Hawkins 1973). In particular, Johannes Andenaes (1966, 1971a, 1974) speculates extensively about the relative effectiveness of deterrent threats for different types of offenses. He (1971a,

538) reasons: "Common sense tells us that the threat of punishment does not play the same role in offenses as different as murder, rape, tax evasion, shoplifting and illegal parking." In rating the deterrability of different offenses, Andenaes (1966, 1971a, 1974) places much importance on whether offenses are (1) rational (i.e., planned or oriented toward economic gain) or emotional (i.e., impulsive or based on some "overwhelming motivating power") and (2) *mala in se* (wrong because they are intrinsically immoral) or *mala prohibita* (wrong only because the law says they are wrong). For *mala in se* offenses (e.g., murder), Andenaes (1966) believes that punishment threats are less effective as deterrents, because even without the force of law, strong moral prohibitions discourage these acts. However, for *mala prohibita* offenses (e.g., illegal parking), he argues that punishment threats are far more important, precisely because "the law stands alone" (i.e., no moral prohibitions encourage forbearance). On the distinction between rational versus emotional offenses, Andenaes (1974) maintains that instances of the former (e.g., tax evasion) are more deterrable than instances of the latter (e.g., rape).

In a related attempt to classify crimes by their deterrability, William Chambliss (1967) distinguishes (1) instrumental offenses (or crimes that are a means to achieve some other goal) from expressive offenses (crimes committed for their own sake, because they are pleasurable in and of themselves) and (2) offenders who are highly committed to crime as a way of life from offenders with low commitments to crime. He hypothesizes that (1) instrumental-low commitment offenses (e.g., parking violations) are most susceptible to deterrence via punishments, (2) expressive-high commitment offenses (e.g., narcotics addiction) are least susceptible to deterrence via punishments, and (3) expressive-low commitment offenses (e.g., most murders) and instrumental-high commitment offenses (e.g., professional theft) occupy a middle range of deterrability.

Much conjecture and some research have also been devoted to the contingent impact of certain sociodemographic variables (e.g., gender, social class, age, and race) on the deterrability of potential or actual offenders (Geerken and Gove 1975; Richards and Tittle 1981, 1982; Tittle 1980b; Zimring and Hawkins 1973). For example, Pamela Richards and Tittle (1981) and Tittle (1980b) argue that because women are more closely supervised by informal social controls (family and friends) than men, their morality tends to be more conventional and conservative. Consequently, women should perceive a higher certainty of punishment risk from formal and informal sanctions than men. Also, because higher-status persons appear to have more to lose (in terms of their reputations and occupations) than lower-status persons in the event of arrest, numerous writers (Geerken and Gove 1975; Richards and Tittle 1982; Tittle 1980b; Zimring and Hawkins 1973) contend that social class should be directly related to deterrability.

One additional contingent factor relating to differences among offenders is the varying effectiveness of deterrence due to the *positioning* of crimes in one's offending "career"—that is, are the offenses the initial deviant acts of novices or the subsequent crimes of more seasoned, chronic offenders? It is likely that deterrence has different effects at different points in an offender's career (see Brennan and Mednick 1991; Geerken and Gove 1975; Smith and Gartin 1989; Tittle 1980b; Tracy, Wolfgang, and Figlio 1990). In considering the positioning of crimes, most writers (Brennan and Mednick 1991; Smith and Gartin 1989; Tittle 1980b; Tracy, Wolfgang, and Figlio 1990) argue that initial offenses are more deterrable by the threat of punishment than subsequent offenses, mostly because initial offenders (1) have stronger stakes in conformity (based on their good community reputations and attachments to family and friends) and (2) perceive a greater certainty of arrest and punishment for committing crime. Michael Geerken and Walter Gove (1975), however, contend that seasoned offenders who have already experienced arrest and punishment may be more deterrable than novices, primarily because the former have firsthand experience with the certainty of punishment.

The analysis of the contingent effects of offense and offender characteristics in deterrence research is strongly recommended by modern rational choice theory (Clarke and Cornish 1985; Cornish and Clarke 1986, 1987; Wilson 1985; Wilson and Herrnstein 1985). As noted in chapter 2, rational choice theory and deterrence arguments closely parallel one another—both depict prospective offenders as decision makers who first weigh the costs and benefits of their actions and then act in ways to minimize costs and maximize benefits. Contemporary rational choice theorists, however, caution that offender rationality is bounded (or limited) by such genetic factors as impulsiveness and low intelligence (Wilson and Herrnstein 1985) and such social factors as constraints on time and access to relevant information (Cornish and Clarke 1986, 1987). Because the degree of rationality varies among decision makers, the effectiveness of punishments as deterrents may vary for different types of offenses and offenders. This suggests that deterrence researchers—and criminal justice policymakers—should develop a "crime-specific" (Cornish and Clarke 1986, 1987) approach to deterrence, by carefully considering how costs and benefits are weighed by different types of offenders committing different types of offenses in different types of situations. For example, if a crime-specific analysis shows that the initial crimes committed by offenders are more susceptible to deterrence than subsequent crimes, this suggests that policies oriented toward deterrence may work for novice offenders, but incapacitation may be the better approach for recidivists (see chapter 5).

Beyond the complex conceptualizations in the deterrence literature that give criminologists migraine headaches when theorizing about deterrence effects, five methodological complications frustrate researchers in their attempts to study the relationship between arrest and punishment threats and crime prevention. First, Gibbs (1975) and Zimring and Hawkins (1973) note that deterrence effects cannot be observed directly, but rather must be inferred through the analysis of legal/formal sanctions and crime rates. Gibbs (1975, 3 [italics deleted]) writes that deterrence is "an inherently unobservable phenomenon. Common sense to the contrary, we never observe someone omitting an act because of the perceived risk and fear of punishment." Because deterrence effects are unobservable, critics can charge that confounding variables other than deterrence are responsible for observed inverse relationships between legal/formal sanctions and crime rates. In particular, incapacitation is frequently mentioned as an important confounding variable (Blumstein, Cohen, and Nagin 1978; Gibbs 1975; Nagin 1978b). The reason that incapacitation effects potentially confound any inferences about the effectiveness of deterrence is that an inverse relationship between imprisonment rates and crime rates could reflect *either* deterrence *or* a reduction in the number of available offenders in the community free to commit crimes (see Blumstein, Cohen, and Nagin 1978; Nagin 1978b).

Another methodological problem that plagues aggregate-level research that uses official data on the rates of crime, arrest, imprisonment, and recidivism centers around the validity of these data (Blumstein, Cohen, and Nagin 1978; Nagin 1978b). Frequent criticisms of police statistics (used to compile official crime rate data) are that they ignore unreported crimes and sometimes reflect different jurisdictional practices (among police departments) in the reporting of offenses. As a result, invalid measures of crime rates could be responsible for the observed inverse relationships between arrest or imprisonment rates and crime rates (Blumstein, Cohen, and Nagin 1978; Nagin 1978b). Furthermore, official statewide data on imprisonment rates are the subject of some criticism (Nagin 1978b); these data usually report only those inmates incarcerated in state penitentiaries, excluding those confined to jails. Consequently, aggregate-level studies that use statewide data on the probability of imprisonment as a measure of punishment certainty (see Gibbs 1968; Tittle 1969a) may be using an invalid indicator for their independent variable.

Aggregate recidivism rates—often cited by critics as an indicator of the failure of prisons to achieve specific deterrence (see Currie 1985; Nagel 1973; Sommer 1976)—are notoriously invalid measures of the effectiveness of punishments (Glaser 1964; Greenberg 1975; Packer 1968; Wilkins 1969; Wright 1992). As noted earlier, the simple analysis of return rates to prison omits any comparison of arrested and punished offenders with those who elude apprehension; despite the existence of high recidivism rates among punished offenders, it is likely that criminals who escape detection continue committing crimes at far higher rates (Packer 1968; Wright 1992). Furthermore, Daniel Glaser's (1964) and David Greenberg's (1975) studies of national samples of parolees reveal that recidivism rates are dramatically inflated by including as "failures" not only prisoners who are reincarcerated for new offenses but also "technical parole violators" (who break such minor parole conditions as changing jobs or traveling out of town without notifying their parole officers) and those arrested for suspicion.

Criminologists have also noted the problems surrounding the clear specification of causal relationships in deterrence research (Blumstein, Cohen, and Nagin 1978; Gibbs 1975; Nagin 1978a, b; Zimring and Hawkins 1973). For example, until the mid-1970s, most deterrence theorists and researchers assumed that various legal/formal sanctions (e.g., arrest or imprisonment rates) could be conceptualized as independent variables affecting crime rates as dependent variables, so that an inverse relationship between sanctions and crime rates could be considered an indicator of deterrence effectiveness. As Daniel Nagin (1978a, b) persuasively contends, however, it is just as reasonable to reverse this causal order by arguing that crime rates are the cause of legal/formal sanctions. Here an inverse relationship could mean that as crime rates rise in particular jurisdictions, criminal justice resources are stretched thin and are overloaded, contributing to the breakdown of punishments (i.e., lowered percentages of offenders who are arrested, convicted, and imprisoned—Nagin 1978a, b; see also Geerken and Gove 1977; Greenberg and Kessler 1982; Greenberg, Kessler, and Logan 1979). The problem of causal ordering between legal/formal sanctions and crime rates has led to the replacement of simple cross-sectional research designs (e.g., Gibbs 1968; Tittle 1969a)—where both variables are examined at the same time—with more sophisticated and time-consuming panel designs (e.g., Greenberg and Kessler 1982; Greenberg, Kessler, and Logan 1979), where legal/formal sanctions are usually measured one, two, or three years earlier than crime rates (so that the latter cannot logically affect the former).

Still another problem in the specification of deterrence causal models that affects both cross-sectional and panel design studies concerns the identification of various exogenous control variables (Blumstein, Cohen, and Nagin 1978; Gibbs 1975; Nagin 1978a, b; Zimring and Hawkins 1973). Early deterrence studies (e.g., Gibbs 1968; Tittle 1969a) assumed the existence of a simple bivariate causal relationship between formal/legal sanctions as independent variables and crime rates as dependent variables. These studies overlooked a variety of exogenous informal sanctions/extralegal factors—ranging from city-wide population densities and police expenditures in aggregate-level actual deterrence studies to one's moral commitment to the law and the condemnation of family and friends for one's deviant behavior in perceptual deterrence studies—that could affect the relationship between legal/formal sanctions and offending patterns (Greenberg and Kessler 1982; Nagin 1978a, b; Tittle 1980b). Researchers who neglect the consideration of various control variables risk a spurious finding of inverse relationships between formal/legal sanctions and criminal behavior (Blumstein, Cohen, and Nagin 1978; Nagin 1978a, b; Greenberg and Kessler 1982; Tittle 1980b).

Still another methodological problem affecting deterrence research emerges in the interpretation of reductions in crime rates following the implementation of justice system crackdowns (Gibbs 1975; Zimring and Hawkins 1973). As Zimring and Hawkins (1973) note, there is a historical tendency for crime rates naturally to fluctuate up and down. Because justice system crackdowns usually are a response to some prolonged increase in crime, any decrease in crime rates following crackdowns could either indicate deterrence effects or reflect so-called regression toward the mean effects, (i.e., natural, cyclical returns to more normal crime rates). Fortunately, it is relatively easy to circumvent regression toward the mean effects if researchers scrupulously choose unexceptional cases or subjects to study—for example, neighborhoods not characterized by conspicuously high or low crime rates.

One final methodological problem that affects specific deterrence research is selectivity in sampling (Gibbs 1975; Sherman and Berk 1984; Tittle and Logan 1973; Wilkins 1969; Wright 1992). Specific deterrence research designs generally compare the recidivism rates between groups of offenders exposed to more severe punishments (e.g., imprisonment) versus groups exposed to less severe punishments (e.g., probation). These studies sometimes show that recidivism rates are higher among the former than the latter (see Gibbs 1975; Hood and Sparks 1970), a finding that superficially contradicts deterrence arguments. However, punishments are seldom randomly assigned to offenders in these studies, which means that higher-risk offenders (with longer prior records and more serious offense histories) who are more likely to recidivate receive the more severe punishments. In this circumstance, differential recidivism rates may be due to the unique characteristics of offenders assigned to research groups rather than to the nature of punishments. Only the random assignment of punishments can protect against selectivity factors in sampling in specific deterrence research.

The remainder of chapter 4 reviews the research findings on the effectiveness of punishments as general and specific deterrents. Because far more criminological research has been devoted to the study of general deterrence effects rather than specific deterrence, my literature review concentrates mostly on the former. Again, I contend that the weight of the research evidence supports the argument that punishments are often at least moderately effective in deterring both potential and actual offenders.

GENERAL DETERRENCE: SOME SPECIFIC FINDINGS

In the last fifty years in criminology, an ocean of research has been done on general deterrence. These studies can be categorized into six waves, depending on the conceptual distinctions made between actual and perceptual deterrence and the nature of the research designs employed: (1) actual deterrence: the early death penalty studies, (2) actual deterrence: recent aggregate-level findings, (3) actual deterrence: natural experiments, (4) perceptual deterrence: cross-sectional studies, (5) perceptual deterrence: panel studies; and (6) qualitative studies of deterrence.

Actual Deterrence: The Early Death Penalty Studies

The earliest empirical studies of general deterrence examine the effects of capital punishment on homicide rates (as examples, see Dann 1935; Savitz 1958; Schuessler 1952; Sellin 1967; Vold 1952; Walker 1965). These studies employ three different research designs. First, Karl Schuessler (1952), Thorsten Sellin (1967), and George Vold (1952) compare the homicide rates between states (or countries) that abolished the death penalty with adjacent retentionist states (or countries). For example, choosing regions of the United States where at least one state practiced executions while another did not, Vold (1952) compares the homicide rates of three groups of contiguous states (with three states in each group) for the years 1933 to 1951. A related research design involves the comparison of homicide rates in various states (or countries) before and after the enactment or abolition of the death penalty (see Schuessler 1952; Sellin 1967; Walker 1965). Here, Sellin (1967) compares the homicide rates in eight states that first abolished, then later reinstated, the death penalty sometime between 1864 and 1958. Finally, Robert Dann (1935) and Leonard Savitz (1958) compare the homicide rates in one city (Philadelphia) immediately before and after well-publicized executions (Dann) or court-imposed death sentences (Savitz). For instance, Savitz (1958) examines the homicide rates in Philadelphia for eight weeks before and four weeks after the handing down of four highly publicized death sentences from 1944 to 1947.

Regardless of these different research designs, the early death penalty studies consistently show that executions have little effect on homicide rates. When these studies first appeared, though, they were widely misinterpreted by criminologists to indicate that *all* punishments fail as general deterrents for *all* types of offenses (see Reckless 1967; Sutherland and Cressey 1966). For example, as Walter Reckless (1967, 508) flatly concludes in his popular criminology textbook, these studies show that "legal" punishment "does not prevent crime in others." As Gibbs (1968) and Tittle (1969a) correctly note, however, the findings of early death penalty/homicide studies cannot be generalized to other forms of punishment (especially imprisonment) and to other types of crimes. Given the highly atypical nature of both the death penalty as a punishment and homicide as a crime, these studies in retrospect appear to tell us virtually nothing about the overall effectiveness of punishments as general deterrents.

Other shortcomings even limit these studies as specific tests of the effectiveness of the death penalty as a deterrent to homicide. For example, the research designs in early death penalty studies permit only an estimation of the effectiveness of the severity of punishments on homicide rates, while ignoring the property of punishment certainty (Gibbs 1968; Tittle 1969a; Tittle and Logan 1973). Deterrence theorists since the time of Beccaria and Bentham, however, have conceded that the severity of punishments is a less important factor in deterrence than punishment certainty. (Parenthetically, though, more recent studies that do examine the certainty of executions on homicide rates still offer little empirical support for the effectiveness of capital punishment as a deterrent to homicide—for a summary of recent research evidence on capital punishment and deterrence, see Zimring and Hawkins 1986.) Also, these studies evaluate only the effectiveness of capital punishment as a marginal deterrent (Gibbs 1968; Tittle and Logan 1973); to study the effectiveness of executions as absolute deterrents, researchers need to compare jurisdictions that execute murderers with other locales where murderers go unpunished. If these comparisons were possible, one can speculate that executions would emerge as powerful deterrents to homicide. In general, the early death penalty studies provide little insight about the overall effectiveness of legal/formal sanctions as general deterrents to crime.

Actual Deterrence: Recent Aggregate-Level Findings

By the late 1960s, some criminologists began to recognize the inadequacy of existing death penalty research for reaching meaningful conclusions about the overall effectiveness of arrest and punishment in reducing the overall crime rate (see Gibbs 1968; Tittle 1969a). This led to a massive new wave of studies that use aggregate-level data to examine the actual general deterrence effects of the certainty and the severity of legal/formal sanctions (e.g., see Bailey, Martin, and Gray 1974; Bowker 1981; Bursik, Grasmick, and Chamlin 1990; Chamlin et al. 1992; Chiricos and Waldo 1970; Decker and Kohfeld 1985; Geerken and Gove 1977; Greenberg and Kessler 1982; Greenberg, Kessler, and Logan 1979; Gibbs 1968; Kohfeld and Sprague 1990; Logan 1972; McGuire and Sheehan 1983; Sampson and Cohen 1988; Tittle 1969a; Tittle and Rowe 1974; Wilson and Boland 1978). These studies use either one of two dependent variables to measure the certainty and the severity of legal/formal sanctions: (1) the probability of imprisonment (certainty) and/or the length of prison sentences (severity), the former usually measured by the annual number of admissions to state prisons, and the latter usually measured by the mean length of time served in state prisons for those convicted of different felonies (see Bailey, Martin, and Gray 1974; Bowker 1981; Chiricos and Waldo 1970; Gibbs 1968; Logan 1972; McGuire and Sheehan 1983; Tittle 1969a), or (2) the probability of arrest (certainty), measured by either police clearance rates (or the number of arrests divided by the number of all known crimes, for particular offenses) for various felonies (see Bursik, Grasmick, and Chamlin 1990; Chamlin et al. 1992; Decker and Kohfeld 1985; Geerken and Gove 1977; Greenberg and Kessler 1982; Greenberg, Kessler, and Logan 1979; Kohfeld and Sprague 1990; Tittle and Rowe 1974) or by police citation rates for traffic violations and disorderly conduct (see Sampson and Cohen 1988; Wilson and Boland 1978). The dependent variable in all of these studies is the crime rate in particular locales, usually measured by the annual number of index crimes reported by the FBI *Uniform Crime Reports*. The units of analysis in these studies range from neighborhoods or census tracts within single cities (e.g., see Bursik, Grasmick, and Chamlin 1990; Chamlin et al. 1992; Kohfeld and Sprague 1990) to comparisons among numerous large cities (see Greenberg and Kessler

1982; Greenberg, Kessler, and Logan 1979; Sampson and Cohen 1988; Wilson and Boland 1978), entire states (Gibbs 1968; Tittle 1969a), or national trend data over time (Bowker 1981; McGuire and Sheehan 1983).

In a recent review of the findings of these studies, Gibbs (1986) observes that they fairly consistently show an *inverse* relationship between the actual certainty of formal/legal sanctions and crime rates, offering support for the argument that punishments are effective as general deterrents. Specifically, cross-sectional studies that examine the effects of the certainty of imprisonment and the length (severity) of prison sentences on crime rates consistently show (1) moderately negative relationships between the certainty of imprisonment and the rates of most index crimes but (2) no relationship between the length (severity) of prison sentences and the rates of index crimes, except for homicide (where there appears to be a weak negative relationship—see Bailey, Martin, and Gray 1974; Chiricos and Waldo 1970; Gibbs 1968; Logan 1972; Tittle 1969a).

Two recent panel design studies (Bowker 1981; McGuire and Sheehan 1983), undertaken to establish a clear causal order between imprisonment rates and arrest rates, are less consistent in their findings. When imprisonment rates from one year are related to crime rates a year or two later, Lee Bowker (1981) finds no consistent correlation between the two, but William McGuire and Richard Sheehan (1983)—in a more methodologically sophisticated study that uses econometric techniques specifically devised for lagged variables—find the anticipated inverse relationship, supporting the deterrence perspective. In analyzing imprisonment rate and crime rate data for the years 1960 to 1979, McGuire and Sheehan (1983) conclude that a 1 percent increase in incarceration rates results in a 0.48 to 1.1 percent reduction in crime rates.

Despite the optimistic assessment of Gibbs (1986), the arrest rate studies offer somewhat less consistent support for deterrence arguments. While early cross-sectional, bivariate studies show a consistent inverse relationship between police clearance rates and crime rates (Geerken and Gove 1977; Tittle and Rowe 1974), later panel design studies (where police clearance rates are measured generally one or more years before crime rates, again to establish a clear causal order) that consider numerous control variables (e.g., population density and unemployment rates in particular locales) find little relationship between arrest certainty and crime rates (see Decker and Kohfeld 1985; Greenberg and Kessler 1982; Greenberg, Kessler, and Logan 1979). Still, two recent studies (Chamlin et al. 1992; Kohfeld and Sprague 1990) that examine the effect of arrest rates on crime rates over shorter time intervals (weeks and months) show strong inverse relationships between arrest certainty and crime rates. Carol

Kohfeld and John Sprague's (1990) extremely sophisticated, recent multivariate panel study, which analyzes the effects of arrest rates for one week on the burglary and robbery rates for the following week for all census tracts in St. Louis during the summer of 1982, shows significant deterrence effects in racially mixed, lower-class neighborhoods (e.g., every ten arrests for burglary in these neighborhoods resulted in eight fewer burglaries). Similarly, Mitchell Chamlin et al.'s (1992) panel study of the effect of arrest rates on crime rates in Oklahoma City for monthly and quarterly intervals over twenty-three years (1967 to 1989) shows significant negative relationships between arrest rates and the rates of robbery and auto theft (in the monthly data) and robbery, auto theft, and larceny (in the quarterly data). These studies strongly suggest that higher arrest rates have an immediate, initial deterrent effect on some types of crimes in some neighborhoods, a finding easily overlooked in multivariate panel studies (e.g., Greenberg and Kessler 1982) that aggregate data citywide and use extremely long lag periods (years) to assess the effect of arrests on crime rates.

One other notable finding in the clearance rate–crime rate studies is some support for the argument that certain thresholds of arrest probability must be achieved before the certainty of arrests inversely affects crime rates (Tittle 1980b; Tittle and Rowe 1974). Tittle and Rowe (1974) compare the relationships between clearance rates and crime rates for larger cities and all counties in Florida for 1971. They found that in data collected from jurisdictions with an arrest certainty of over 30 percent for all index crimes, the inverse relationship was much stronger between clearance rates and crime rates than in jurisdictions where arrest certainty fell under 30 percent. It is still unclear if some threshold of imprisonment certainty must be attained for incarceration rates to affect crime rates inversely.

Two studies examine the effect of aggressive, high-visibility, "proactive" styles of policing on robbery rates in numerous large U.S. cities (Sampson and Cohen 1988; Wilson and Boland 1978). These studies measure proactive law enforcement styles by comparing the police citation rates for high-visibility traffic and disorderly conduct offenses in thirty-five cities (Wilson and Boland 1978) and 171 cities (Sampson and Cohen 1988). Both studies show that robbery rates are significantly lower where the police maintain a high-visibility street presence. James Q. Wilson and Barbara Boland (1978) and Robert Sampson and Jacqueline Cohen (1988) speculate that proactive police styles are instrumental in increasing the perceived certainty of arrest among citizens on the streets, which in turn contributes to lower robbery rates.

Although general deterrence arguments admittedly are supported inconsistently by studies relating arrest clearance rates to crime rates, the imprisonment rate studies (more central to the argument of this book) offer moderately strong support that the certainty—but not the severity—of punishments deters crime. As noted earlier, however, five important criticisms have been made of aggregate-level studies of the actual deterrence effects of imprisonment: (1) both official police statistics and state imprisonment records may be invalid measures of (respectively) crime rates and imprisonment certainty (Blumstein, Cohen, and Nagin 1978; Nagin 1978b), (2) these studies to date have not clearly separated deterrence effects from incapacitation effects (crime rates may be lower in states with high incarceration rates only because more chronic offenders in these states have been taken off the streets—Gibbs 1986; Gibbs and Firebaugh 1990), (3) states with higher crime rates naturally may have lower imprisonment rates because criminal justice resources are stretched thin, contributing to a breakdown in the delivery of punishments (here, the inverse relationship between imprisonment rates and crime rates might reflect the statewide efficiency of criminal justice agencies rather than the effectiveness of actual deterrence—Greenberg and Kessler 1982; Greenberg, Kessler, and Logan 1979; Nagin 1978a, b), (4) other, unknown exogenous variables still unspecified in causal models may render spurious the inverse relationship between imprisonment rates and crime rates (Gibbs and Firebaugh 1990), and perhaps most importantly (5) these studies fail to consider how individual *perceptions* of the certainty and the severity of punishments affect individual decisions to commit crime (Chiricos and Waldo 1970; Tittle 1980b; Waldo and Chiricos 1972). The latter criticism in recent years has led deterrence researchers to de-emphasize aggregate-level studies of actual deterrence, in favor of perceptual deterrence studies that use individuals as the unit of analysis.

Actual Deterrence: Natural Experiments

One final group of actual deterrence studies includes natural experiments, or studies of the effects of policy changes or other interventions that occur in real world settings (see Gibbs 1975; Sherman 1990; Zimring 1978; Zimring and Hawkins 1973). Natural experiments on the actual deterrence effects of punishments customarily examine the impact of some newly implemented get-tough policy on the behavior of a specific group of offenders committing specific types of offenses. Measurements of the rates of offending are taken before and after policy implementation;

decreases in the rates of offending following policy implementation are usually considered to be an indicator of actual deterrence effects.

Many natural experiments have analyzed the effectiveness of new get-tough policies or threatened punishments on many different types of offenders in real world settings (for literature reviews of these studies, see Gibbs 1975; Sherman 1990; Zimring 1978; Zimring and Hawkins 1973). Some specific offenses analyzed in this research include drunk driving (Ross 1973, 1984; Ross, Campbell, and Glass 1970), parking violations (Chambliss 1966), income tax evasion (Schwartz and Orleans 1967; Klepper and Nagin 1989), domestic assault (Jolin 1983), cable television signal theft (Green 1985), skyjacking (Chauncey 1975), military draft evasion (Blumstein and Nagin 1977), and the failure of ex-husbands to make court-mandated child-support payments (Lempert 1981-1982). These studies consistently show that various get-tough policies and punishment threats produce significant initial deterrent effects but are much less successful in achieving long-term, residual deterrence (i.e., the immediate actual deterrent effects of policy implementations and punishment threats tend to decay over time).

Numerous natural experiments have been conducted over the years on get-tough policies enacted to combat drunk driving (see Ross 1984 for a summary of this research). Perhaps the most sophisticated of these studies were conducted by H. Laurence Ross, Donald Campbell, and Gene Glass (1970) and Ross (1973) on the 1967 British Road Safety Act—a well-publicized get-tough law that for the first time in England (1) authorized police to use on-the-scene breathalyzer tests to check for drunk driving, and (2) prescribed a blood alcohol content level of .08 percent for a drunk driving conviction (notably, punishments for drunk driving were not increased by the law). Ross, Campbell, and Glass (1970) examined the initial deterrent effects produced by the enactment of the law; Ross (1973) focused more on the law's residual deterrent effects. Both studies are models for natural experiments research—the authors go to great lengths to rule out the influences of exogenous variables (e.g., time-of-day, day-of-week, or seasonal fluctuations in accident rates and other legal changes, including a new tire inspection law) in their studies. Deterrence effects were primarily measured by examining the number of traffic fatalities that occurred in the months before and after the law took effect on 9 October 1967.

The Ross, Campbell, and Glass (1970) and Ross (1973) studies show that statistically significant declines in traffic fatalities in general, and alcohol-related traffic fatalities in particular, occurred in England in the months immediately following the enactment of the Road Safety Act. Initial deterrent effects were especially strong for weekend nights (Friday and Saturday, from 10:00 P.M. to 4:00 A.M.), when traffic deaths declined by an impressive 40 to 45 percent. However, Ross's (1973) subsequent analysis shows that the law's deterrent effects were short-lived; by the middle of 1968, traffic fatalities were again on the rise (at a statistically significant rate). In general, the British Road Safety Act apparently resulted in notable initial deterrent effects on drunk driving, but these early effects rapidly decayed, producing few residual deterrent benefits.

Ross's (1984) extensive summary of similar get-tough laws enacted to deter drunk driving in countries ranging from France to the United States and New Zealand confirms the view that these laws are more effective in achieving initial, rather than residual, deterrence. He explains this finding by arguing that the media attention and publicity surrounding new drunk driving laws create an immediate exaggerated estimation of the certainty of arrest among potential drunk drivers. Once drivers realize that they are still not likely to be apprehended despite these tough new laws, they return to their before-enactment driving practices. Although laws and publicity that increase the public estimates of the certainty of punishments for drunk driving appear to be effective as initial (but not residual) deterrents, Ross (1984) also concludes that laws that increase the severity of punishments for drunk driving have no initial or residual deterrent effects.

Most of the other natural experiments that examine the impact of new get-tough policies or punishment threats on other offenses concentrate on the initial deterrent effects of legal/formal sanctions. For example, Chambliss (1966) interviewed a random sample of forty-three faculty at a large state university about their on-campus parking violations following the enactment of a tough new university regulation to ticket and fine faculty parking offenders (before the new regulation, the campus police largely overlooked faculty parking violations). Those interviewed reported committing significantly fewer parking violations after the enactment of the regulation than before, a finding that suggests that "an increase in the certainty and the severity of punishment deters [the] violation of parking regulations" (Chambliss 1966, 74).

Research also shows that punishment threats are effective in deterring income tax evasion (Schwartz and Orleans 1967; see also Klepper and Nagin 1989). With the cooperation of the Internal Revenue Service, Richard Schwartz and Sonya Orleans (1967) interviewed a random sample of 263 taxpayers from high-income neighborhoods in a large city, shortly before they submitted their 1962 federal income tax returns. The interviewees were randomly assigned to either one of two experimental groups (one experimental group was informed of the legal penalties for false income tax returns, and the other was reminded of their moral obligations to file honest tax returns) or a control group (these respondents were interviewed but were not informed about possible legal penalties or their moral obligations). When comparing the 1961 and 1962 federal income tax returns submitted by the taxpayers interviewed in the study, Schwartz and Orleans (1967) found that those in *both* experimental groups reported significantly more adjusted gross income, declared significantly fewer deductions, and paid significantly more income tax (after deduction credits) than those in the control group in their 1962 income tax returns (no differences among the groups were found in the 1961 tax returns).

In yet another natural experiment, Annette Jolin (1983) examined the effect of the enactment of the 1977 Abuse Prevention Act in Oregon, a get-tough law on domestic violence that requires police to arrest all assailants, unless their victims object. Before the passage of this law, Jolin (1983) notes that Oregon police seldom intervened in domestic assault incidents. To determine the impact of the law on domestic violence, the number of domestic homicides (killings of spouses and lovers) was analyzed from 1975 through 1981. Jolin (1983) reports that significantly fewer domestic homicides occurred in the four years after the passage of the act (eighty-nine killings), compared with the three years before passage (ninety-eight killings), a particularly impressive finding considering that the overall rate of nondomestic homicides increased dramatically in Oregon during these years.

As one final example of a natural experiment on actual deterrence, Gary Green (1985) studied cable television signal thefts of Home Box Office (HBO) transmissions in a small midwestern city from 1984 to 1985. Outside-the-home inspections of the 3,500 households in the community that subscribed to cable television services uncovered 67 homes where HBO signals were being illegally "pirated." In cooperation with HBO and the local cable television company, Green (1985) sent first-class, personal letters to all 67 pirates, warning them of the maximum penalties (a $1,000 fine and one year in prison) for those convicted of cable television signal theft and informing them that an outside-the-home audit of their cable television lines would occur within two weeks to check for illegal HBO signal descramblers (as a preliminary step toward the prosecution of violators). In addition, the letter offered amnesty from prosecution for all pirates who either disconnected their own descramblers or voluntarily contacted the local cable television company for disconnection. Forty-two of the pirates accepted the amnesty offer; more importantly, a six-month follow-up, outside-the-home audit of cable television lines revealed that only two of the ex-pirates later reconnected descramblers to their lines.

In general, the natural experiments conducted on the actual deterrent effects of get-tough policy implementations or punishment threats offer moderate support for the argument that the certainty (but perhaps not the severity) of punishments has an initial (but perhaps not residual) deterrent effect on crime. Furthermore, these actual deterrence effects appear to be fairly *noncontingent* with respect to different types of offenses, contradicting the arguments of Andenaes (1966, 1971a, 1974) and Chambliss (1967). For example, natural experimental studies report significant actual deterrence effects for both rational/planned offenses (e.g., income tax evasion and cable television theft) and emotional/impulsive offenses (e.g., domestic assault and, to a lesser extent, drunk driving), *mala in se* offenses (e.g., domestic assault) and *mala prohibita* offenses (e.g., parking violations), and instrumental offenses (e.g., income tax evasion) and expressive offenses (e.g., domestic assault). Despite the important contributions that natural experiments have made to the deterrence literature, however, these studies still largely ignore how individual perceptions of the certainty and the severity of legal/formal sanctions influence behavior, topics considered by two more waves of deterrence research.

Perceptual Deterrence: Cross-Sectional Studies

During the 1970s, the focus of deterrence research gradually shifted from the analysis of actual deterrence effects to the consideration of perceptual deterrence effects. The major cause of this shift was a growing realization among criminologists that decisions to commit crimes are less influenced by the real, objective probabilities of the certainty and the severity of punishments than by one's personal estimations of the likelihood of the certainty and the severity of punishments (Chiricos and Waldo 1970; Geerken and Gove 1975; Gibbs 1975; Tittle 1980b; Waldo and Chiricos 1972; Zimring and Hawkins 1971, 1973). The measurement of perceptual deterrence effects requires the abandonment of aggregate-level studies (that analyze the relationships between clearance rates or imprisonment rates and crime rates over large geographical areas) in favor of survey research (that examines how individual estimations of the certainty and the severity of punishments affect self-reported past deviance or the future likelihood that one will commit crime). The first wave of perceptual deterrence studies (published from 1969 through the mid-1980s) used cross-sectional survey designs, asking respondents (usually random samples of university students or the local residents of university towns) to report their current perceptions of punishment certainty and severity for committing specified offenses (as independent variables) and their past histories or future probabilities of committing the same specified offenses (as dependent variables).

An immense number of perceptual deterrence studies using cross-sectional research designs were published during this era (see Anderson, Chiricos, and Waldo 1977; Bailey and Lott 1976; Erickson, Gibbs, and Jensen 1977; Grasmick and Appleton 1977; Grasmick and Bryjak 1980; Grasmick and Green 1980, 1981; Grasmick, Jacobs, and McCollom 1983; Grasmick and Milligan 1976; Jensen 1969; Jensen, Erickson, and Gibbs 1978; Meier and Johnson 1977; Parker and Grasmick 1979; Silberman 1976; Richards and Tittle 1981, 1982; Tittle 1980b; Waldo and Chiricos 1972). Although the sheer number of these studies prohibits any attempt to analyze their findings individually, fortunately several fairly clear trends emerge when these studies are considered as a group.

First, these studies fairly consistently show that the perceived certainty of legal/formal sanctions (usually measured by one's estimation of the likelihood that he or she would be arrested or imprisoned for committing some offense) and the perceived severity of legal/formal sanctions (measured by one's estimation of the extent to which he or she would be punished for committing some offense) exert independent effects on self-reported rates of deviance (although Grasmick and Bryjak [1980] reject this view, claiming that the perceived severity of punishments deters self-reported offenses only when high thresholds of the perceived certainty of punishments are attained). Furthermore, these studies consistently show that while the perceived certainty of legal/formal sanctions is moderately inversely related to self-reported deviance, the perceived severity of legal/formal sanctions has little effect on self-reported deviance (suggesting once more that the effectiveness of general deterrence occurs because of the certainty, but not the severity, of punishments—see, e.g., Anderson, Chiricos, and Waldo 1977; Bailey and Lott 1976; Silberman 1976; Tittle 1980b; Waldo and Chiricos 1972).

Many of these studies have also employed multivariate research designs to separate the perceived certainty of legal/formal sanctions from the influence of the perceived certainty of informal sanctions/extralegal factors (e.g., the probable condemnation of family, friends, and the wider community to the public disclosure of one's deviance or the strength of one's moral commitment to the law) on one's self-reported deviant behavior (e.g., see Anderson, Chiricos, and Waldo 1977; Bailey and Lott 1976; Grasmick and Appleton 1977; Grasmick and Green 1980, 1981; Jensen, Erickson, and Gibbs 1978; Meier and Johnson 1977; Silberman 1976; Tittle 1980b). Some multivariate studies (see Anderson, Chiricos, and Waldo 1977; Meier and Johnson 1977; Silberman 1976) find interactive effects between perceived legal/formal sanctions and perceived informal sanctions/extralegal factors (i.e., the perceived certainty of legal/formal sanctions largely influences self-reported deviance *through* the intervening variables of perceived informal sanctions/extralegal factors). However, most researchers assume that perceived legal/formal sanctions and perceived informal sanctions/extralegal factors exert independent effects on self-reported deviance (see Bailey and Lott 1976; Grasmick and Appleton 1977; Grasmick and Green 1980, 1981; Jensen, Erickson, and Gibbs 1978; Tittle 1980b). The latter studies consistently show that the perceived certainty of legal/formal sanctions has *less* influence on self-reported deviance than various perceived informal sanctions/extralegal factors. This suggests that although the perceived certainty of punishment prevents crime, it does so less effectively and less reliably than the anticipated opinions of one's family and friends or the strength of one's moral commitments.

Perhaps the most important contribution of cross-sectional perceptual deterrence research is the light that it sheds on the contingent effects of the perceived certainty of punishments on different types of offenses and offenders. With respect to *types of offenses*, a few studies (see Waldo and Chiricos 1972; Jensen, Erickson, and Gibbs 1978) find modest contingent effects on the influences of perceived legal/formal sanctions. For example, Waldo and Chiricos (1972) conclude that the perceived certainty of punishment exerts a stronger negative effect on self-reported marijuana use than self-reported theft. In contrast, Gary Jensen, Erickson, and Gibbs (1978) find that the perceived certainty of punishments has a more negative effect on self-reported property offenses than "victimless" crimes (e.g., marijuana use). In general, though, the majority of cross-sectional perceptual deterrence studies (like natural experiments) show that certainty of punishment effects are fairly noncontingent on different types of offenses (Paternoster 1987); in other words, there are weak-to-moderate inverse relationships between the perceived certainties of punishment and self-reported behaviors for all different types of crimes studied by researchers.

Cross-sectional perceptual deterrence studies also offer some tentative findings about the contingent effects of the certainty of punishments on different *types of offenders*. For example, the age of offenders appears to exert some influence on the effectiveness of punishments as deterrents (Grasmick and Milligan 1976). In an analysis of the influence of the perceived certainty of punishments on speeding violations, Harold Grasmick and Herman Milligan (1976) conclude that younger drivers are less deterred by the threat of legal/formal sanctions than older drivers.

Furthermore, social class apparently has some effect on the relationship between the perceived certainty of punishments and self-reported offenses—three studies (Grasmick, Jacobs, and McCollom 1983; Richards and Tittle 1982; Tittle 1980b) find that social class is inversely related to the perceived certainty of punishment for committing various offenses (however, Jensen, Erickson, and Gibbs [1978] report no social class effects in their study). Finally, the findings are inconclusive on the effects of gender on the perceived certainty of sanctions: Richards and Tittle (1981) and Tittle (1980b) find that women are more responsive to legal/formal sanction threats than men; Linda Anderson, Chiricos, and Waldo (1977) and Jensen, Erickson, and Gibbs (1978) find no gender effects; and Matthew Silberman's (1976) data show that men are more responsive to legal/formal sanction threats than women.

To summarize, cross-sectional perceptual deterrence studies in many ways confirm the earlier findings of actual deterrence research (both aggregate-level studies and natural experiments). Together, these studies show that (1) there is a moderate inverse relationship between the certainty of punishment (both actual and perceived) and crime rates (both aggregate-level and self-reported by individuals), (2) the certainty of punishments is a far more effective deterrent to crime than punishment severity, and (3) the effectiveness of the certainty of punishments is noncontingent on different types of offenses (i.e., certainty of punishment appears to deter all different types of crimes relatively equally). Cross-sectional perceptual deterrence studies, however, add two new findings to the literature: (1) legal/formal sanctions appear to be less influential in preventing crime than informal sanctions/extralegal factors and (2) the effectiveness of legal/formal sanctions as deterrents may be contingent on one's age and social class, but probably not one's gender.

Despite these important contributions to the deterrence debate, cross-sectional perceptual deterrence studies have been sharply criticized for causal model specification problems (Lundman 1986; Minor and Harry 1982; Paternoster 1987; Saltzman et al. 1982). These studies typically relate *current* perceptions of the certainty and the severity of punishments to *past* self-reported deviant behavior. As a consequence, the causal order of the relationship is unclear—perceptions of the certainty and the severity of punishments may negatively affect one's deviant behavior (a deterrence effect), or one's deviant behavior may negatively affect perceptions of the certainty and the severity of punishments (what Saltzman et al. 1982 call an "experiential effect"). Experiential effects may undermine the effectiveness of punishments as deterrents, because these effects suggest that individuals lower their estimations of the certainty and the severity of punishments after they begin committing deviant behavior (i.e., once they see that they are not likely to be apprehended, novice offenders dismiss the effectiveness of punishments, which then contributes to further deviant behavior—see Paternoster 1987; Paternoster et al. 1985). To disentangle this causal order confusion—and to separate deterrence effects from experiential effects in perceptual deterrence research—suggests the replacement of cross-sectional research designs (which measure perceptions of punishment threats and self-reported deviant behavior at the same time) with panel research designs (where perceptions of punishment threats are measured before one's self-reported deviant behavior to establish a clear and unambiguous causal order).

Related to the causal order specification problem is another possible flaw in cross-sectional perceptual deterrence research—the assumption that perceptions of the certainty and the severity of punishments remain unchanged over time (Lundman 1986; Minor and Harry 1982; Paternoster 1987; Saltzman et al. 1982). For cross-sectional perceptual deterrence researchers to argue that current perceptions of punishment threats affect past deviant behavior, the perceptions of punishment threats must be invariant. However, this may be a dubious assumption; as Linda Saltzman et al. (1982) note, it is likely that perceptions of punishment threats change over time with one's experience in committing deviant behavior. These criticisms have resulted in still another wave of deterrence research: panel design perceptual deterrence studies.

Perceptual Deterrence: Panel Studies

During the last decade, numerous panel design studies have been undertaken to separate experiential effects from deterrence effects in the perceptual deterrence literature (see Bishop 1984a, b; Meier, Burkett, and Hickman 1984; Minor and Harry 1982; Nagin and Paternoster 1991; Paternoster 1987; Paternoster et al. 1983, 1985; Piliavin et al. 1986; Saltzman et al. 1982). Saltzman et al.'s (1982) study is the model for most of this research; the authors twice interviewed (between January and June 1975 and again between January and June 1976) 300 students randomly chosen from the incoming freshman class at a large state university. The respondents (during both time periods) were asked (1) if (and how often) they committed five minor offenses (e.g., marijuana use, petty theft, and writing bad checks) and (2) their perceived risk of the likelihood that they (or others) would be arrested for committing these offenses. The authors measured experiential effects by relating *Time 1* (January through June 1975) perceptions of arrest certainty to self-reported deviant behavior during the past year (i.e., from January through June 1974 to January through June 1975). Deterrent effects were measured by relating *Time 1* perceptions of arrest certainty to *Time 2* self-reported deviant behavior during the past year (i.e., from January through June 1975 to January through June 1976). While the authors found significant inverse relationships supporting the existence of both experiential effects and deterrent effects, the experiential effects were about twice as strong as the deterrent effects. Furthermore, in a later multivariate analysis of these data—where informal sanctions/extralegal factors were added to the causal model—no support whatsoever was found for perceptual deterrence effects, although the experiential effects remained statistically significant (Paternoster et al. 1983).

Most subsequent panel perceptual deterrence studies have also found moderate support for the existence of experiential effects but little or no support for the existence of deterrence effects (see Meier, Burkett, and Hickman 1984; Minor and Harry 1982; Nagin and Paternoster 1991; Paternoster 1987; Paternoster et al. 1985; Piliavin et al. 1986). One important exception to these findings is Bishop's (1984a, b) panel studies of a sample of 2,147 Virginia high school students. Using a similar research design as Saltzman et al. (1982) and Raymond Paternoster et al. (1983), Bishop (1984a, b) found moderate support for the existence of both experiential effects and deterrence effects, even when informal sanctions/extralegal factors were included in a multivariate analysis. In addition, Bishop (1984a, b) found that for certain subgroups within her sample (notably black males), the deterrent effects actually were stronger than the experiential effects.

One additional important finding in panel perceptual deterrence studies is that the perceptions of arrest certainty among respondents appear to change significantly over time (Minor and Harry 1982; Paternoster et al. 1983, 1985; Saltzman et al. 1982). This finding contradicts the assumption of the stability of perceptions of arrest certainty so essential to cross-sectional perceptual deterrence studies. The support for both experiential effects and changes over time in estimations of arrest certainty suggests that as new offenders begin committing criminal behavior, they lower their perceptions of arrest certainty. In general, the findings of panel perceptual deterrence studies show that "illegal behaviors and perceptions of risk mutually affect each other over time" (Minor and Harry 1982, 201).

Notwithstanding the notable exception of Bishop's (1984a, b) studies, panel perceptual deterrence research appears to deliver an enormous blow to the argument that the certainty of punishments can deter subsequent criminal behavior. Unlike cross-sectional perceptual deterrence studies, panel perceptual deterrence research establishes a clear and unambiguous causal order between current perceptions of the certainty of punishments and subsequent deviant behavior. When this causal order is adequately specified, perceptual deterrence effects virtually disappear. In what seems to be a major understatement, William Minor and Joseph Harry (1982) observe that this finding is "bad news" to deterrence supporters.

Or is it? Several shortcomings in existing panel perceptual deterrence studies suggest that the findings in this research must be viewed with much caution. For example, Richard Lundman's (1986) reanalysis of Saltzman et al.'s (1982) and Minor and Harry's (1982) data suggests that perceptions of the certainty of arrest are (after all) reasonably stable. Saltzman et al. (1982) and Minor and Harry (1982) used a five-point scale (ranging from "very likely" to "very unlikely") to measure one's estimated probability of arrest certainty for committing an offense. As a result, trivial changes in responses (say, from estimating that it is "very likely" that one would be arrested for writing bad checks, to later estimating that it is "likely") were coded as shifts in perceived arrest certainty. In recalculating Saltzman et al.'s (1982) and Minor and Harry's (1982) data, Lundman (1986) uses a two-point scale ("high" or "low" estimations of the likelihood of arrest) as measures of changes in perceived arrest certainty. These recalculations show that perceived arrest certainty changes little over time among respondents, suggesting that Saltzman et al.'s (1982) and Minor and Harry's (1982) findings of shifts in perceived arrest certainty are merely statistical artifacts.

Further recalculations of their data suggest that Saltzman et al. (1982) and Minor and Harry (1982) exaggerate their estimations of experiential effects in their findings (Lundman 1986). Lundman's reanalyses of these data show that most persons who lower their perceptions of arrest certainty for a particular offense between *Time 1* and *Time 2* observations *do not commit the offense during this period* (disputing the notion of experiential effects). In addition, Lundman's (1986) recalculation of the data for one offense examined in Minor and Harry's (1982) study—drunk and disorderly conduct—shows that respondents who committed this offense between *Time 1* and *Time 2* observations usually revised their perceptions of arrest certainty *upward*.

Not only do panel perceptual deterrence studies overestimate experiential effects, but there are reasons to believe that they *underestimate* deterrence effects. To measure deterrence effects, these studies use long lag periods between data collections (typically nine months to one year). For example, Saltzman et al. (1982) measure deterrence effects by relating perceptions of arrest certainty at one time period to self-reported deviant behavior committed over the next year. However, implicit in deterrence arguments is the notion that perceptions of the certainty and the severity of punishments should virtually *instantaneously* influence behavior; as Derek Cornish and Ronald Clarke (1986, 1987) observe, offender decision making is characterized by limitations on time, involving spur-of-the-moment estimations of risk that almost immediately affect behaviors. Recall that in their aggregate-level studies of the relationships between arrest rates and crime rates using short time intervals (of one week or one month), Kohfeld and Sprague (1990) and Chamlin et al. (1992) found strong deterrent effects in St. Louis and Oklahoma City neighborhoods. To measure deterrence effects adequately, panel perceptual deterrence researchers would need somehow to design lag periods around minutes, hours, days, and weeks, rather than around months and years.

Finally, as Williams and Hawkins (1986) argue, *both* multivariate cross-sectional perceptual studies and multivariate panel perceptual studies probably underestimate deterrence effects by misspecifying the causal relationship between legal/formal sanctions and informal sanctions/extralegal factors. Virtually all multivariate perceptual deterrence studies assume in their model specifications that legal/formal sanctions and informal sanctions/extralegal factors exert *independent* effects on self-reported deviant behavior. For example, the perceived certainty of arrest (as a legal/formal sanction) for committing theft is analytically separated from the perceived certainty of the social condemnation of one's family and friends (as an informal sanction) for committing theft in most multivariate perceptual deterrence studies. These studies then go on to conclude that informal sanctions/extralegal factors are much more influential in controlling behavior than legal/formal sanctions, a finding often interpreted as contradicting deterrence arguments. As noted earlier, however, Williams and Hawkins (1986) contend that the relationship between legal/formal sanctions and informal sanctions/extralegal factors is *interactive*; specifically, they claim that legal/formal sanctions affect informal sanctions/extralegal factors, which in turn affect behavior. Williams and Hawkins's (1986) interactive model appropriately recognizes that the perceived certainties of arrest and imprisonment for committing theft are probably what *trigger* the perceived certainty of the social condemnation of one's family and friends for committing theft. Or as English jurist James Fitzjames Stephens (quoted in Andenaes 1974, 21) more colorfully wrote in 1863:

Some men [*sic*], probably, abstain from murder because they fear that if they committed murder they would be hanged [a legal/formal sanction]. Hundreds of thousands abstain from it because they regard it with horror [an extralegal factor]. One great reason why they regard it with horror is that murderers are hanged with the hearty approbation of all reasonable men [*sic*—the interactive effect].

In general, it appears that multivariate panel perceptual deterrence researchers have an elegant grasp of research methods but little appreciation for the nuances inherent in the deterrence perspective. Until these researchers solve the theoretically based problems of excessively long lagged observation periods and the probable misspecification of the causal relationship between legal/formal sanctions and informal sanctions/extralegal factors, there is good reason to accept provisionally the earlier findings of simple bivariate perceptual deterrence studies that the certainty (but not the severity) of punishments deters crime.

Qualitative Studies of Deterrence

A handful of qualitative studies offers some insight on the effectiveness of punishments as general deterrents (see Adler 1985; Adler and Adler 1983; Ekland-Olson, Lieb, and Zurcher 1984; Glassner et al. 1983; Shover 1983). For example, Barry Glassner et al.'s (1983) intriguing field study of an unspecified number of older juvenile offenders from upstate New York suggests that punishment threats help to deter these youths from committing adult crime. The authors try to explain why the youth interviewed in their study usually curtailed their criminal activities at approximately age sixteen. *Two-thirds* of the subjects in the study noted their fear of the harsher penalties (especially imprisonment) imposed by the criminal justice system on adults (in comparison to the lenient treatment of younger offenders by the juvenile justice system) as their reason for desisting in crime. Glassner et al. (1983, 221) conclude that most older youth make a "conscious decision" based on a rational calculation of risk to quit criminal involvement, largely "because they feared being jailed if apprehended as adults."

A few additional field studies that examine the careers of middle- and upper-level drug dealers support the argument that an interactive relationship exists between legal/formal sanctions and informal sanctions/extralegal factors (Adler 1985; Adler and Adler 1983; Ekland-Olson, Lieb, and Zurcher 1984). In Sheldon Ekland-Olson, John Lieb, and Louis Zurcher's (1984, 160) six-year intensive field study of thirty-four drug dealer "middlemen" in central Texas, they observe that criminal justice "sanctions are perceived as more severe the more they threaten to disrupt the subject's life." The authors contend that both novice and more seasoned drug dealers fear legal sanctions mostly because of the impact of these sanctions on their relationships with friends, families, and drug-dealing associates. Novice drug dealers fear arrest because it threatens their relationships with "straight" friends and relatives; more seasoned drug dealers are concerned about the impact of an arrest on their network of relationships with other drug dealers.

Ekland-Olson, Lieb, and Zurcher (1984) note that over time, the fear of arrest among drug dealers contributes to a general sense of paranoia, causing them to distrust strangers and restrict their drug sales to known associates. Eventually the social networks of long-term drug dealers narrow to the point that they interact only with a small group of trusted fellow drug dealers and users; this ironically restricts their ability to sell drugs, decreasing both sales and profits. In other words, among seasoned drug dealers, the fear of arrest (as a legal/formal sanction) causes the fear of strangers and the restriction of social networks (as informal sanctions/extralegal factors), which contribute to partial deterrence.

Patricia Adler's (see Adler 1985; Adler and Adler 1983) six-year field study of a network of sixty-five top-level drug dealers and smugglers operating in southern California corroborates the existence of interactive deterrence effects. Adler (1985, 115) contends that upper-level drug dealers primarily fear arrest and imprisonment because of social opprobrium; her drug-dealing respondents viewed arrest "as a 'status transformation,' a ceremonial rite that downgraded individuals in the eyes of significant others." Adler (1985, 115) continues that among drug dealers, "being arrested suggested that they might be informing to the narcs. Temporarily, at least, they ceased to be desirable business connections. Thus, in the drug business, locked up often meant locked out from all those who had come to constitute their circle of friends." Drug dealers sever their associations with arrested compatriots mostly because they fear the "heat" of police investigations; Adler and Peter Adler (1983, 204) remark that "arrested individuals were so 'hot' that few of their former associates would deal with them."

Because few qualitative criminological researchers to date have deigned to write on the topic of deterrence, it is unclear if the microstructural interactive deterrence mechanisms that appear to operate among higher-level drug dealers can be generalized to other types of criminal offenders. Nevertheless, at least among upper-echelon drug dealers, the fear of punishment seems to have some partial deterrence benefits, largely because it contributes to the fear of stigmatization from one's family, friends, and business associates. These studies suggest again that criminologists who conceptualize an independent relationship between legal/formal sanctions and informal sanctions/extralegal factors underestimate the effectiveness of punishments as deterrents.

General Deterrence: Some Concluding Remarks

Despite the many waves of research on general deterrence, the complexities of the topic have blocked criminologists from reaching many firm conclusions. Still, a number of reasonably clear inferences emerge from a review of this literature:

—A moderate inverse relationship exists between both the actual and perceived certainties of punishment and crime rates.

—There is little relationship between both the actual and perceived severities of punishment and crime rates.

—The perceived certainty of punishments is a more significant factor in deterring crime than the actual certainty of punishments.

—Get-tough criminal justice policies that increase the perceived certainty of punishments to potential offenders have a moderate initial deterrent effect on crime rates but little residual deterrent effect.

—Although the causal model specification of the relationship between legal/formal sanctions and informal sanctions/extralegal factors and deterrence remains subject to dispute, it is likely that the relationship is interactive rather than independent. This suggests that legal/formal sanctions exert much of their influence on individual behavior through the intervening variables of informal sanctions/extralegal factors.

—There is little empirical evidence to suggest that deterrence effects are contingent for different types of offenses; that is, the certainty of punishment appears to exert weak to moderate deterrent effects for *all* types of offenses.

—Finally, there is some empirical evidence to suggest that deterrence effects are contingent for different types of offenders. Specifically, lower-class persons and older persons appear to be more deterred by the certainty of punishment than the affluent and the young.

Clearly much more research remains to be done on the effectiveness of punishments as general deterrents. In particular, it is imperative that future researchers disentangle the complex relationship between legal/formal sanctions and informal sanctions/extralegal factors. Nevertheless, it is fair to conclude even now that the actual and perceived certainty of punishment (both arrest and imprisonment) is moderately effective as a general deterrent to crime.

SPECIFIC DETERRENCE: SOME GENERAL IMPRESSIONS

Although an ocean of research exists on the topic of general deterrence, only a small stream of studies exists on the effectiveness of punishments as specific deterrents. Perhaps because of the scarcity of actual research on the topic, the debate on specific deterrence has been strongly influenced by the two major opposing theoretical perspectives on the individual outcomes of punishment—labeling theory and rational choice theory (see chapters 2 and 6). The proponents of labeling theory argue that punishments are counterproductive because they stigmatize individual offenders and sever their contacts with conventional society. This contributes to the formation of deviant self-identities and deviant subcultures that reinforce one's commitment to deviant values and behaviors. Labeling theorists concur that "less is better" when it comes to formal criminal justice interventions in the lives of individual offenders; in other words, offenders are less likely to recidivate if they are left alone by the criminal justice system. Labeling theorists in particular view prisons as "crime schools," because they segregate offenders from conventional society and immerse offenders in a criminal subculture that perpetuates deviant values and behaviors (see Currie 1985; Lemert 1967; Schur 1973; Sommer 1976; chapter 6).

In contrast, rational choice theorists argue that individual offenders are decision makers who weigh the probable benefits and costs of criminal activities before committing crimes (see Becker 1968; Clarke and Cornish 1985; Cornish and Clarke 1986, 1987; Wilson 1985; Wilson and Herrnstein 1985). Rational choice theorists contend that punishments are important factors that influence the calculations of the benefits and costs attached to prospective criminal activities by offenders. Implicit in these arguments is the assumption that formal criminal justice sanctions are essential mechanisms in convincing offenders that "crime doesn't pay." Because labeling theorists believe that imprisonment breeds future crime, they mostly dismiss the effectiveness of incarceration as a specific deterrent to crime. Rational choice theorists, however, consider general deterrence to be the most important social outcome of imprisonment and consider specific deterrence as the cardinal individual outcome of imprisonment (Becker 1968; Wilson 1985; Wilson and Herrnstein 1985). Chapter 6 reviews a number of research studies that compare the contradictory predictions regarding the individual outcomes of punishment made by labeling theorists versus rational choice theorists.

Those sympathetic to labeling arguments often cite simple recidivism rates to support their claim that imprisonment fails to achieve specific deterrence (see Currie 1985; Sommer 1976). Currie (1985, 70), for example, concludes that "high recidivism rates are a troubling, stubborn prima facie case that if imprisonment deters individual criminals at all, it clearly doesn't do so reliably or consistently." As noted earlier in this chapter, however, there is a variety of reasons why the simple analysis of return rates to prison is probably an invalid indicator of the effectiveness of criminal justice sanctions. Fortunately, a small, but fairly sophisticated, specific deterrence literature now exists that goes beyond the study of simple prison recidivism rates. These studies evaluate the effectiveness of specific deterrence by comparing the subsequent crime rates of groups of offenders who receive either more lenient or harsher criminal justice sanctions. In some cases, the research designs in these studies include the random assignment of offenders to various research groups (see Berk and Newton 1985; Sherman and Berk 1984), which ensures that higher-risk offenders (who are more likely to recidivate) are not more likely than lower-risk offenders to receive harsher punishments (a research design flaw that can predetermine the finding of the failure of punishments as specific deterrents). In general, specific deterrence studies that employ comparison groups and the random assignment of offenders to different punishment alternatives offer moderate support for the rational choice argument that legal/formal sanctions deter future individual offending.

I next review the admittedly scattered and scarce empirical studies of the effectiveness of legal/formal sanctions as specific deterrents, categorized in six areas: (1) cohort studies, (2) domestic assault studies, (3) shoplifting studies, (4) drunk driving studies, (5) partial deterrence/suppression effects studies, and (6) perceptual specific deterrence studies. Some general conclusions are made about the relative effectiveness of the certainty and the severity of punishments as specific deterrents and about contingent specific deterrence effects for different types of offenders and offenses.

Cohort Studies

Cohort studies in criminology usually examine a group of persons born in the same year, using official police data to follow their offense histories over a number of years (say, until their eighteenth birthdays). In the process of tracking delinquent/criminal histories, some of these studies analyze the effects of arrest and punishment on subsequent offending patterns among members of the cohort (see Brennan and Mednick 1991; Smith and

Gartin 1989; Tracy, Wolfgang, and Figlio 1990; Wolfgang, Figlio, and Sellin 1972). These studies offer some important insights on the effectiveness of formal/legal sanctions on offender recidivism.

In two separate cohort studies in Philadelphia, Marvin Wolfgang, Robert Figlio, and Sellin (1972) and Paul Tracy, Wolfgang, and Figlio (1990) followed the delinquent careers of boys who continuously resided in the city from their tenth to their eighteenth birthdays (see chapter 5). The earlier study followed 9,945 boys born in Philadelphia in 1945; the later study tracked 13,160 boys born in Philadelphia in 1958. Among the many topics analyzed in these complex studies are the effects of "remedial" dispositions (where apprehended offenders are merely warned by the police, without being arrested and processed through the juvenile justice system) versus official arrest and court processing on the subsequent behavior of young offenders. For youth apprehended for serious, Federal Bureau of Investigation (FBI) index crimes in the 1945 cohort, those who received arrest/court dispositions had slightly *higher* index crime recidivism rates than youth processed informally (Wolfgang, Figlio, and Sellin 1972). In the 1958 cohort, however, the *opposite* proved true; among boys apprehended for index offenses, those who received the more punitive disposition of arrest/court processing had substantially *lower* index offense recidivism rates than youths who were only warned (Tracy, Wolfgang, and Figlio 1990). For example, among boys apprehended for index crimes for their first official offense in the 1958 cohort, those receiving a remedial disposition had a 66 percent probability of recidivism (defined as at least one subsequent index offense apprehension before their eighteenth birthdays); in contrast, boys receiving an arrest/court disposition had a 52 percent probability of recidivism. Data from the 1958 cohort of Philadelphia boys clearly support the specific deterrence/rational choice argument that more punitive arrest/court processing for youth apprehended for serious offenses is associated with lower rates of subsequent offending.

One additional important finding in the Philadelphia cohort studies concerns the contingent effects of arrest/court dispositions depending on the positioning of an offense in one's delinquent career. It appears that an inverse relationship exists between the length of delinquent careers and the effectiveness of arrest/court sanctions; that is, novice offenders are more deterred by more punitive dispositions than chronic offenders (who have numerous previous apprehensions). For example, among boys apprehended for three previous index offenses in the 1958 cohort, the selection of dispositions had much less impact on whether the boys were apprehended for a fourth offense; here, boys receiving remedial dispositions had an 84 percent probability of recidivism, while boys receiving arrest/court dispositions had an 81 percent recidivism probability (Tracy, Wolfgang, and Figlio 1990). Although these data suggest that the effectiveness of punishments appears to weaken with each subsequent arrest, note that the direction of these percentages remains consistent with specific deterrence predictions.

Douglas Smith and Patrick Gartin's (1989) reanalysis of Lyle Shannon's (1982, 1988) cohort studies (see chapter 5) of 325 males born in Racine, Wisconsin, in 1949 who were apprehended for at least one misdemeanor or felony before their twenty-fifth birthdays supports Tracy, Wolfgang, and Figlio's (1990) 1958 cohort findings. Like the Philadelphia cohort researchers, Smith and Gartin (1989) compare the impact of arrest/detention dispositions versus nonarrest/warning dispositions on the subsequent apprehension records of their Racine offenders. Controlling for the age of offenders and the seriousness of their offenses, the authors conclude that (1) arrested/detained first offenders in the cohort were significantly *less likely* to have future police contacts than the nonarrested first offenders and (2) although the beneficial effects of arrest/detention diminished with each subsequent apprehension, *they remained statistically significant.* These findings again suggest that legal/formal sanctions have important specific deterrent effects but that these effects are contingent on the positioning of offenses and sanctions in one's offending career.

Finally, Patricia Brennan and Sarnoff Mednick (1991) study the effect of criminal justice sanctions in a cohort of 28,879 males born in Copenhagen, Denmark, between 1 January 1944 and 31 December 1947 (and followed until their twenty-sixth birthdays). Among the 6,579 males in the cohort who had at least one nontraffic-related arrest, Brennan and Mednick (1991) compare the relative impact of "nonsanction" dispositions (where charges were dropped and offenders were released) versus "sanction" dispositions (where offenders were punished through probation, fines, or imprisonment). As in the 1958 Philadelphia and Racine, Wisconsin, cohort studies, the authors found that sanctioned offenders had significantly lower recidivism rates than nonsanctioned offenders, controlling for the variables of age, social class, and previous arrests (but not for the seriousness of offenses). In addition the data again show that although an inverse relationship exists between the number of one's previous arrests and the effectiveness of sanction dispositions, the specific deterrent effect of sanction dispositions remains statistically significant, at least among offenders with as many as four career arrests.

It is important to note that the cohort studies reviewed here mostly support the argument that the certainty of legal/formal sanctions (arrest, court processing, and brief detention) deters subsequent individual offending, not the severity of legal/formal sanctions. For example, in Brennan and Mednick's (1991) study, no differences were found in the recidivism rates among differentially sanctioned offenders (those receiving probation, fines, or imprisonment), although the authors did not control for the seriousness of offenses (so perhaps offenders who were imprisoned had similar recidivism rates as those who received probation only because the former were higher-risk offenders). Notwithstanding this research design shortcoming, cohort studies seem to suggest that Draconian legal/formal sanctions (involving long prison terms) are unnecessary to achieve specific deterrence benefits; arrests followed by short periods of detention are sufficient to discourage at least some subsequent offending. This conclusion is further supported by domestic assault research.

Domestic Assault Studies

Perhaps the most important studies of the effectiveness of punishments as specific deterrents examine the impact of various punishments on males apprehended for assaulting their wives or lovers (see Berk et al. 1992; Berk and Newton 1985; Dunford, Huizinga, and Elliott 1990; Pate and Hamilton 1992; Sherman et al. 1991; Sherman and Berk 1984; Sherman and Smith 1992; Steinman 1991). These domestic assault studies offer crucial insights into the specific deterrence process because *all* (except Steinman 1991) use research designs where offenders are randomly assigned to alternative law enforcement "strategies," ranging from ordering offenders to leave the premises for a few hours, to arrest and short-term detention. The random assignment of alternative apprehension strategies in domestic assault research excludes the possibility of selectivity factors in the assignment of punishments, where only high-risk offenders who are more likely to recidivate receive the harsher punishments.

The exemplary study on which subsequent domestic assault research is modeled is Lawrence Sherman and Richard Berk's (1984) evaluation of the effectiveness of different domestic assault apprehension strategies pursued by the Minneapolis Police Department in the early 1980s. For eighteen months, a special unit of the Minneapolis police force randomly assigned one of three apprehension strategies—advice and mediation, ordering offenders to leave the premises for eight hours, or arrest and short-term detention—to all male offenders in misdemeanor domestic assault cases. The 314 randomly assigned cases were then followed by Sherman and Berk (1984) for six months to determine if male offenders experienced a subsequent police contact for domestic assault and if interviewed female victims reported subsequent assaults. Both police-contact and victim-interview data show that offenders who were arrested and detained were significantly *less* likely to recidivate than those who were informally processed, a finding that supports the argument that arrest and brief detention have a significant specific deterrent effect on male offenders apprehended for domestic assault.

Numerous domestic assault studies have attempted to replicate Sherman and Berk's (1984) original findings, using samples of 783 offenders in one southern California county (Berk and Newton 1985), 330 offenders from Omaha, Nebraska (Dunford, Huizinga, and Elliott 1990), 907 offenders from Miami (Pate and Hamilton 1992), 1,200 offenders from Milwaukee (Sherman et al. 1991; Sherman and Smith 1992), and 1,658 offenders from Colorado Springs, Colorado (Berk et al. 1992). The research designs in each of these studies closely parallel the design originally used by Sherman and Berk in Minneapolis (including the random assignment of domestic assault cases to different apprehension strategies, and follow-up analyses of recidivism rates using police-contact and victim-interview data). In one of the replications (Berk and Newton 1985), arrested and detained offenders were again found to be significantly less likely to recidivate than offenders who were processed informally, while in the Omaha study (Dunford, Huizinga, and Elliott 1990), no differences were found among offenders receiving different apprehension strategies. The other studies (Berk et al. 1992; Pate and Hamilton 1992; Sherman et al. 1991; Sherman and Smith 1992) are somewhat less straightforward in interpretation; in general, they show that punitive arrest and detention strategies deter only women batterers who have stronger attachments and commitments to the community. Specifically, arrest and detention *decrease* the rates of recidivism in domestic assault cases among employed males (Berk et al. 1992; Pate and Hamilton 1992; Sherman and Smith 1992) and possibly also among married males (Sherman and Smith 1992) but sometimes *increase* the rates of recidivism among males who are unemployed and unmarried.

It bears reiterating that because these domestic assault studies randomly assign offenders to different apprehension strategies, they offer invaluable insight on the effectiveness of legal/formal sanctions as specific deterrents. These studies now appear to offer strong support for Williams and Hawkins's (1986) interactive effects model of the relationship between legal/formal sanctions and informal sanctions/extralegal factors—women-batterers who fear reprisals from employers and family members are more deterred by punishments than offenders without these social attachments and commitments. Because judges understandably are reticent to assist researchers by randomly imposing sentences for other types of offenses (can you imagine the public furor if a judge randomly assigned warnings or life sentences to offenders convicted of murder?), it is unclear if these findings can ever be replicated and generalized much beyond domestic assault cases. Still, a handful of studies on both shoplifters and drunk drivers that employ less rigorous research designs confirms the argument that arrests sometimes deter subsequent individual offending, especially among those who fear informal sanctions.

Shoplifting Studies

Several studies attempt to assess the impact of apprehension on future offending patterns among shoplifters (Cameron 1964; Klemke 1978; Kraut 1976). In a comparison of "pilferers" (amateur, mostly female shoplifters from relatively "respectable" backgrounds) with "boosters" (professional, male and female shoplifters who are committed to shoplifting as a way of life) either apprehended in one Chicago department store between 1943 and 1950 or charged with petty larceny/shoplifting and processed through Chicago courts between 1948 and 1950, Mary Owen Cameron (1964) concludes that apprehension has an important deterrent effect among the former, but not the latter. Recidivism among pilferers is rare: "Once arrested, interrogated, and in their own perspective, perhaps humiliated, pilferers apparently stop pilfering. The reward of shoplifting, whatever it is, is not worth the cost of [the loss of one's] reputation and self-esteem" (Cameron 1964, 151). Boosters, however, apparently remain undaunted by arrest and imprisonment: "He [sic] does, of course, make every possible effort to talk his [sic] way out of the [arrest] situation. But once he [sic] finds that this is impossible, he [sic] accepts jail and its inconveniences as a normal hazard of the trade" (Cameron 1964, 142).

Cameron's (1964) study not only corroborates that arrest and the threat of incarceration deter some types of individual offending but also suggests again that interactive effects exist between legal/formal sanctions and informal sanctions/extralegal factors. Pilferers seem to be deterred by arrests for shoplifting because they fear informal sanctions (e.g., public humiliation/stigmatization and the loss of respectable community reputations). Probably because they have no upstanding community reputations to protect, boosters are little deterred by the sting of either formal or informal sanctions.

Two additional studies examine the effectiveness of the apprehension of shoplifters on their subsequent shoplifting activities, using self-report data collected from samples of students (see Klemke 1978; Kraut 1976). Robert Kraut's (1976) survey of a random sample of 606 university students shows that respondents who reported shoplifting usually perceived a low certainty of punishment for the offense, unless they were once apprehended for shoplifting. Students apprehended for shoplifting not only perceived a significantly higher certainty of punishment for the offense but also apparently committed fewer offenses after apprehension than before. Notably, though, apprehension resulted in only partial specific deterrence: apprehended shoplifters still reported committing an average of five shoplifting offenses following their apprehension. Nevertheless, Kraut (1976, 365) concludes that his data are "consistent with a [specific] deterrent model: the decision to steal is an inverse function of the perceived risks associated with stealing."

In contrast, Lloyd Klemke's (1978) survey of shoplifting patterns among 1,189 high school students suggests that apprehended offenders may be *more* likely to recidivate than those who elude detection. The relationships reported by Klemke (1978), however, are barely statistically significant. Furthermore, Klemke does not control for the frequency of shoplifting episodes *before* offender apprehension—as a result, it is probable that apprehended offenders committed higher rates of shoplifting than those who escaped detection not only after, but also before, apprehension (which may explain why they were apprehended in the first place). In fact, it is quite possible that Klemke's apprehended shoplifters—like those in Kraut's study—committed fewer offenses after apprehension than before, a conclusion that again would support the argument that apprehension for shoplifting achieves partial specific deterrence.

The important distinction in shoplifting studies between amateur offenders (including Cameron's pilferers and undoubtedly most of Kraut and Klemke's student shoplifters) and professional boosters suggests that *specific* deterrence effects may be contingent on a factor mentioned by Chambliss (1967)—the offender's degree of commitment to crime as a way of life. Because amateur shoplifters have little commitment to crime as a career, the informal sanctions of conventional society still retain much influence over their behavior (which enhances the deterrent effectiveness of legal/formal sanctions). The high commitment to crime among boosters, however, probably diminishes the strength of conventional informal sanctions, concomitantly diminishing the specific deterrent effectiveness of apprehension. This may help to explain why deterrence effects are related to the positioning of offenses in one's criminal career—chronic offenders (like Cameron's boosters) are less deterrable because they are more committed to the life of crime.

Drunk Driving Studies

In response to the growing public concern over the number of alcohol-related traffic accidents and deaths, many states and foreign countries have adopted new get-tough laws for those convicted of drunk driving (Wheeler and Hissong 1988). While most of the studies of the impact of these laws evaluate their effectiveness as general deterrents, a few focus instead on the effect of various punishment options on the subsequent behavior of those convicted for drunk driving (see Ross 1984; Shapiro and Votey 1984; Wheeler and Hissong 1988). The latter studies offer mixed support for the effectiveness of legal/formal sanctions for drunk drivers; although the mere arrest of drunk drivers appears to exert some deterrent effect on their later drinking and driving behavior, tougher penalties (e.g., fines and jail) seem to have little added impact (beyond arrest) in deterring drunk driving.

Perry Shapiro and Harold Votey (1984) compare the relative effects of arrests, fines, and jail sentences on the subsequent arrest patterns of all 46,000 males apprehended for drunk driving in Sweden from 1976 through 1979. Using complex econometric estimation procedures, the authors conclude that each arrest for drunk driving appeared to decrease significantly the likelihood that an offender would be subsequently arrested for drunk driving. Additional penalties imposed on persons convicted for drunk driving (i.e., fines and/or jail sentences), however, had no statistically significant impact on the future probability of arrest.

The specific deterrent effects of a tough new Texas law requiring mandatory seventy-two–hour jail sentences for a first conviction for drunk driving are examined by Gerald Wheeler and Rodney Hissong (1988). The authors analyze the subsequent arrest patterns over a three-year period in a random sample of 397 persons convicted for drunk driving in Houston, Texas, in January 1984 (after the new law took effect). Interestingly, despite the new law, only 12 percent of the first-time offenders in the authors' sample received the supposedly "mandatory" jail sentence. In their comparisons of the failure rates over three years among convictees who received either probation, fines, or jail sentences, Wheeler and Hissong (1988) found no statistically significant differences either in one's probability for a subsequent arrest or in the average time-to-failure for persons subsequently arrested. Although these findings fail to support the effectiveness of harsher punishments for individuals convicted of drunk driving, the authors attribute this failure in part to the low certainty of mandatory jail sentences (Wheeler and Hissong note that most convictees viewed the new law as a "sham"). It is also likely that the 12 percent of first-time drunk driving convictees who received jail sentences were high-risk offenders who were more likely to recidivate than the majority of offenders who received either probationary sentences or fines. In general, the drunk driving studies suggest once more that the certainty of punishments—but not punishment severity—plays some role in deterring future offending.

Partial Deterrence/Suppression Effects Studies

Although scattered evidence that supports the effectiveness of punishments in achieving partial (rather than absolute) specific deterrence (by decreasing the frequency of individual offending after the punishment compared with before) is found in the cohort, domestic assault, and shoplifting research, two studies (Klein 1974; Murray and Cox 1979) examine partial deterrence in considerable detail. Malcolm Klein (1974) compares the recidivism rates of juvenile offenders in thirteen of forty-nine Los Angeles County police departments, selected on the basis of their extreme differences in diversion practices. Eight departments were identified as "high diversion agencies," because they screened away most arrested young offenders from juvenile court processing. The other five departments were "low diversion agencies," which frequently resorted to more formal and punitive juvenile court and reformatory processing for offenders. Klein (1974) followed the recidivism rates for thirty months of the first 100 youths arrested in the thirteen departments during 1969.

Interestingly, no differences were found in the simple recidivism rates between high diversion and low diversion police departments—the percentages of juvenile offenders who had at least one subsequent arrest were almost identical in the different departments. When Klein (1974) compared the number of offenders with *multiple* subsequent arrests in high diversion and low diversion departments, however, he found significantly lower recidivism rates in the *low* diversion departments. This study suggests that while legal/formal sanctions may have no apparent impact on the prevalence of simple recidivism (defined here as one subsequent arrest), they significantly reduce the rate of multiple offending (or the frequency of subsequent arrests).

This interpretation is corroborated by Charles Murray and Louis Cox's (1979) longitudinal study of the criminal careers of 317 male juvenile offenders in Chicago. The researchers examined offender arrest records for one year before, and seventeen months after, each received his first prison sentence (the average age of offenders was sixteen, and the average time spent in prison was ten months). The offenders selected for the study were hard-core delinquents, averaging thirteen arrests prior to incarceration. Murray and Cox (1979) found that on the average, the 317 offenders were arrested 6.3 times each in the year before imprisonment, but only 2.9 times each during the seventeen months following release. The authors coined the term *suppression effects* to refer to the reduced levels of offending apparently brought about by imprisonment. Note that an analysis of the simple recidivism rates in this study would reach the erroneous conclusion that incarceration failed as a specific deterrent (because most offenders were subsequently rearrested following imprisonment). The much more important conclusion supporting partial specific deterrence is that offenders had far fewer arrests after imprisonment.

The critics of prisons are quick to repudiate the Murray and Cox (1979) study (see Currie 1985). Currie (1985) correctly observes that the findings in this study may be the spurious result of regression toward the mean effects (Gibbs 1975; Zimring and Hawkins 1973) rather than specific deterrence. Assuming that delinquent careers naturally fluctuate between periods of high-rate and low-rate offending, it is possible that Murray and Cox's hard-core delinquent offenders committed an uncharacteristically large number of offenses immediately before incarceration but then returned to more normal rates of offending upon release from prison. It is possible that imprisonment may have had nothing to do with this natural fluctuation in offending patterns. Because the Klein (1974) study, however, does not include only high-rate offenders in its sample, it is extremely unlikely that regression toward the mean effects influenced his findings. It is interesting to note that when Currie (1985) disputes partial deterrence/suppression effects research, he conveniently omits any discussion of Klein's (1974) study.

In general, some research evidence suggests that legal/formal sanctions (including arrests, court processing, and brief detention/short prison sentences) exert important partial deterrence effects on subsequent offending patterns. Idealists who desire absolute solutions to the crime problem may be frustrated that punishments sometimes merely lower the rates of future offending; however, in the real world of nonlinear criminal justice, partial victories are a cause for celebration.

Perceptual Specific Deterrence Studies

A final topic that has received some attention by specific deterrence researchers is the effect of legal/formal sanctions on an offender's perceived certainty of punishment for subsequent offenses (see Bridges and Stone 1986; Horney and Marshall 1992; Thomas and Bishop 1984). Recall that several perceptual *general* deterrence researchers who have undertaken panel design studies argue that the experience of committing crimes causes many offenders to lower their perceived certainty of punishment for subsequent offenses (Minor and Harry 1982; Paternoster 1987; Paternoster et al. 1983, 1985; Saltzman et al. 1982). These experiential effects (Saltzman et al. 1982) suggest that some offenders gradually learn over time through committing various offenses that the actual likelihood that they will be apprehended and punished for any given crime is very low. Recognition of the low certainty of *actual* punishment may eventually cause offenders to lower their estimations of the *perceived* certainty of punishments, possibly contributing to additional criminal activity. But once offenders finally *are* apprehended and punished, what effect does this have on their perceived certainty of punishment for future offenses?

A number of early studies of chronic offenders with long arrest histories (see chapter 5) suggest that even offenders who have been apprehended and punished continue to perceive a low certainty of punishment for offending (Chaiken and Chaiken 1982; Peterson, Braiker, and Polich 1981). Three recent studies that attempt to shed additional light on the effect of legal/formal sanctions on the perceived certainty of punishment are Charles Thomas and Bishop (1984), George Bridges and James Stone (1986), and Julie Horney and Ineke Marshall (1992). Thomas and Bishop (1984) study the effect of police apprehension on estimations of the perceived certainty of punishment in a sample of 2,147 Virginia high school students. Surveys measuring the students' perceptions of punishment certainty and self-reported rates of offending for thirteen offenses (ranging in seriousness from truancy to assault with a weapon) were administered at the beginning and again at the end of the school year. At the time of the second survey, students were also asked to report their number of police contacts since the first survey. Controlling for a variety of factors (including the age, gender, race, and self-reported number of offenses of respondents), Thomas and Bishop (1984) found no significant changes in the perceived certainty of punishment among those students with recent police contact experience. Furthermore, the authors found evidence supporting the experiential effect—that is, inverse relationships between the number of self-reported offenses and the perceived certainty of punishment for offenses—controlling for police contact experience. Bishop and Thomas's (1984) study suggests that while experience committing crime causes juvenile offenders to revise *downward* their estimations of punishment risk, police apprehension does not cause juvenile offenders to revise these estimations back *upward*. (Interestingly, this contradicts Kraut's [1976] earlier finding that apprehension increases the perception of the certainty of punishment among amateur shoplifters.)

In a study of 550 inmates incarcerated in a men's federal prison, Bridges and Stone (1986) try to clarify further the relationship between the punishment experiences of offenders and their perceptions of the certainty of punishment. Bridges and Stone (1986) relate the number of self-reported crimes committed by inmates and their self-reported punishment histories—including the number of prior convictions, the total length of time served in prison, and the actual certainty of punishment throughout their own criminal careers (measured by dividing each offender's total number of reported convictions by his total number of reported offenses)—to their perceived certainty of punishment for numerous offenses. The authors found an inverse relationship between an offender's number of self-reported offenses and estimations of the certainty of punishment (again supporting the experiential effect). In addition, while the number of prior convictions and the length of time served in prison were not related to perceptions of punishment certainty in Bridges and Stone's (1986) inmate sample, the actual certainty of punishment in one's own criminal career was moderately positively related to perceptions of punishment certainty.

Finally, in a study of the relationships among arrest histories, perceived certainties of punishment, and self-reported offenses among 1,046 male inmates in Nebraska, Horney and Marshall (1992) confirm most of Bridges and Stone's (1986) findings. Horney and Marshall asked inmates to report (1) how often they had been arrested for nine offenses (including robbery, burglary, assault, and drug deals), (2) the estimated likelihood of arrest for each of these offenses, and (3) the number of each of these offenses they had committed for three years prior to incarceration. Importantly, the authors found a significant direct relationship between the ratio (or certainty) of actual arrests for each offense and the inmates' perceived certainties of arrest and a significant negative relationship between the perceived certainties of arrest for each offense and the inmates' reported frequencies of committing each offense.

In general, perceptual specific deterrence research supports the experiential effect argument that novice offenders perceive a greater certainty of punishment than chronic offenders. This research also suggests that the simple experience of apprehension and punishment will not necessarily cause an offender to perceive a greater certainty of punishment for subsequent offenses, unless one's recent apprehension and punishment experience is part of a high ratio of actual apprehension/punishment throughout one's offending career. Perceptual specific deterrence studies appear to offer striking support for rational choice arguments—offenders apparently base their estimations of punishment risk on a fairly complex assessment of their own perceived offense, apprehension, and punishment histories, so that perceptions of punishment certainty mirror the actual certainty of apprehension and punishment in one's own criminal career.

Specific Deterrence: Some Concluding Remarks

Although the research on specific deterrence is rather sparse, a few general conclusions still can be reached from a survey of this literature:

—Legal/formal sanctions—including arrest, court processing, and brief periods of detention—appear to be moderately inversely related to subsequent individual offending, in support of specific deterrence/rational choice arguments. There is no evidence, however, to suggest that severe punishments (i.e., long prison terms) are more effective as specific deterrents than milder punishments (short-term detention).

—Legal/formal sanctions may fail to lower the absolute (or simple) recidivism rates among individual offenders and yet still achieve important partial specific deterrence benefits by reducing the overall rates (or frequencies) of offending among individual offenders (the suppression effect).

—The effectiveness of legal/formal sanctions in deterring individual offending is contingent on the positioning of offenses in one's offending career. Punishments are more effective in deterring future offending the earlier that they occur in one's offending career, although some specific deterrence benefits are still apparent in the punishment of chronic offenders.

—Perceptions of the certainty of punishment are also contingent on the positioning of offenses in one's offending career. Specifically, novice offenders usually perceive a greater certainty of punishment for their offenses than chronic offenders.

—The perceived certainties of punishment among offenders are contingent on their actual certainties of punishment (or their objective likelihoods of arrest and imprisonment throughout their offending careers).

—The effectiveness of legal/formal sanctions as specific deterrents may be contingent on the degree of an offender's commitment to his or her offending career. Specifically, professional offenders who are committed to crime as a way of life appear to be less deterred by punishments than amateur offenders.

—Finally, an interactive relationship appears to exist between legal/formal sanctions and informal sanctions/extralegal factors as specific deterrents. Punishments are more effective in deterring future individual offending the more that one worries about reprisals from one's friends and family and/or the loss of one's job or good community reputation.

In the near future, criminologists must conduct more research on the effectiveness of punishments as specific deterrents. For example, some of the conclusions noted above are based on research evidence from only a few studies; replication studies of previous specific deterrence research findings are of utmost importance. In particular, to enhance the generalizability of specific deterrence research, studies involving the random assignment of offenders to different punishment options are needed for offenses other than domestic assault. As with general deterrence, much more specific deterrence research also needs to examine the likely interactive effects among legal/formal sanctions, informal sanctions/extralegal factors, and subsequent patterns of individual offending. Still, it is fair to conclude even at this early juncture that legal/formal sanctions (including arrest and mild punishments) are moderately effective as specific deterrents to crime.

FINIS DETERRENCE, ENTREE INCAPACITATION

After this whirlwind review of the dizzying array of deterrence studies in criminology, some readers may feel overwhelmed with details. Despite the somewhat obscure nature of the literature, I believe that four palpable lessons of crucial relevance to policymakers can be distilled from deterrence studies:

—Apprehension and punishment appear to be moderately effective in achieving both general and specific deterrence.

—The certainty of punishment is a far more important factor in deterring crime than the severity of punishment. To discourage most people from committing crimes, long prison sentences are unnecessary. An essential goal of policymakers and criminal justice officials should be to increase the certainty of arrest, conviction, and mild punishment/short detention for most offenders.

—Individual perceptions play a crucial role in deterring crime. The perceived certainty of punishment is more important than the actual certainty of punishment in convincing most people to behave themselves. This suggests that policymakers and criminal justice officials should place great importance on conveying the message to the public that crime does not pay. High-profile, well-publicized anticrime campaigns are an essential component for deterring crime in America. Criminal justice officials should take a lesson from the notebooks of politicians that imagery often is more important than substance (Edelman 1988); photo opportunities of flashy police crackdown operations (that make the local evening news) may be far more beneficial in keeping the average citizen honest than countless low-profile undercover investigations.

—While average citizens and novice offenders can be deterred by well-publicized anticrime campaigns, chronic offenders usually won't be. For offenders with much crime experience, the perceived certainty of punishment mirrors the actual certainty of punishment: because experience has taught them that actual punishments are rare, chronic offenders often perceive that crime in fact *does* pay. Assuming the accuracy of the interactive effects model of the relationship between legal/formal sanctions and informal sanctions/extralegal factors, chronic offenders will also be less deterred by legal/formal sanctions because they have fewer ties to conventional society (through attachments to "square" friends and family members) and no "good" community reputations to protect. This suggests that policymakers and criminal justice officials should de-emphasize deterrence for chronic offenders, in preference to incapacitation strategies. This is the subject of chapter 5.

Chapter Five

Positive Support for Prisons, II: Incapacitation

In an interview shortly before his execution, Gary Gilmore (quoted in Mailer 1980, 906) offered this explanation for the murders of two Provo, Utah, men that he didn't even know.

I was always capable of murder. There's a side of me that I don't like. I can become totally devoid of feelings for others, unemotional. I know I'm doing something grossly fucking wrong. I can still go ahead and do it.

Specific deterrence clearly failed for Gary Gilmore; despite his imprisonment for nineteen of the twenty-two years before his execution, he inevitably returned to sprees of alcohol abuse, robbery, and assault almost immediately upon release from prison.

Although there is reasonably compelling evidence that arrest and incarceration can deter certain potential and actual offenders, deterrence is clearly no panacea; some criminals—like Gilmore—"may be beyond the pale of appeals to conventional rationality" (Wright 1992, 105). Criminologists have for some time acknowledged the problem of "chronic" or "habitual" offenders—or a small number of criminals who commit a great number of crimes. As noted in chapter 4, punishments are only minimally effective in deterring these criminals. For example, from his interviews with sixty older chronic offenders (who collectively reported committing 48,626 offenses in their criminal careers), Kenneth Tunnell (1990, 687–688; see also Bridges and Stone 1986; Horney and Marshall 1992) concludes that these offenders "view themselves as immune from criminal sanction[s], and hence are undeterred." The offenders in this study offered three reasons why legal sanctions failed to prevent them from committing crimes: (1) they believed that they would not be apprehended for their offenses, (2) they thought that if they were apprehended, at worst they would receive only short prison sentences, and (3) previous incarceration experience led them to conclude that prison was a "nonthreatening," tolerable environment. For these reasons, and perhaps others—including genetic impulsivity, a hardheaded temperament, inadequate socialization, raging sociopathy (à la Gilmore), superior intelligence and wit that lead them to believe they can elude the police, and/or inferior reasoning abilities that prevent them from learning from past mistakes—chronic offenders do not fear the threat of punishments sufficiently to forgo the pleasures of crime. For the chronic offender, incarceration serves the important purpose of protecting society from the crimes they would commit if free. Chapter 5 shows that prisons are at least modestly successful in achieving incapacitation as a utilitarian social outcome.

THE CHRONICLES OF THE CHRONICS

A plethora of criminological studies recently has been devoted to examining the problem of chronic offenders. For the most part, these studies have explored this topic through longitudinal analyses of (1) police department records of offender arrests (see Hamparian et al. 1978; Shannon 1982, 1988; Tracy, Wolfgang, and Figlio 1990; Wolfgang, Figlio, and Sellin 1972; Wolfgang, Thornberry, and Figlio 1987) or offender convictions (see West 1969, 1982; West and Farrington 1973, 1977) or (2) the self-reported offenses of juvenile offenders (see Dunford and Elliott 1984) or adult prisoners (see Chaiken and Chaiken 1982, 1984; Greenwood 1982; Horney and Marshall 1991; Petersilia, Greenwood, and Lavin 1977; Peterson and Braiker 1980; Peterson, Braiker, and Polich 1981). Despite the different research designs of these studies, all attempt to distinguish categories of offenders on the basis of their *frequencies* (or rates) of individual offending; frequency calculations on the average annual rates of individual offending while on the streets now by convention are referred to by the Greek letter lambda (λ) by criminologists (see Blumstein et al. 1986; Blumstein, Cohen, and Farrington 1988a, b). These studies consistently show that offender samples can be subdivided into a low-frequency category (comprised of a large number of "occasional" offenders) versus a high-frequency category (comprised of a small number of chronic offenders).

Among the publications that rely on police records of arrests, the landmark studies of Marvin Wolfgang and his associates (Tracy, Wolfgang, and Figlio 1990; Wolfgang, Figlio, and Sellin 1972; Wolfgang, Thornberry, and Figlio 1987) using cohorts of Philadelphia youth have been pivotal in drawing systematic attention to the existence of chronic offenders. Initially, Wolfgang, Robert Figlio, and Thorsten Sellin (1972) examined the nontraffic-related arrest records of 9,945 Philadelphia boys born in 1945 who maintained continuous residence in the city from their tenth to their eighteenth birthdays. Although 34.9 percent of these boys were arrested at least once before turning eighteen, most (28.6 percent) were arrested four or fewer times. However, 6.3 percent of the boys were classified by the authors as chronic offenders (with five or more arrests); these boys were responsible for an astonishing 51.9 percent of the total arrests in the study. In addition, a subsequent study that traced the arrest records of a random sample of 975 males from the 1945 cohort until they turned thirty revealed that almost half (45.2 percent) of those who were chronic juvenile offenders became chronic adult offenders (again, with five or more arrests—see Wolfgang, Thornberry, and Figlio 1987).

In a replication of the original Wolfgang, Figlio, and Sellin study (1972), Paul Tracy, Wolfgang, and Figlio (1990) examined the nontraffic-related arrest records of a cohort of 13,160 Philadelphia boys born in 1958 and followed until their eighteenth birthdays. Again, important differences were found between nonchronic and chronic offenders; while 32.8 percent of the boys had at least one arrest before turning eighteen, 25.3 percent were arrested four or fewer times, and 7.5 percent were arrested five or more times. Once again, the small group of chronic offenders accounted for the majority (60.6 percent) of the total arrests among the boys born in 1958.

Lyle Shannon's (1982, 1988) studies of the arrest and court records of three cohorts (born in 1942, 1949, and 1955) of males and females from Racine, Wisconsin ($n = 4,079$), support the argument for the existence of a small number of chronic offenders. When data on the arrest records of males under eighteen years old are considered (combining all three cohorts), approximately 32 percent had at least one misdemeanor or felony arrest by the age of eighteen. Males with four or more arrests in the three cohorts, however, represented only 7 percent of the sample but accounted for 50 percent of the total arrests.

Yet another longitudinal study profiling 1,138 juveniles arrested at least once for violent offenses who were born from 1956 to 1960 in Columbus, Ohio, offers additional evidence concerning chronic offenders (see Hamparian et al. 1978). As with the other studies, a small number of the

Columbus violent offenders (31 percent) were classified as chronics (with five or more arrests for all types of crimes). Once again, the chronic offenders accounted for a majority (this time, two-thirds) of the arrests for the entire cohort.

One final group of studies of chronic offenders that relies on official criminal justice statistics is Donald West and David Farrington's longitudinal analyses of the conviction records of a group of 396 London boys born between 1951 to 1954 (see West 1969, 1982; West and Farrington 1973, 1977). The authors followed the criminal records of these males until their twenty-fifth birthdays. Although 34.3 percent of the males had one or more convictions by age twenty-five, only 5.8 percent of the sample were chronic offenders (with six or more convictions). Again, the researchers found that the chronic offenders were responsible for almost half of the crime convictions in the studies.

The longitudinal studies of police records summarized above draw important distinctions between the *prevalence* of offending (or the proportion of the population with one or more arrests or convictions) versus offense frequency (Blumstein et al. 1986; Blumstein, Cohen, and Farrington 1988a, b). These studies show that while delinquent and criminal offending is fairly prevalent (i.e., perhaps one-third of any given cohort has at least one arrest), high-frequency, chronic offending is comparatively rare (roughly 7 percent of any cohort can be classified as chronic offenders).

Several recent reanalyses of Wolfgang et al.'s Philadelphia data and West and Farrington's London data support the argument that offender samples can be divided between low-frequency, occasional offenders and high-frequency, chronic offenders (see Barnett, Blumstein, and Farrington 1987, 1989; Blumstein, Farrington, and Moitra 1985). These reanalyses suggest that the lambda values (here defined as the probability of annual arrests or convictions for individual offenders) and the probabilities of desistance (or the likelihood of the termination of one's criminal career) can be modeled (or estimated) in a relatively homogeneous and stable fashion for both occasional and chronic offenders. In other words, once one's offending career begins, arrest/conviction and desistance rates remain relatively constant over time within subgroups of occasional and chronic offenders. For example, in Arnold Barnett, Alfred Blumstein, and Farrington's (1987, 101) reanalysis of the London cohort data, chronic offenders were estimated to have "a high annual conviction rate (1.14) and a low probability of termination [desistance] after each conviction (.10), [while the occasional offenders] had a low annual conviction rate (.41) and a high probability of termination (.33)." In general, the longitudinal studies of offender cohorts using arrests or conviction data suggest that early, prospective identification of potential chronic offenders may prove to be a worthwhile strategy for preventing crime in society at large.

Studies examining the self-reported offenses committed by juveniles and adults also support the argument that offender populations can be divided into groups of occasional and chronic offenders. An analysis of data from the National Youth Survey—a study of a national random sample of 1,389 male and female youth ages eleven to seventeen who were interviewed annually for five years (from 1977 to 1981) concerning their delinquent activities during the previous year—again shows that while many youth commit delinquency, only a small number can be classified as chronic offenders (Dunford and Elliott 1984). Using both offense frequency (lambda) and offense seriousness during the previous year to classify youthful (mis)behavior, Franklyn Dunford and Delbert Elliott (1984) were able to separate so-called noncareer offenders (who mostly commit trivial delinquent offenses at low rates) from "nonserious career offenders" (who mostly commit trivial delinquent offenses at high rates) and "serious career offenders" (who commit trivial and serious delinquent offenses at high rates). For example, for the year 1977, 51.5 percent of the 1,389 youths were classified in one of these three categories (a prevalence measure), but only 10 percent (7.5 percent "nonserious" and 2.5 percent "serious") were classified as "career offenders." Furthermore, data for the years 1976 and 1978 show that some of these juvenile offenders were very busy indeed—6.5 percent of the entire sample reported committing at least 200 offenses during these two years.

Finally, studies of the self-reported offenses of samples of prison inmates are an invaluable source of data on chronic offenders. In particular, research conducted by the California-based Rand Corporation suggests that prisoner populations can also be divided into low-frequency and high-frequency offending groups (see Chaiken and Chaiken 1982, 1984; Greenwood 1982; Petersilia, Greenwood, and Lavin 1977; Peterson and Braiker 1980; Peterson, Braiker, and Polich 1981). In the most ambitious Rand Corporation study, 2,190 incarcerated prisoners in three states—California, Michigan, and Texas—who were surveyed in 1978 were asked to report all of the serious offenses that they committed while on the streets during the two previous years (see Chaiken and Chaiken 1982, 1984; Greenwood 1982). In their analyses of these data, Jan Chaiken and Marcia Chaiken (1982, 1984) isolated a subgroup of the 2,190 offenders whom they classified as "violent predators"—or chronic offenders who reported extraordinarily high rates of assault, robbery, and drug deals. For example, in one year of street time, the average violent predator reported committing eight assaults, sixty-three robberies, 1,252 drug deals, 172 burglaries, and 214 "miscellaneous" thefts (Chaiken and Chaiken 1982, 1984). For these chronic offenders, street time represents a constant hustle from one crime to another, day in and day out.

Another way to examine the problem of chronic offenders using the Rand Corporation inmate survey is to compare the median and ninetieth percentile lambda scores of inmates who reported committing selected offenses (see Chaiken and Chaiken 1982; Greenwood 1982). For example, among burglars and robbers, the median number of reported annual offenses was 5.5 and 5.0, respectively. The most active 10 percent of burglars and robbers, however, reported committing 232 and 87, respectively, of these crimes per year. Using more conservative estimates of offender responses on these questionnaires (for data that were missing and for inmate responses that were ambiguous), Christy Visher's (1986) reanalysis of the Rand survey still shows that chronic offenders commit crimes at very high rates. Visher's (1986) conservative recalculations estimate the ninetieth percentile lambda scores to be 195.9 for burglars and 71.6 for robbers. A replication of the Rand inmate survey on a sample of 403 Nebraska prisoners in 1988 and 1989 further corroborates that chronic burglars and robbers report committing offenses at high rates; here, the self-reported lambda scores among the most active 10 percent of offenders were 112.3 for burglars and 74.3 for robbers (Horney and Marshall 1991).

These studies offer convincing evidence that a small group of chronic offenders is responsible for an immense amount of delinquency and crime in America. In an extensive review of chronic, "career" offender studies, Blumstein et al. (1986) conclude that the lambda scores (for all offenses) for the most active 10 percent of offenders nationally are probably about 100 offenses. While prisons may fail to deter these chronic offenders, they can still serve the essential purpose of protecting law abiding citizens from the crimes of the chronics.

THE FORMS OF INCAPACITATION

Incapacitation as a utilitarian social outcome of punishment refers to the prevention of crime through the use of various punishment restraints to debilitate or remove criminals from circulation in free society (see Barnett and Hagel 1977; Blumstein et al. 1986; Blumstein, Cohen, and Nagin 1978; Cohen 1978, 1983; Currie 1985; Greenberg 1975; Greenwood 1982; Greenwood and Turner 1987; Hospers 1977a, b; Visher 1987; van den Haag 1975; von Hirsch 1985; Wilson 1985; Wright 1992).

Historically, four types of punishments have been used to achieve incapacitation: execution, corporal punishment, banishment, and imprisonment. Although it is unquestionably the "only total, permanent, and irrevocable" means for incapacitation (van den Haag, 1975, 51), execution today is invoked only in particularly heinous murder cases. For example, in his summation at Gary Gilmore's sentencing hearing—where he recommended the death penalty for Gilmore—prosecutor Noall Wooton (quoted in Mailer 1980, 439) remarked: "[If Gilmore is] ever free again, nobody who ever comes in contact with him is going to be safe. . . . Even the other prisoners, if you tell us to send him to prison, cannot be guaranteed safety from his behavior."

Executions were far more commonly used for the purpose of incapacitating serious offenders in Europe and Asia during the Middle Ages. For those committing lesser offenses, however, corporal punishments were preferred for the purposes of both retribution and incapacitation. Some typical forms of incapacitating mutilations included castration for male adulterers, the disfiguration of the faces of female adulterers and prostitutes, the amputation of the hands of thieves, and the tearing out of the tongues of liars (see Bowker 1982; Ives [1914] 1970; Newman 1978).

Banishment also was an important historical conduit of incapacitation. Although, in recorded history, banishment appears first to have been used by the ancient Greeks, the transportation of disreputables and criminals to isolated penal colonies, remote islands, and frontier outposts emerged as a common form of incapacitation in Europe and Asia from the sixteenth to the twentieth centuries (Barnes 1930; Bowker 1982; Sellin 1976). Until the American Revolution, the English used the colonies of Georgia and North and South Carolina as dumping grounds for undesirables; from 1787 to 1867, the English transported an additional 135,000 prisoners to the Tasmanian and Norfolk islands off the coast of Australia. In addition, it is estimated that the French banished 70,000 prisoners to Devil's Island off the coast of French Guiana from 1791 to 1953, while the Russians and later the Soviets exiled millions to Siberia, beginning in 1753 (Barnes 1930; Bowker 1982; Murton 1989; Sellin 1976).

For the most part, execution, mutilation, and banishment are unacceptable as instruments of incapacitation in modern civilizations because each offends the normative sensibilities of modern cultures (Garland 1990). The use of imprisonment for incapacitation, however, still seems compatible with modern sensibilities and values. In recent years, criminologists have distinguished between two different ways in which prisons can be used as forms of incapacitation—*collective incapacitation* versus *selective incapacitation* (Blumstein et al. 1986; Blumstein, Cohen, and Nagin 1978;

Cohen 1978, 1983; Currie 1985; Greenberg 1975; Greenwood 1982; Visher 1987; von Hirsch 1985; Wright 1992). Collective incapacitation refers to preventing crimes in society at large through traditional forms of prison sentencing, which mostly emphasize the seriousness of the current offense and, to a lesser extent, one's prior criminal record. Sentencing policies based on collective incapacitation make little attempt to predict the future crime risk of offenders. In contrast, selective incapacitation is intended to prevent crime by targeting imprisonment toward those classes of chronic offenders who appear to pose the greatest potential crime risk to the larger community (Wright 1992). The creation of predictive instruments that can identify likely chronic offenders prior to sentencing is essential in the implementation of selective incapacitation policies. The remainder of chapter 5 examines the current effectiveness and future promise of using prisons to achieve collective and selective incapacitation.

THE CURRENT EFFECTIVENESS OF COLLECTIVE INCAPACITATION: GREENBERG, ZEDLEWSKI, AND THE THREE BEARS

Critics are quick to cite evidence purporting to show that prisons are largely ineffective as instruments of collective incapacitation. They contend that prisons not only fail to protect law-abiding citizens from criminal offenses but also have little effect on the overall crime rate in society. For example, Thomas Mathiesen (1990, 87) contends that research on incapacitation offers "no defense" for prisons and adds that implementing even the sternest collective incapacitation policies would have "only a marginal incapacitative effect, and would not in any significant way increase the safety of . . . citizens." In his summary of the research on collective incapacitation, Elliott Currie (1985) concludes that prisons have a "disturbingly small" effect on the crime rate.

Indeed, some research seems to support the claims made by Mathiesen (1990) and Currie (1985). Using 1971 data on those arrested for serious offenses in California, David Greenberg (1975) concludes that a one-year, across-the-board increase in prison sentences for all inmates in California would result in only a 3 to 4 percent reduction in the crime rate. A similar article by Stephan van Dine, Simon Dinitz, and John Conrad (1977), using data on adults arrested for violent felonies in Columbus, Ohio, in 1973, estimates that mandatory five-year prison sentences for all felons in the Columbus area (even those convicted for less serious offenses) would result in only a 4 percent reduction in the rate of violent felonies.

Interestingly, some of the most partisan defenders of prisons cite remarkably contradictory evidence that suggests that even current collective incapacitation policies prevent an immense number of crimes and save the economy billions of dollars annually (Reynolds 1990; Zedlewski 1987, 1989). Morgan Reynolds (1990) and Edwin Zedlewski (1987, 1989) estimate that the incarceration of every 1,000 felons prevents 187,000 crimes per year and the annual financial loss of $430,100,000. (If these estimates are accurate, Zimring and Hawkins [1988] skeptically observe that an increase in the incarceration rate by 221,768 offenders in 1984 would have resulted in the elimination of *all* of the crime in the United States.) Reynolds (1990) and Zedlewski (1987, 1989) use their "evidence" to support proposals for drastic increases in the current levels of imprisonment. How can one make sense of these wildly divergent claims about the effectiveness of prisons as instruments of collective incapacitation?

As Blumstein et al. (1986), Blumstein, Jacqueline Cohen, and Daniel Nagin (1978), Cohen (1983), Christy Visher (1987), James Q. Wilson (1985), and Franklin Zimring and Gordon Hawkins (1988) correctly note, these absurdly contradictory estimates of the effectiveness of collective incapacitation are based on highly questionable assumptions about the lambda values among incarcerated inmates. Cohen (1983), Visher (1987), and Wilson (1985) criticize the Greenberg (1975) and van Dine, Dinitz, and Conrad (1977) incapacitation studies for assuming in their estimations of lambda that offenders commit only the crimes for which they are arrested. Because only a small fraction of the total crimes committed in the United States ends in arrest (see Dunford and Elliott 1984), the use of arrest data results in conspicuous underestimates of lambda scores (Cohen 1983; Visher 1987; Wilson 1985). For example, on the basis of his California arrest data, Greenberg (1975) estimated the minimum value of lambda to be 0.5 offenses per year and the maximum value to be 3.3 offenses. Assuming the accuracy of these lambda (under)estimates, Greenberg (1975) incredibly contends that the total elimination of prisons in the United States would result in only a 1.2 to 8.0 percent increase in the rate of index crimes.

While the Greenberg (1975) and van Dine, Dinitz, and Conrad (1977) estimates of lambda are far too low, the Reynolds (1990) and Zedlewski (1987, 1989) estimates are far too high (see Zimring and Hawkins 1988). Using the self-reported data from the Rand Corporation survey of 2,190 inmates in three states (see Chaiken and Chaiken 1982; Greenwood 1982), Reynolds (1990) and Zedlewski (1987, 1989) estimate the lambda score for the average incarcerated offender to be 187 offenses (the mean number of crimes that the inmates in the survey reported committing annually). As

Zimring and Hawkins (1988) correctly note, however, this is certainly an overestimate of lambda—the mean number of offenses reported in the Rand survey is severely distorted by the highly skewed nature of offending patterns among the 2,190 inmates. The fact that a small number of chronic offenders in the study reported committing offenses at extremely high rates dramatically inflates the mean as a summary statistic, rendering it nonsensical as an estimate of lambda for the "typical" offender. By more reasonably using the median offender score of reported crimes from the Rand survey as an assumed lambda score (here, $\lambda = 41.6$), Reynolds's (1990) and Zedlewski's (1987, 1989) estimates of the crime reduction benefits of incapacitation would be cut by over 400 percent.

Although Greenberg's (1975) and van Dine, Dinitz, and Conrad's (1977) lambda porridge is too cold, and Reynolds's (1990) and Zedlewski's (1987, 1989) lambda porridge is too hot, luckily there are other estimates that appear to be just right. In one of the first papers to offer mathematical models to estimate the effectiveness of incapacitation policies, Shlomo Shinnar and Reuel Shinnar (1975) treat lambda as a constant, with a conservatively estimated value of 10. Using data on the incarceration rates and probabilities of going to prison in New York State, the authors estimate that the imprisonment of 12,500 inmates in the state correctional system during 1970 resulted in a 20 percent reduction of "safety crimes" (violent offenses and burglary). Interestingly, Cohen's (1978) recalculation of Greenberg's (1975) data using Shinnar and Shinnar's (1975) more reasonable lambda value increases Greenberg's estimates of the effectiveness of incapacitation to a *24 percent* reduction in the crime rate (for one additional year of prison for all inmates).

Four extensive reviews of the literature (see Blumstein et al. 1986; Cohen 1983, 1986; Visher 1987) corroborate the probable accuracy of the estimate of an approximate 20 percent reduction of the crime rate at current levels of imprisonment, assuming a conservative lambda value of approximately 10. For particular types of offenses and offenders, the collective incapacitation effects of imprisonment may be greater; assuming a slightly higher lambda score of 15.4 in an analysis of Uniform Crime Report and incarceration data for 1973 and 1982, Blumstein et al. (1986) report that imprisonment reduced the rates of robbery by 33.4 percent (1973) and 42.5 percent (1982) and burglary by 25.7 percent (1973) and 34.7 percent (1982). (The increase in collective incapacitation effects from 1973 to 1982 can largely be attributed to a doubling in the number of inmates imprisoned in the United States during this period.) Using examples of real offenses, this means that incarceration in 1973 averted an estimated 92,000 robberies and 487,000 burglaries (Visher 1987).

Although the critics of prisons might scoff that a 20 percent reduction in the crime rate based on an estimated lambda score of 10 suggests only a "marginal" (Mathiesen 1990) or "disturbingly small" (Currie 1985) collective incapacitation effect, this extent of incapacitation prevents literally millions of offenses annually, given the high crime and imprisonment rates in America. One way to estimate the overall effectiveness of collective incapacitation policies is to project the estimated 20 percent reduction in the crime rate into the total number of offenses committed annually in the United States. National Crime Survey data show that 34,800,000 serious offenses were committed in the United States in 1990 (Bureau of Justice Statistics 1991), so that an estimated 20 percent reduction in the crime rate would mean that collective incapacitation via imprisonment in 1990 averted 6,960,000 offenses. Another way to estimate the overall effectiveness of collective incapacitation is to multiply the assumed conservative lambda value of 10 by the number of inmates incarcerated in state and federal prisons. Given that 771,243 inmates were imprisoned in the United States by the end of 1990 (Bureau of Justice Statistics 1991), this suggests that collective incapacitation policies averted 7,712,430 crimes during the year. On the basis of these two estimates, one can conservatively conclude that the use of imprisonment for the purposes of collective incapacitation prevented approximately 7 million serious crimes nationally in 1990. Certainly this suggests that prisons are at least moderately successful in achieving the utilitarian social outcome of collective incapacitation.

It is important to note that I have purposely chosen a conservative estimate of the lambda score for the typical offender in order to arrive at a conservative estimate of the overall collective incapacitation benefits of imprisonment. Numerous writers (see Blumstein 1983; Blumstein et al. 1986; Blumstein, Cohen, and Nagin 1978; Cohen 1983, 1986; Visher 1987) argue that all estimates of the effectiveness of collective incapacitation are suspect because they debatably assume that (1) all subpopulations of offenders (from first-time juvenile delinquents to professional thieves and Mafia bosses) are equally subject to arrest and imprisonment, (2) incarcerated offenders are not replaced by new criminal recruits on the streets who continue committing similar crimes, and (3) incarcerated offenders are not part of larger criminal groups/organizations that persist in criminal conduct despite the imprisonment of one (or more) of their members. Because these assumptions are undoubtedly wrong for some offenses and offenders (e.g., there is much evidence to suggest that the replacement by new recruits on the streets is common following the arrest and imprisonment of drug dealers), the use of conservative lambda scores in the estimates of the collective incapacitation effectiveness of prisons is required to offset the problems inherent in these assumptions.

Several authors have called for large-scale future increases in the rates of imprisonment to enhance the overall crime reduction benefits from collective incapacitation (see Reynolds 1990; Shinnar and Shinnar 1975; Zedlewski 1987, 1989). For example, Shinnar and Shinnar (1975) estimated that implementing a policy where all convicted felons received at least one-year prison sentences would have increased the prison population of New York State from 12,500 in 1970 to approximately 35,000 by the late 1970s but would have resulted in a dramatic 75 percent reduction in safety crimes in the state. Using a preposterously inflated lambda value ($\lambda = 187$), both Reynolds (1990) and Zedlewski (1987, 1989) similarly contend that large increases in future prison populations would result in astonishing decreases in the crime rate. Policies favoring the even more extensive use of imprisonment for the purposes of collective incapacitation, however, appear to be ill-advised. As numerous criminologists have noted (see Blumstein et al. 1986; Blumstein, Cohen, and Nagin 1978; Cohen 1978, 1983; Greenwood 1982; Visher 1987; Zimring and Hawkins 1988), a law of diminishing returns unquestionably applies to collective incapacitation policies. As imprisonment rates increase, more and more chronic offenders with high lambda scores inevitably find themselves behind bars, leaving fewer and fewer high-rate offenders in free society. As a result, additional increases in imprisonment rates would end up incarcerating too many low-rate offenders, producing only a minimal reduction in the overall crime rate. For example, based on crime rate and imprisonment data from 1981, Blumstein et al. (1986) estimate that a 10 to 20 percent increase in the imprisonment rate would be necessary to achieve an extremely modest 1 percent reduction in the crime rate. This law of diminishing returns suggests the importance of shifting future imprisonment policies from an emphasis on collective incapacitation to one of selective incapacitation, where imprisonment is specifically targeted toward potential high-rate, chronic offenders.

SELECTIVE INCAPACITATION: ACUTE PUNISHMENT FOR THE CHRONIC OFFENDER

In order to increase the incapacitation effectiveness of prisons much beyond its current level—without substantial increases in the rates of imprisonment—policies providing for the selective incapacitation of chronic offenders must be considered. As the first part of chapter 5 documents, there is abundant evidence that a small number of chronic offenders commits an immense number of crimes. Although singling out these criminals for long prison terms appears to hold some promise for reducing the overall crime rate in society, chronic offenders must be identified prospectively through valid and reliable predictive instruments for selective incapacitation policies to be effective (see Blumstein 1983; Blumstein et al. 1986; Blumstein, Cohen, and Nagin 1978; Cohen 1983, 1986; Gottfredson and Gottfredson 1986; Greenwood 1982; Greenwood and Turner 1987; Visher 1987; von Hirsch 1985; Wilkins 1969).

Prediction (defined as the estimation of the probability of future behaviors—Gottfredson and Gottfredson 1986) is an essential element in many stages of criminal justice processing (including bail decisions, sentencing, prison classification, and parole). In modern criminal justice systems, prediction takes two forms: "intuitive" (also called "clinical" or "subjective") prediction (where decision makers use their own professional training, experiences, and hunches to make judgments) and "actuarial" (also called "statistical") prediction (where decisions are made based on statistical "experience" tables that summarize the factors known to be associated with recidivism among earlier samples of offenders—see Cohen 1983; Gottfredson and Gottfredson 1986; Wilkins 1969). Although intuitive prediction has been used far more extensively than actuarial prediction in criminal justice processing throughout the twentieth century, there is persuasive empirical evidence to show the superiority of actuarial instruments in the prediction of offender recidivism (see Forst 1984; Glaser 1955, 1962; Gottfredson and Gottfredson 1986; Loeber and Dishion 1983; Wilkins 1969).

Among the first criminologists to devise actuarial prediction instruments were Edwin Burgess (1928) and Sheldon and Eleanor Glueck (1930). From his study of parole violators in Illinois, Burgess (1928) isolated numerous factors associated with parole failure and success. He combined these factors into offender "experience tables," assigning positive points to factors associated with parole failure and negative points to factors associated with parole success (see Wilkins 1969). A final tally of these points resulted in a risk assessment prediction (of probable parole violation or nonviolation) for each offender.

To devise their actuarial instrument, the Gluecks (1930) studied the recidivism patterns among 510 offenders released from a Massachusetts reformatory from 1921 to 1922. Recidivism rates were examined for a minimum of five years following the release of each offender. From these data, the Gluecks calculated correlation coefficients on numerous factors that they suspected were associated with recidivism. The final prediction instrument that they compiled contained the six factors that were most strongly associated with offender recidivism—offender work habits, the seriousness of previous offenses (prior to incarceration), the frequency of previous offenses (prior to incarceration), a previous arrest for the same offense for which one was incarcerated, previous time served in prison, and the offender's employment record (prior to incarceration—see Wilkins 1969).

Burgess (1928) reported surprising success in predicting the recidivism rates of parolees through the use of his simple experience tables. For example, in a study of inmates from Joliet Prison, Leslie Wilkins (1969, 66) notes that Burgess found "that among men with between 16 and 21 favorable points, only 1.5 percent violated [on parole], whereas for men with only 2 to 4 favorable points the rate of violation was 76 percent." Ironically, the more sophisticated actuarial predictive instrument devised by the Gluecks (1930)—and still more sophisticated later instruments that relied on multivariate statistics (e.g., multiple regression or discriminant analysis techniques)—have been found to be little more accurate in predicting offender recidivism than simple Burgess scales (Blumstein et al. 1986; Wilkins 1969).

Three recently devised actuarial instruments have elicited widespread comment and debate among criminologists, criminal justice practitioners, and policymakers: (1) Peter Greenwood's selective incapacitation instrument, developed for the Rand Corporation (see Blumstein 1983; Blumstein et al. 1986; Cohen 1983, 1986; Gottfredson and Gottfredson 1986; Greenwood 1982; Greenwood and Turner 1987; Miranne and Geerken 1991; Visher 1986, 1987; Wilson 1985), (2) the instrument developed by INSLAW, Incorporated, to assist federal prosecutors in the risk assessment of offenders (Blumstein et al. 1986; Forst 1984; Forst et al. 1983; Wilson 1985), and (3) the Salient Factor Score, developed as a risk assessment scale for the U.S. Parole Commission (Blumstein et al. 1986; Gottfredson and Gottfredson 1986; Hoffman 1983; Janus 1985). Detailed familiarity with these instruments is an important prerequisite to comprehending the debates over the relative merits of selective incapacitation proposals.

Perhaps the best known and most controversial of these scales is Greenwood's (1982) selective incapacitation instrument. In an analysis of the Rand self-report survey of the crimes committed by 2,190 inmates in three states, Greenwood (1982) isolated seven factors that could be used to identify low-, medium-, and high-rate offenders: (1) a prior conviction for the same offense for which one was currently incarcerated, (2) incarceration for more than 50 percent of the two previous years, (3) a conviction before the age of sixteen, (4) time served in a state juvenile reformatory, (5) illegal drug use during the two previous years, (6) illegal drug use as a juvenile, and (7) unemployment for more than 50 percent of the two previous years. Greenwood used a positive response to four or more of these factors as the cut point for discriminating between high-rate and low- and medium-rate offenders. On the basis of this cut point criterion, Greenwood's scale correctly identified 45 percent of the self-reported chronic offenders in the study (see Cohen 1983; Greenwood 1982; Visher 1986).

In addition, Greenwood's (1982) analysis of the California inmate self-reports revealed that by implementing a selective incapacitation sentencing policy that specifically targeted long (eight-year) prison sentences to predicted chronic robbers and burglars (and short one-year sentences to predicted low- and medium-rate offenders), the robbery rate in California could be reduced by 20 percent and the burglary rate by 12 percent (without any increase in the number of incarcerated inmates). Reanalyses of these data (see Cohen 1983; Visher 1986), however, have reduced Greenwood's estimated crime reduction benefits for his proposed selective incapacitation policy by between one-third (Cohen 1983) to one-half (Visher 1986). (These reanalyses called attention to the fact that in his original study, Greenwood failed to recognize that some chronic offenders would terminate their criminal careers before completing their eight-year sentences. Cohen [1983] and Visher [1986] also reduced the lambda scores that Greenwood attributed to chronic offenders, noting that he neglected to consider that some chronic offenders in his study were crime "spurters," who committed an uncharacteristically large number of crimes just before incarceration. By projecting the inflated self-reported lambda scores of some crime spurters throughout his proposed eight-year prison sentences for all chronic offenders, Greenwood exaggerated the crime reduction benefits of his model.)

A lesser-known, but possibly more powerful selective incapacitation instrument designed to assist federal prosecutors in identifying chronic offenders was developed in the early 1980s by the Washington, D.C.,– based INSLAW research corporation (see Forst 1984; Forst et al. 1983; Janus 1985). The INSLAW instrument was devised from a five-year retrospective study of the recidivism trends among a sample of 1,708 federal inmates released from prison in 1970 (Forst et al. 1983). Using multiple regression techniques, these researchers identified nine factors that were associated with high-rate offender recidivism (see Forst et al. 1983): (1) heavy use of alcohol, (2) heroin use, (3) age at the time of the most recent arrest (offenders under twenty-two were predicted to have higher recidivism rates), (4) the length (in years) of one's criminal career, (5) the number of arrests during the previous five years, (6) the length of one's longest previous prison sentence, (7) the number of one's previous probation sentences, (8) one's most recent arrest was for a crime of violence, and (9) one's most recent arrest was for a nonviolent offense (this factor was negatively related to recidivism). Using these factors, the INSLAW researchers devised a weighted point system to assign predictive risk assessment scores for each offender. (E.g., evidence of heroin use resulted in a score of "+10"; age of forty-three or above at the time of one's most recent arrest was scored "-14"—Forst et al. 1973.) The cut point of forty-seven was used to identify chronic offenders (Forst et al. 1983).

The INSLAW factors identified 200 chronic offenders (or 11.7 percent) from the original sample of 1,708 federal parolees. Of those predicted to be chronic offenders, 170 (85 percent) recidivated during the five-year follow-up period (530—or 35 percent—of those predicted to be nonchronics recidivated). Importantly, arrest data showed that the 200 persons identified as chronic offenders by the scale averaged committing *ten times* the number of offenses per person compared with those identified as nonchronics. By using the INSLAW prediction scale to ensure that all predicted chronic offenders receive prison sentences, Forst (1984) estimates that prosecutors and the judiciary could reduce the federal crime rate by 5 to 10 percent annually (or by 22,500 to 45,000 crimes). Although the INSLAW instrument appears to offer much promise for identifying chronic offenders, the estimates of the accuracy of the scale must be viewed with some caution, since this instrument has received far less critical scrutiny than the one devised by Greenwood.

Yet another prediction instrument—this one designed to aid in the risk assessment of federal parolees—is the Salient Factor Score used by the U.S. Parole Commission (Blumstein et al. 1986; Gottfredson and Gottfredson 1986; Hoffman 1983; Janus 1985). This scale was developed through a two-year study of the recidivism rates among 902 federal parolees released from prison during the first six months of 1970; the instrument was adopted for national use in 1973 (Gottfredson and Gottfredson 1986). Although the original Salient Factor Score instrument relied on nine risk assessment factors, including such social history items as an offender's employment record and the stability of his or her family relations, the most recent (1981) revision includes six factors: (1) the number of prior convictions (or adjudications for juveniles), (2) the number of prior prison, jail, or probation commitments of over thirty days, (3) one's age at the time of the current offense (older offenders are rated as better risks, unless they have five or more previous commitments), (4) one episode of prison, jail, or probation commitment for over thirty days during the last three years, (5) a probation, parole, confinement, or escape status at the time of one's current offense, and (6) a history of heroin or opiate dependence (see Blumstein et al. 1986; Gottfredson and Gottfredson 1986; Hoffman 1983; Janus 1985). These factors are used to rate the likelihood of each offender's success on parole in one of four categories: "poor," "fair," "good," or "very good."

Michael Janus (1985) correctly notes that the use of the Salient Factor Score among federal inmates for almost two decades represents a de facto policy of selective incapacitation; offenders predicted by the instrument to be poor risks are more likely to be denied parole for the sake of protecting the community. Importantly, research suggests that the Salient Factor Score is a fairly accurate predictor of future criminality. Janus (1985) examined the effectiveness of the instrument in predicting recidivism in a sample of 2,385 federal offenders released from prison during the first half of 1978. The arrest records of these parolees were followed for three years. Notably, 65.5 percent of the 493 parolees rated as poor risks had at least one subsequent arrest for a serious offense during the study period; only 22.0 percent of the 722 parolees rated as very good risks had a subsequent arrest. Janus (1985) also notes that if the 493 parolees identified as poor risks by the Salient Factor Score in 1978 had remained in prison during the three-year study period, 757 arrests would have been averted (only 285 arrests would have been averted if the 722 very good risks remained in prison).

While there appears to be substantial evidence that the use of prisons for collective incapacitation is at least modestly successful in preventing crime in the community, the debates over the merits of selective incapacitation are more heated. The critics of selective incapacitation have raised methodological, legal, and ethical concerns about the accuracy of predictive instruments in prospectively identifying chronic offenders. Most of these criticisms center around the problem of "false positives" in prediction—or the fact that numerous persons predicted to be chronic offenders do not become chronic offenders (see Blumstein 1983; Blumstein et al. 1986; Cohen 1983, 1986; Currie 1985; Forst 1984; Gottfredson and Gottfredson 1986; Greenwood 1982; Greenwood and Turner 1987; Mathiesen 1990; Visher 1986, 1987; von Hirsch 1985, 1988).

Most of the methodological criticisms of selective incapacitation instruments have focused on Greenwood's (1982) scale developed for the Rand Corporation (see Blumstein 1983; Blumstein et al. 1986; Cohen 1983, 1986; Gottfredson and Gottfredson 1986; Greenwood and Turner 1987; Visher 1986, 1987; von Hirsch 1985). For example, Blumstein et al. (1986), Cohen (1983, 1986), Stephen Gottfredson and Don Gottfredson (1986), Visher (1986, 1987), and Andrew von Hirsch (1985) correctly observe that before much importance can be attached to Greenwood's scale, it must be validated through replication on additional samples of offenders. Recently, however, Alfred Miranne and Michael Geerken (1991) applied Greenwood's self-report instrument to a sample of 200 male inmates in New Orleans who had at least one conviction for burglary. The study was conducted in 1986 using individual interviews to minimize the ambiguity in inmate responses and polygraph tests of inmates to maximize response validity. Miranne and Geerken's (1991) findings regarding the predictive accuracy of the instrument are remarkably similar to those of Greenwood—while in his original study, Greenwood's instrument correctly classified 50 percent of low-, medium-, and high-rate offenders, the New Orleans replication correctly classified 49 percent of the offenders. Importantly, the authors conclude that their "results offer support for the generalizability of Greenwood's predictive scale, at least to inmate self-report samples" (Miranne and Geerken 1991, 511).

Another common validation criticism of the Greenwood study is that he used *retrospective* data (on the self-reported crimes of offenders during the previous two years) to devise a *prospective* scale (see Blumstein 1983; Blumstein et al. 1986; Cohen 1983, 1986; Currie 1985; Mathiesen 1990; Visher 1986, 1987; von Hirsch 1985). Mathiesen (1990, 94) complains that "the Rand studies are strictly speaking 'postdiction' rather than "prediction" studies, because the criminal behavior which is to be predicted has already been committed, and is reported in an interview." However, several years *before* Mathiesen's criticism, the Rand Corporation published two prospective replications of the original Greenwood scale (see Greenwood and Turner 1987; Klein and Caggiano 1986). Greenwood and Susan Turner (1987) examined the *pre*dictive accuracy of the scale on two samples—2,355 male juvenile and criminal offenders processed through California Youth Authority facilities from 1966 to 1971, and 192 burglars and robbers from California who participated in the original Greenwood study. In the former sample, Greenwood and Turner (1987) used California Youth Authority records to reconstruct a prediction score for each offender at the time of incarceration; the accuracy of these scores was then evaluated through a ten-year follow-up of the arrest records for each offender. In the latter sample, the researchers reinterviewed offenders about their self-reported crimes four years after the assignment of the original prediction scores.

Although the Greenwood instrument had only modest success in predicting future arrests in the California Youth Authority sample (44 percent of the predictions for low, medium, and high arrest rates were accurate when compared with the actual arrests of offenders), predicted high-rate offenders still on the average were arrested 2.5 times more often during the ten-year follow-up period than predicted low-rate offenders. More importantly, the Greenwood scale fared much better in predicting the *self-reported* offenses in the reinterviewed sample of 192 offenders from the original study. When predicted and actual low- and medium-rate offenders were combined and compared with predicted and actual high-rate offenders in the original retrospective Greenwood study (1982), 67 percent of the burglars and 72 percent of the robbers were correctly classified. In the follow-up prospective study, these figures emerged virtually unchanged—65 percent of the burglars and 70 percent of the robbers went on to commit *actual* crimes at their *predicted* rates (Greenwood and Turner 1987). These data strongly suggest that as a prospective instrument, the Greenwood scale is more accurate in predicting self-reported offenses than future arrests (primarily because high-rate offenders appear to have a lower probability of arrest for each of their offenses than low- and medium-rate offenders—see Greenwood and Turner 1987). The S. Klein and M. Caggiano (1986) study for the Rand Corporation confirms this interpretation: using subsequent arrest rate and reincarceration data as measures of recidivism on the same group of offenders from the original Greenwood study (1982) who were reinterviewed by Greenwood and Turner (1987), Klein and Caggiano (1986) found that the Greenwood scale had only limited success in prospectively predicting rearrests and reincarcerations. For example, although 80.0 percent of the predicted high-rate offenders in the original Greenwood scale experienced a subsequent arrest during a two-year follow-up period, 70.4 percent of the predicted low- and medium-rate offenders were also rearrested during this period (Klein and Caggiano 1986).

Another common methodological criticism of selective incapacitation prediction instruments is that criminal justice decision makers (e.g., prosecutors and judges) may not have accurate data on all of the factors included in prediction scales (Blumstein 1983; Blumstein et al. 1986; Blumstein, Cohen and Nagin 1978; Cohen 1983; Gottfredson and Gottfredson 1986; von Hirsch 1985, 1988). For example, "rap sheets" may include incomplete information on an offender's arrest history, especially in jurisdictions that prohibit the merging of juvenile and adult court records (Blumstein et al. 1986; Blumstein, Cohen, and Nagin 1978). Furthermore, data may be missing on an offender's employment history and drug use, two factors often included in prediction scales (Blumstein et al. 1986; Cohen 1983; von Hirsch 1985). Although accurate record keeping is an absolute prerequisite for reliable prediction, this does not pose an insurmountable hurdle for the implementation of selective incapacitation policies. As Blumstein (1983) notes, in criminal justice jurisdictions where probation officers do thorough presentence investigation reports, all of the social history factors necessary for selective incapacitation sentencing (including the offender's employment and family histories, drug use, and school records) should routinely be at the judge's disposal at the time of sentencing.

Finally, numerous critics of selective incapacitation have claimed that the false positive rates of current prediction instruments are probably unacceptably high (Blumstein et al. 1986; Cohen 1983, 1986; Visher 1987) and that there is little reason to believe that more valid and reliable instruments (comprised of more accurate prediction factors) will be formulated in the future (Currie 1985; Irwin 1980; Mathiesen 1990; von Hirsch 1985). Certainly false positives are a nagging problem in selective incapacitation instruments—in the original Greenwood study (1982), 55 percent of the respondents were falsely predicted to be chronic offenders. Research on the INSLAW (Forst et al. 1983) and Salient Factor Score (Janus 1985) instruments indicates that, respectively, 15 percent and 35.5 percent of predicted high-risk offenders were not subsequently arrested during five-year (INSLAW) and three-year (Salient Factor Score) follow-up periods. High false positive rates invariably are a problem in predicting rare events (see Blumstein et al. 1986; Cohen 1983; Gottfredson and Gottfredson 1986; Wilkins 1969)—just as weather forecasters have trouble predicting blizzards and tornados, crime forecasters find it difficult to predict the 7 percent or so of criminals who will go on to become chronic offenders.

It is important to reiterate, however, that actuarial instruments are superior to either chance (Loeber and Dishion 1983) or intuitive predictors (Forst 1984; Glaser 1955, 1962; Gottfredson and Gottfredson 1986; Wilkins 1969) in forecasting recidivism. For example, Rolf Loeber and Thomas Dishion (1983) devised a formula to calculate "relative improvement over chance" (RIOC) scores for comparing the prediction success of various actuarial instruments. In their comparisons of twenty-nine different actuarial instruments, Loeber and Dishion (1983) found that *all* instruments predicted recidivism better than chance predictions (the RIOC scores for the various instruments ranged from 15.3 percent to 78.0 percent). RIOC scores calculated for the original Greenwood data (1982) and on Janus's (1985) evaluation of the Salient Factor Score reveal that the former predicts chronic offenses 35 percent better than chance (Greenwood and Turner 1987) while the latter predicts recidivism 38 percent better than chance (Blumstein et al. 1986). As Brian Forst (1984, 157–158 correctly observes, this evidence shows that actuarial selective incapacitation instruments "not only do not 'cause' false positives where none existed before," but, more importantly, "generally *reduce* the rate of false positives."

The critics are undoubtedly wrong when claiming that new and improved actuarial instruments that further reduce the rate of false positives cannot be devised (see Ashford and LeCroy 1990; Blumstein et al. 1986; Gottfredson and Gottfredson 1986; Klein and Caggiano 1986; Loeber and Dishion 1983; Visher 1987; Visher, Lattimore, and Linster 1991). José Ashford and Craig LeCroy's (1990) study offers compelling evidence that some actuarial instruments designed to predict parole failure risk among juvenile offenders are superior to others. They compared the accuracy of three instruments—the Contra Costa (California) Risk Assessment Instrument, the Orange County (California) Risk Assessment Instrument, and the Arizona Juvenile Risk Assessment Form—in predicting the likelihood of recidivism for a follow-up period of thirty-one months in a random sample of 107 juveniles paroled from Arizona reformatories between 1963 and 1967. Ashford and LeCroy (1990, 446) found significant differences in the false positive rates among the three instruments—the proportions of false positives among offenders were 52.1 percent for the Contra Costa instrument, 45.8 percent for the Orange County instrument, but only 26.8 percent for the Arizona instrument (the latter includes nine prediction factors: "age, prior referrals, prior parole violations, runaway behavior, offense type, school [records], peer associations, alcohol or drug abuse, and family dynamics").

Furthermore, Visher, Pamela Lattimore, and Richard Linster (1991) evaluated the effectiveness of a new and apparently more accurate actuarial model designed to predict parole failure among juvenile offenders. The Visher, Lattimore, and Linster (1991) instrument differs from previous scales by placing much importance on two prediction factors—the school problems of adolescents (including school dropout and disciplinary problems) and ecological factors (including the violent and property crime rates in the neighborhoods in which youth reside). The authors examined the effectiveness of their instrument in predicting recidivism for a three-year period in a random sample of 1,949 males released on parole by the California Youth Authority from 1 July 1981 to 30 June 1982. The new instrument appears to be notably more successful than previous actuarial scales in predicting short-term offender recidivism—during the first thirty-six weeks of release, the false positive rate for the 5 percent of offenders classified as high-risk was only 15 percent, while the RIOC score was an impressive 71 percent. These data are strong evidence that better actuarial instruments comprised of more accurate prediction factors can be devised in the future.

Besides the inclusion of new and more powerful prediction factors, there are a number of other ways that actuarial instruments can be improved (Gottfredson and Gottfredson 1986). Perhaps most importantly, selective incapacitation instruments should be tailored to the specific characteristics of particular offenders in particular jurisdictions (Ashford and LeCroy 1990; Blumstein et al. 1986; Cohen 1983, 1986; Gottfredson and Gottfredson 1986; Greenwood 1982; Visher 1987). For example, Greenwood's (1982) original instrument proved to be more accurate in predicting chronic offenders and reducing the estimated crime rates in his subsample of California inmates than in his subsamples of Michigan and Texas inmates. In jurisdictions where most chronic offenders are already incarcerated (as in Greenwood's Texas inmate sample), probably only extremely discriminating instruments that include a wide array of prediction factors will have any beneficial impact on identifying additional chronic offenders at sentencing.

In addition, Gottfredson and Gottfredson (1986) recommend hybrid "bootstrapping" techniques—that rely on multiple forms of prediction—to increase the accuracy of selective incapacitation instruments. One bootstrapping technique is to subdivide various categories of offenders (e.g., drug-related offenders, violent offenders, and property offenders) within particular sentencing jurisdictions so that separate actuarial prediction tables are created for different types of offenders. Another form of bootstrapping that shows some promise is the combination of actuarial prediction instruments with intuitive predictors (Gottfredson and Gottfredson 1986). The future use of bootstrapping techniques in prediction scales could reduce further the rates of predicted false positives.

Perhaps a more serious area of criticism regarding the use of actuarial prediction instruments for the purposes of selective incapacitation sentencing centers around the legality of these practices (see Blumstein 1983; Ewing 1991; Forst et al. 1983; Janus 1985; von Hirsch 1985, 1988). Some civil libertarians contend that incarcerating offenders on the basis of predictions of their *future* dangerousness—rather than on the basis of the seriousness and number of their *past* crimes—amounts to cruel and unusual punishment (in violation of the Eighth Amendment to the Constitution) and the denial of equal protection under the law (in violation of the Fourteenth Amendment—see Ewing 1991; von Hirsch 1985, 1988). Especially problematic is the use of various social history factors (e.g., unemployment and family histories, school records, and neighborhoods of residence) as predictors of future criminality: one can reasonably contend that sentencing certain offenders to long prison terms because of their poor work habits, family disputes, difficulties with teachers, and high-crime neighborhoods of residence not only is cruel and unusual but also treats offenders unequally.

Somewhat surprisingly, U.S. courts for the most part have been unsympathetic to these arguments (see Ewing 1991; Janus 1985). Janus (1985) notes that the Salient Factor Score used by the U.S. Parole Commission has withstood numerous court challenges since its implementation in 1973 (although in 1981 the scale was revised to exclude data on unemployment and family histories, and school records—see Blumstein et al. 1986; Gottfredson and Gottfredson 1986). Charles Ewing (1991) also observes that recent U.S. Supreme Court decisions have consistently upheld the use of both actuarial *and* intuitive predictions of future dangerousness in cases involving so-called preventive detention (where offenders are denied bail or other forms of pretrial release because they pose a future threat to the community) and preventive execution (where offenders are sentenced to death because they pose a future threat to the community). Despite being well informed in appellate arguments about false positives and other problems associated with prediction, the Supreme Court ruled in *Schall v. Martin* (1984) that preventive detention is constitutional for juveniles and in *United States v. Salerno* (1987) that preventive detention is constitutional for adults. The Court also upheld the constitutionality of preventive execution on the basis of predictions of future dangerousness in its *Jurek v. Texas* (1976) and *Barefoot v. Estelle* (1983) decisions. The reasoning of the justices in these cases is that prediction instruments should be admissible in the courtroom because prosecutors and judges routinely must make judgments about the future dangerousness of offenders for the purposes of protecting the community (Ewing 1991). In general, these Supreme Court decisions offer little solace to those who question the constitutionality of the use of prediction instruments in support of selective incapacitation policies.

Among the most intransigent criticisms surrounding selective incapacitation proposals are ethical concerns. Most of these criticisms focus on the purported lack of justice or fairness in selective incapacitation sentencing: it is argued that these policies would make a mockery of commensurate deserts by incarcerating offenders for who they are or what they may become, rather than for what they have done (Cohen 1983; von Hirsch 1985, 1988).

First, several authors offer ethical reservations about the type of factors that might comprise selective incapacitation instruments (see Blumstein 1983; Blumstein et al. 1986; Cohen 1983; von Hirsch 1985, 1988).

Particularly repugnant is the possibility that certain ascribed statuses (that individuals inherit at birth)—especially race and sex—might be included. Although no currently proposed actuarial instrument includes race and sex as prediction factors, several other social history variables (including unemployment histories, school records, and neighborhoods of residence) may also be ethically suspect because they are highly correlated with race (Cohen 1983). Policymakers who are considering implementing selective incapacitation programs must be cautioned to remain vigilant about the impact of ascribed statuses on prediction scales.

A number of writers also express ethical concerns about the number of false positives that will inevitably emerge through the use of prediction instruments for selective incapacitation purposes (see Blumstein 1983; Blumstein et al. 1986; Cohen 1983; von Hirsch 1985, 1988). As Blumstein (1983, 105) notes:

One of the fundamental concerns that pervades all decisions in the criminal justice system is the avoidance of "false positives," that is, subjecting someone to punishment when it is not warranted. This concern is reflected in the requirement for conviction of "guilty beyond a reasonable doubt," and in the principle that "better a hundred guilty men [*sic*] go free than one innocent man [*sic*] be punished."

The existence of fairly high rates of false positives in all prediction instruments absolutely guarantees that in selective incapacitation sentencing, many convictees will be wrongly branded as chronic offenders.

Once more, though, one must recall that despite the high rates of false positives in actuarial scales, these instruments predict future behavior better than intuitive predictors (based on the "informed hunches" of prosecutors, judges, and probation and parole officers—see Forst 1984; Glaser 1955, 1962; Gottfredson and Gottfredson 1986; Loeber and Dishion 1983; Wilkins 1969). As a result, one can reason that using actuarial scales for sentencing purposes is *more* ethical than relying on intuitive prediction, because the former actually *reduce* the rates of false positives when compared with the latter (Forst 1984; Wright 1992). As Gottfredson and Gottfredson (1986, 275) conclude:

Decisions will be made in criminal justice settings with or without the aid of statistical [i.e., actuarial] prediction tools. Those who make the decisions—the parole board members, the judges, the prosecutors, and others—typically receive no training with respect to the difficult problems confronting them. [The criminology] . . . literature very strongly suggests that in comparison even with trained decision makers, statistical tools are more accurate. On simply an accuracy consideration, [the use of actuarial scales] . . . would seem to be preferred.

I would add to this quote that actuarial instruments may even be preferable on *ethical* considerations.

Finally, the supporters of the recompense social outcomes of punishment—and especially retribution—have criticized the ethical fairness of incapacitative forms of sentencing because these strategies stray from the principle of commensurate deserts (see Blumstein, Cohen, and Nagin 1978; Cohen 1983; von Hirsch 1985, 1988). Recall that retributive theorists emphasize that punishments should fit the seriousness of one's current offense; they argue that crime seriousness should be determined by the extent of harm suffered by the victim and the degree of culpability (or blameworthiness) of the offender. "Deserved" punishments should be oriented solely toward undoing past wrongs and not toward modifying or controlling the future behavior of the offender (see chapter 3). For the retributivist, incapacitative sentencing policies raise the ugly specter of undeserved punishment; as von Hirsch (1985, 129) pointedly observes: "Selective incapacitation strategies potentially involve [a] drastic infringement on the ordinal proportionality requirements of desert."

Passionate advocates of recompense and retribution frankly can never be persuaded that incapacitation is a just social outcome of punishment. For those more open-minded on the issue, however, remember the problems associated with implementing retributive policies (reviewed in chapter 3). Devising a scientific sentencing system where the seriousness of crimes is matched neatly to the severity of punishments to date has remained about as elusive as the search for the Holy Grail. On balance, the empirical evidence suggests that criminologists—working in conjunction with policymakers—will have more success in formulating reasonably valid and reliable actuarial prediction instruments that support modestly effective selective incapacitation policies, rather than in creating scientific presumptive sentencing guidelines in support of retributive policies.

One new form of incapacitation that appears to mollify some of the retributivist criticisms of collective and selective incapacitation is so-called categorial (or charged-based) incapacitation, recently proposed by Cohen (1983; see also Visher 1987; von Hirsch 1985). Because lambda scores vary widely for different categories (or types) of offenses and offenders, Cohen (1983) suggests linking incapacitative sentences to particular offense types where offenders have conspicuously high lambda rates (for all crimes), rather than to the characteristics and behaviors of individual offenders. For example, if pickpockets are found to commit many more serious crimes than "boosters" (professional shoplifters), convicted pickpockets *all* could be targeted uniformly with longer prison sentences than convicted boosters. Categorial incapacitation overcomes the usual ethical objections of retributivists to the fairness of other forms of incapacitation, because it applies a commensurate deserts principle to all offenders convicted for certain types of offenses (see von Hirsch 1985).

Cohen (1983) contends that because of the high lambda scores among convicted robbers and burglars, these are the logical offenses for implementing categorial incapacitation policies. She proposes an additional two-year prison sentence for all offenders convicted of robbery and burglary. Because categorial incapacitative sentences would not be tailored to the social histories of individual offenders, no actuarial prediction instruments would be needed.

Through her study of 1,543 adults arrested for FBI index crimes in Washington, D.C. in 1973, Cohen (1983) estimates that the enactment of her policy recommendation would have resulted in an 8 percent reduction in the robbery rate and a 6 percent reduction in the burglary rate in the city (although there would have been substantial increases in the District's prison population—a 7 percent increase in the number of incarcerated robbers and a 21 percent increase in the number of incarcerated burglars). As a result, although Cohen's categorial incapacitation proposal appears to sidestep some of the ethical controversies surrounding selective incapacitation, it would have the disadvantage of increasing (perhaps dramatically) the number of prisoners, requiring the construction of additional prison space. In contrast, selective incapacitation policies ideally promise to reduce crime rates with no increase in prison populations (see Forst 1984; Forst et al. 1983; Greenwood 1982).

In general, the studies reviewed here of the Rand, INSLAW, and Salient Factor Score actuarial prediction instruments suggest that sentencing policies based on such instruments offer the hope for the more efficient use of available prison space and the prospect for modest reductions in the overall crime rate. Selective incapacitation certainly is no foolproof solution for the crime problem; in the real world of human fallibility and caprice, no prediction instrument will ever prospectively diagnose chronic offenders with absolute certainty and accuracy. However, selective incapacitation policies hold promise for bringing incrementally more efficiency and rationality to criminal justice decision making. In a nonlinear criminal justice system characterized by bounded rationality, such small successes are perhaps the most that policymakers should expect.

FROM THE POSITIVE TO THE NEGATIVE SUPPORT FOR PRISONS

To conclude, the empirical evidence reviewed in chapters 4 and 5 offers positive support for the past, present, and future effectiveness of incarceration in reducing crime rates. While prisons fail to meet the social outcomes of rehabilitation, retribution, and social solidarity, they nonetheless appear to be modestly effective in meeting the outcomes related to deterrence and incapacitation. In a society like the United States where the culture places a tremendous premium on such values as competition, progress, achievement, and success (Williams 1970), quick fixes typically are demanded even for hard problems like reducing the crime rate. Because few persons are satisfied with imperfect social institutions that only modestly succeed, numerous proposals have been made for curtailing the use of imprisonment.

Chapter 6 examines the "less punishment is better" alternative of "noninterventionism" for offenders. I contend that existing empirical evidence suggests that implementing this alternative would be *less* effective than current policies of incarceration. The failure of nonintervention offers important negative support for the retention of imprisonment policies.

Chapter Six

Negative Support for Prisons: The Failure of Nonintervention

By the time you get out [of prison]—*if* you get out—you are capable of *anything*, any crime at all (Abbott 1982, 145).

In this powerful statement, convict-writer Jack Henry Abbott summarizes the archetypical indictment against prisons: the prison experience corrupts inmates, making them more predisposed to commit crimes *after* imprisonment than before. Countless writers have made this indictment; it is a common "wisdom" shared by many criminal justice practitioners, criminologists, and convicts. Some of the earliest jail and prison reformers were the first to make the indictment; John Howard ([1777] 1929, 8) remarked that eighteenth-century English "bridewells" (jail-like workhouses that detained debtors and other "riffraff") were "seminaries of idleness and every vice." In the nineteenth century, Jeremy Bentham ([1802] 1931, 351) argued that the "ordinary prison is a school in which wickedness is taught by surer means than can ever be employed for the inculcation of virtue."

Twentieth-century criminologists have also been quick to condemn prisons for making inmates worse rather than better. Donald Clemmer concludes his classic *The Prison Community* (1940, 316)—the 1930s study of Menard State Penitentiary, a maximum security men's prison located in southern Illinois—by proclaiming that prisons "work immeasurable harm on the men [*sic*] held in them." In his 1980s study of California jails, John Irwin (1985) similarly argues that jails psychologically, culturally, and socially prepare detainees for a "rabble" existence. (He defines the rabble as lower-class disreputables who commit offensive but not particularly dangerous crimes—e.g., public intoxication or drug possession.) Irwin (1985, 98) contends that because they provide "novices with ties to . . . the deviant world of the rabble," jails are "the primary socializing institution of the rabble existence."

Convicts likewise echo these sentiments. Washington, D.C., street hustler John Allen (1978, 19) comments on some of the specific crime skills that he acquired during his first stay in reform school:

I learned a lot of things at Junior Village—mostly more bad than good. I learned the right way to go about housebreaking, the right way to get away from the truant officers, the right way to steal from the Safeway. My fighting became much better because I did it more often. Lying. I used to lie, but before then I was no expert at lying. I became an expert liar. I learned how to hot-wire cars right there in the place—on the superintendent's car.

Far worse than teaching *the skill* to commit crimes is the claim by some convicts that prisons teach "*the will* to commit crimes," by "blackening" the hearts of inmates (Abbott 1982, 144). Imprisoned for a sodomy conviction in 1895, British playwright and satirist Oscar Wilde observes in his epic poem "The Ballad of Reading Gaol" ([1898] 1973, 249):

The vilest deeds like prison weeds,
Bloom well in prison-air;
It is only what is good in Man
That wastes and withers there.

Lester Douglas Johnson (1970, 6)—imprisoned for thirty years at Kansas State Penitentiary in Lansing—similarly notes that years ago prisons "failed to improve the attitudes of men [sic] and served to carve more bitterness on what were already sorely wounded hearts." Johnson (1970, 219) ominously concludes that when prisoners "were mistreated, they made up their minds that when they got out, someone was going to have to pay for it."

The deterrence and incapacitation research summarized in chapters 4 and 5, however, suggests that these anecdotal arguments are misleading when applied to contemporary prisons in the United States, because these arguments create the erroneous impression that prisons cause more crime in the aggregate than they prevent. British criminologist Gordon Hawkins (1976) bluntly calls the "prisons are crime schools" indictment a pernicious "myth" that contributes to unworkable social policy. Perhaps the worst policy that has emerged from the crime school myth is "non-interventionism"—or the idea that because "less is better" when it comes to punishing criminals (see Currie 1985), offenders should be "turned away" from traditional forms of justice system processing (Klein 1979). Chapter 6 reviews the "failure of noninterventionism" by examining (1) the labeling theory of deviance and its empirical shortcomings, (2) the dismal record of noninterventionist policy implementations in the areas of mental illness and juvenile delinquency, and (3) the empirical inadequacies of the "prisonization" hypothesis (or the argument that prisons are criminogenic institutions because they expose inmates to corrosive subcultures that teach deviant attitudes, norms, and values).

LABELING THEORY: WHEN STRONG CONVICTIONS MEET WEAK DATA

Noninterventionist social policies have been endorsed most enthusiastically by psychologists, social workers, sociologists, and criminologists who embrace one of the many variations of the labeling theory of deviance. Although labeling theory is a complex and highly nuanced perspective (Wright 1990), the various renditions of the theory generally share two propositions about the nature of deviant labels (see Paternoster and Iovanni 1989; Tittle 1980a): (1) the wealthy and the powerful are more likely to assign deviant labels, while the poor and the powerless are more likely to be assigned deviant labels and (2) the assignment of labels by social control agencies creates additional deviance by promoting deviant self-identities and deviant subcultures. The latter "secondary deviation" proposition is the theoretical linchpin in the argument by noninterventionists that less is better when punishing criminals. It is also important to note that this secondary deviation proposition *directly* contradicts the claim by deterrence/rational choice theorists that punishments prevent crime (Tittle 1980b).

Three of the most influential labeling theorists in criminology are Edwin Lemert (1951, 1967), Howard Becker (1963), and Edwin Schur (1965, 1971, 1973, 1979). In his book *Social Pathology* (1951), Lemert was the first to make the crucial labeling theory distinction between primary and secondary deviations. Primary deviations are the initial deviant actions of individuals, which are caused by countless social, psychological, and physiological factors (Lemert 1951, 1967). Persistent primary deviation results in the social imposition of deviant labels and the subsequent differentiation and isolation of offenders from conventional society. Negative social reactions over time cause the emergence of deviant roles and eventually secondary deviations, or offenses which are "a means of defense, attack, or adjustment" to negative social reactions and deviant roles (Lemert 1951, 76). Lemert (1967) singles out imprisonment as the pivotal labeling agent that contributes to secondary deviation.

It is important to emphasize that Lemert sees secondary deviations as the outcome of the social penalties imposed on earlier primary deviations. This implies the existence of a "snowballing effect" (Schur 1979, 241) between crime and punishment—continued primary deviation results in gradual increases in rejection, isolation, stigmatization, and related penalties, which eventually lead to more serious secondary deviation. Lemert essentially suggests that societies bring a certain amount of crime on themselves by choosing to respond punitively to primary deviation; in Leslie Wilkins's (1964) words, punishments cause "deviance amplification."

Becker's major contributions to labeling theory appear in his book *Outsiders* (1963), a collection of essays that examine the emergence of deviant "careers" among marijuana users and jazz musicians. Becker contends that the commitment to deviant motives, identities, and life-styles emerges in a step-by-step, careerlike progression, beginning with the commission of a deviant act. Public disclosure of the deviant act results in the "branding" of the offender with the deviant label and the severing of ties with conventional, conforming groups. Now shunned by conventional society, the deviant turns to various "organized deviant groups" for friendship and support. The creation of these groups results in the formation of deviant subcultures, which develop well-articulated roles and "self-justifying rationales" (i.e., a deviant ideology). Deviant subcultures foster the "solidification" of a deviant identity, so that it "is far more likely than ever before [that the deviant will] continue in his [*sic*] deviant ways" (Becker 1963, 39).

Crucial to the development of deviant careers is the fact that deviant identities are often "master statuses" that "override most other status considerations in most other situations" (Becker 1963, 33). For example, a woman who is identified publicly as a prostitute becomes socially defined mostly by this status—her other statuses as a daughter, sister, mother, next-door neighbor, feminist, or college student are diminished in importance. Becker (1963, 34) contends that the deviant label/master status "produces a self-fulfilling prophecy," or a conspiracy "to shape the person in the image [that] people have of him [*sic*]." Again, deviance amplification is the outcome of labeling: the deviant "finds it difficult to conform to other rules which he [*sic*] had no intention or desire to break" (Becker 1963, 34).

Becker (1963) also argues that certain members of the upper class in the United States are "moral entrepreneurs" who develop careers in crusading against deviance. Moral entrepreneurs see the world as sharply divided between good and evil and right and wrong; they have deeply held ethical and religious convictions that they wish to impose on the rest of society. In their crusade to "stamp out evil," moral entrepreneurs instigate the creation of numerous puritanical laws—prohibiting such vices as drugs, alcohol, gambling, prostitution, and homosexuality—that the police have great difficulty in enforcing. These laws contribute not only to the labeling of deviance but also to the creation and perpetuation of deviant identities, life-styles, behaviors, and careers. Becker implies that non-interventionism should extend to the laws prohibiting various vices; this anticipates later proposals to legalize public order offenses.

Easily the most prolific labeling theorist is Schur (1965, 1971, 1973, 1979), whose major contributions to the perspective center around its policy implications. For the most part, Schur's specific labeling model parallels the earlier arguments of Lemert, Becker, and other theorists. He contends that three social "mechanisms" transfer deviant labels and deviant identities to individuals (Schur 1971). These mechanisms include "stereotyping" (where the disclosure of the deviant label becomes a powerful stigmatizing cue that results in "a more general picture of 'the kind of person' with whom one is dealing"—Schur 1971, 52); "retrospective interpretation" (here the deviant's personal history is reinterpreted and rewritten to conform to the deviant label; Lofland [1966] earlier referred to this process as "biographical reconstruction"); and "negotiation" (or bargaining over the assignment of deviant labels; success in bargaining is affected by one's power, wealth, and other personal resources). The outcome of stereotyping, retrospective interpretation, and negotiation is "role engulfment" (where one becomes completely immersed in a deviant role, so that it is the most salient part of one's personal identity). The concept of role engulfment closely parallels Becker's notion of the deviant identity as a master status. Like Lemert and especially Becker, Schur concludes that the social mechanisms involved in the labeling process—along with the outcome of role engulfment—cause deviant labels to become self-fulfilling prophecies.

Of more interest are Schur's policy recommendations based on his labeling arguments. In his early work *Crimes Without Victims* (1965), Schur criticizes the continued criminalization of numerous public order offenses. He contends that homosexuality, drug offenses, and abortion (which at the time was illegal) are "victimless" crimes, because they involve "willing exchanges" of desired illegal goods and services. Schur argues that the laws controlling these offenses are unenforceable for two reasons: (1) there is tremendous demand for these illegal goods and services, and (2) there are no complainants to report the offenses. For the police, the enforcement of these laws is expensive and time-consuming and often involves questionable investigative techniques (including entrapment and the use of informers). The police also sometimes are bribed to ignore these offenses, which leads to scandals and public disrespect for the law. Even worse, keeping these offenses illegal contributes to widespread secondary deviation; an example is the stereotypical female dope addict who turns to streetwalking to support her habit. Schur (1979, 452) concludes that keeping victimless crimes illegal on balance causes society "*more harm than good*"; his ambitious proposal is to legalize these offenses.

In his book *Radical Nonintervention* (1973), Schur's recommendations for the processing of juvenile offenders are equally ambitious and cut to the heart of the policy implications of labeling theory. Because "a great deal of the labeling of delinquents is socially unnecessary and counterproductive," Schur (1973, 23) reasons that less state intervention in the lives of juvenile offenders must be better. He urges decision makers to pursue a policy of radical nonintervention for juvenile offenders. Here, in a spirit of "tolerance for diversity," the state would "define away" (i.e., legalize and ignore) most delinquent acts by limiting the jurisdiction of juvenile courts to only the most serious offenses. Schur (1973, 170) adds that the "ultimate goal" of policymakers should be the "abolition of treatment institutions" for juveniles (i.e., reformatories), to be replaced with various "noninstitutional and voluntary" treatment programs. In general, the guiding principle to a policy of radical nonintervention is to "*leave kids alone whenever possible*" (Schur 1973, 155).

When reading the works of Lemert, Becker, and Schur, one is struck by the fact that they are long on convictions but short on hard data. Early labeling theorists either rely on modest studies of a handful of deviants to reach some very immodest conclusions (à la Becker) or seem content to cite the largely untested arguments of other labeling theorists as "evidence" to support their own claims (à la Schur). Fortunately, beginning in the early 1970s, other sociologists using more systematic methods began to test the two pivotal labeling theory propositions. Here I review primarily the empirical evidence relating to the second proposition, that deviant labels contribute to the creation of secondary deviation. (Parenthetically, though, it should be noted that several literature reviews—see Hagan 1974; Paternoster and Iovanni 1989; Tittle and Curran 1988—offer little empirical support for the first proposition, that the assignment of deviant labels is largely determined by one's wealth and power. For example, in his review of twenty previous studies, Hagan [1974] concludes that "extralegal offender characteristics," including social class and race, contribute little to explaining differences in judicial sentencing. More recently,

Tittle and Curran's [1988] meta-analysis of thirty-five previous studies indicates that only 29 percent find evidence that social class and race significantly affect the processing of juvenile offenders.)

The first empirical tests of the secondary deviation proposition in labeling theory used samples of patients in mental hospitals rather than criminals (see Gove 1970, 1980a; Gove and Fain 1973; Gove and Howell 1974). Labeling theorists argued that institutionalization in mental hospitals is extremely stigmatizing, resulting in social isolation, a loss of self-esteem, and further deterioration in one's mental health (see Goffman 1961; Laing 1967; Rosenhan 1973; Scheff 1966, 1974; Szasz 1961, 1970a, 1970b). In effect, these theorists contend that the label of mental illness is itself the cause of mental illness; in Thomas Scheff's (1966, 92–93 [italics deleted]) words: "Among [mental patients as] residual rule breakers, labelling [sic] is the single most important cause of careers of residual deviance." Supposedly, institutionalization in mental hospitals contributes to mental illness by exposing the otherwise "sane" patient to degradation and insanity within the hospital; in a famous article, labeling theorist D. L. Rosenhan (1973) bluntly refers to mental hospitals as "insane places." The implication is that one "becomes insane" by exposure to the "insane institution."

The extensive research on mental patients by Walter Gove and his associates (Gove 1970, 1980a; Gove and Fain 1973; Gove and Howell 1974) shows there is little empirical support for these arguments. Gove and his colleagues gathered extensive data on 429 mental patients both before and one year after they were released from a large state mental hospital (Gove and Fain 1973; Gove and Howell 1974). For all the background measures examined by the researchers—including such factors as the relations with one's spouse and the abilities to maintain employment, to manage one's finances, and to manage a household—hospitalization resulted in a marked *improvement* in the capacities of most ex-mental patients to function normally in society. Even the ex-patients themselves believed that hospitalization on balance had more positive than negative effects; Gove (1980a, 83) notes that "a substantial majority of the patients saw their ability to handle problems as improved and saw their general situation as better than it was prior to hospitalization." In a seven-year study of the recurrent episodes of mental illness among schizophrenics, William Eaton (1974, 258) similarly concludes that the labeling/stigmatization incurred from institutionalization, "if operative at all, is a trivial factor in the recurrence of episodes of schizophrenia."

Abundant later research using samples of juvenile delinquents and adult offenders also offers little support for the secondary deviation proposition (see Berk et al. 1992; Berk and Newton 1985; Brennan and Mednick 1991; Coates, Miller, and Ohlin 1978; Dunford, Huizinga, and Elliott 1990; Farrington 1977; Fisher and Erickson 1973; Grasmick and Milligan 1976; Horwitz and Wasserman 1979; Klein 1974; Klemke 1978; Pate and Hamilton 1992; Paternoster and Iovanni 1989; Rausch 1983; Sherman et al. 1991; Sherman and Berk 1984; Sherman and Smith 1992; Smith and Gartin 1989; Steinman 1991; Thomas and Bishop 1984; Tittle 1975, 1980a, b; Tracy, Wolfgang, and Figlio 1990; Wolfgang, Figlio, and Sellin 1972; and chapter 4). Importantly, a search of *Sociological Abstracts* and *Criminal Justice Abstracts* for the years 1971 to 1990 helped to uncover eighteen studies—Richard Berk et al. (1992); Berk and Phyllis Newton (1985); Patricia Brennan and Sarnoff Mednick (1991); Robert Coates, Alden Miller, and Lloyd Ohlin (1978); Franklyn Dunford, David Huizinga, and Delbert Elliott (1990); Allan Horwitz and Michael Wasserman (1979); Malcolm Klein (1974); Lloyd Klemke (1978); Antony Pate and Edwin Hamilton (1992); Sharla Rausch (1983); Lawrence Sherman et al. (1991); Sherman and Berk (1984); Sherman and Douglas Smith (1992); Smith and Patrick Gartin (1989); Michael Steinman (1991); Charles Thomas and Donna Bishop (1984); Paul Tracy, Marvin Wolfgang, and Robert Figlio (1990); and Wolfgang, Figlio, and Thorsten Sellin (1972)—that use research designs and samples that permit a comparison of the relative merits of labeling theory versus the specific deterrence/rational choice argument that formal justice system processing reduces the recidivism rates of offenders (see chapter 4). Each of these studies compares the recidivism rates among samples of offenders who were arrested and detained versus other offenders who were handled informally (through warnings or mediation), controlling for a variety of factors (including the social and demographic characteristics of offenders, the nature of the current offense, and offense seriousness). I used the conventional "ballot box" technique (see Hagan 1974; Paternoster and Iovanni 1989; Tittle and Curran 1988)—where one simply tallies statistically significant and non-significant findings—as the burden of proof in evaluating the labeling versus specific deterrence/rational choice argument.

Only four of the eighteen studies (or 22.2 percent—see Klemke 1978; Pate and Hamilton 1992; Sherman and Smith 1992; Wolfgang, Figlio, and Sellin 1972) report some evidence in support of the secondary deviation proposition that formal justice system processing results in deviance amplification. As noted in chapter 4, in their cohort study of Philadelphia boys born in 1945, Wolfgang, Figlio, and Sellin (1972) found higher recidivism rates among offenders apprehended for index crimes who received arrest and court dispositions than among those who received informal remedial dispositions (a finding consistent with labeling theory). Tracy, Wolfgang, and Figlio's (1990) cohort study of Philadelphia boys born in 1958, however, produced the *opposite* results (consistent with specific deterrence arguments). Given that the data from the latter study are more recent, they undoubtedly are more relevant to understanding the effectiveness of justice system sanctions on contemporary juvenile offenders.

Klemke's (1978) self-report study of shoplifting among 1,189 high school students shows that apprehended offenders are more likely to recidivate than those who escape detection (by store personnel, their parents, and/or the police). The relationships examined by Klemke, however, are extremely weak, barely achieving statistical significance. As mentioned in chapter 4, there are also a number of serious shortcomings in Klemke's research design; for example, he does not control for the frequency of shoplifting episodes *before* offender apprehension. Consequently, it is probable that apprehended offenders committed higher rates of shoplifting than those who eluded detection not only after, but also before, apprehension. If this is true, Klemke's conclusion that apprehended shoplifters are somewhat more likely to recidivate may be spurious.

Two of the domestic assault studies discussed in chapter 4 (see Pate and Hamilton 1992; Sherman and Smith 1992) ironically show support for *both* labeling and specific deterrence arguments for different types of offenders. Sherman and Smith's (1992) study of the random assignment of various law enforcement strategies—from warnings to arrest and "long" custody (eleven hours)—to 1,200 Milwaukee males apprehended for domestic assault shows that arrest and detention increased the likelihood of subsequent police reports of women battering among unemployed and unmarried males but decreased the likelihood of recidivism among employed and married males. Using a similar research design involving the random assignment of apprehension strategies among 907 Miami males who committed domestic assault, Pate and Hamilton (1992) replicated Sherman and Smith's (1992) employment—but not marriage—findings. (Specifically, the most punitive arrest and fifteen-hour detention strategy resulted in higher six-month recidivism rates for women battering among unemployed Miami males but lower rates among employed males. No significant differences were found when comparing married and unmarried Miami offenders.) Importantly, though, because the majority of males in most communities who are apprehended for domestic assault probably are *employed*, Berk et al. (1992, 706) conclude that "[specific] deterrence may be effective for a substantial segment of the offender population."

The specific deterrence hypothesis fares much better in its head-to-head comparisons with labeling theory. Twelve of the eighteen studies—Berk et al. (1992); Berk and Newton (1985); Brennan and Mednick (1991); Coates, Miller, and Ohlin (1978); Klein (1974); Pate and Hamilton (1992); Sherman et al. (1991); Sherman and Berk (1984); Sherman and Smith (1992); Smith and Gartin (1989); Steinman (1991); and Tracy, Wolfgang, and Figlio (1990)—or fully 66.7 percent, report statistically significant findings that recidivism rates are *lower* among most offenders who are formally processed through the justice system compared with most who are ignored or handled informally. Furthermore, six of the seven studies (Berk et al. 1992; Berk and Newton 1985; Pate and Hamilton 1992; Sherman et al. 1991; Sherman and Berk 1984; Sherman and Smith 1992) that employ the most sophisticated research designs—that is, the random assignment of warnings or arrest and detention to individual offenders—show support for the specific deterrence argument for at least some types of offenders (the exception not supporting specific deterrence is Dunford, Huizinga, and Elliott 1990).

Considering the often ambiguous and inconclusive research findings on most topics in criminology, the studies comparing labeling and specific deterrence/rational choice arguments are fairly straightforward and persuasive: there is virtually no empirical support for the labeling theory secondary deviation proposition, but there is modest empirical support for specific deterrence. In other words, there is little evidence that formal justice system intervention causes offender recidivism, and there is some evidence that formal intervention in fact deters recidivism. Importantly, these findings suggest that noninterventionism may contribute to recidivism—not providing needed hospitalization to mental patients or equally needed punishment for delinquents and criminals may cause their behavior to deteriorate. This hints that implemented policies of noninterventionism could risk disastrous consequences for society.

Still another important shortcoming of labeling theory is that it ignores the incapacitation and general deterrent benefits of imprisonment. As the Pate and Hamilton (1992) and Sherman and Smith (1992) domestic assault studies attest, aggregate data research admittedly can hide the fact that judicial interventions make some offenders worse; the convict quotations cited in the beginning of this chapter are convincing additional anecdotal evidence of this. When commenting on the effects of his twenty years of imprisonment, Abbott (1982, 49 [italics deleted]) makes this point eloquently by paraphrasing Ho Chi Minh: "Hardships have tempered and strengthened me, and turned my mind to steel." Still, keeping unrepentant "outlaw" convict types like Abbott behind bars prevents crime in society at large through incapacitation. Abbott's own tragic life demonstrates the point: soon after the publication of his book *In the Belly of the Beast* (1982), he was paroled from prison through a campaign led by novelist Norman Mailer. Within a matter of weeks, Abbott murdered waiter Richard Adan outside the Binibon restaurant in Manhattan, New York (see Farber 1981; Montgomery 1982). Secondary deviation cannot occur on the streets when chronic offenders like Abbott are securely incapacitated in prison.

Imprisonment also ironically may have the beneficial social outcome of promoting general deterrence in society at large, even while it is causing some secondary deviation among certain inmates (Thorsell and Klemke 1972; Tittle 1969a, 1975, 1980a; Tittle and Logan 1973). Although incarceration occasionally "blackens" (Abbott 1982) or "wounds" (Johnson 1970) the hearts of some convicts, the example of the punishment of these offenders unquestionably convinces others in the wider society that crime does not pay (see chapter 4). It probably is rational social policy for society to risk a certain amount of future secondary deviation from "labeled" convicts (once they are released from prison) in order to achieve the immediate benefits of deterring primary deviation from prospective offenders outside the prison walls. Importantly, deterring primary deviation *now* would have the additional benefit of eliminating the possibility of secondary deviation *later*; even most labeling theorists would agree that secondary deviation is unlikely to occur if one does not commit the initial acts of primary deviation (although Becker [1963] contends that some secondary deviation may occur among "innocents" who have been "falsely accused").

THE IMPLEMENTATION OF NONINTERVENTIONISM: RISKY POLICIES BECOME DISASTROUS REALITIES

Despite the fact that there is virtually no empirical support for the secondary deviation proposition in labeling theory, and there is some evidence that certain forms of intervention/labeling actually improve the behavior of those who are labeled, noninterventionist policies have had a profound impact on the treatment of some types of deviants in the last thirty years in the United States. Policies of noninterventionism have been (1) implemented widely in the treatment of the mentally ill, (2) implemented much more selectively among juvenile offenders, and (3) endorsed enthusiastically—but seldom implemented to date—for adult offenders. Criminologists, criminal justice practitioners, and policymakers especially can draw important inferences about the risks to implementing noninterventionist policies among juvenile and adult offenders by considering the disastrous example of noninterventionism among the mentally ill.

At about the same time that criminologists Lemert, Becker, and Schur were proposing labeling arguments to explain the creation of deviant identities among juvenile and adult offenders, similar arguments were being made by psychiatrists (Laing 1965, 1967; Szasz 1961, 1963, 1970a, b, 1976), psychologists (Rosenhan 1973), and sociologists (Goffman 1961; Scheff 1966, 1974) to explain mental illness. For example, in his book *The Politics of Experience* (1967), R. D. Laing denies that schizophrenia is a form of insanity; rather he claims that it is a "mystical apprehension" of reality, which he calls "hypersanity." Laing argues that the condition of insanity does not exist in reality; insanity is merely a label created by psychiatrists to justify the power that they wield over patients. In a series of influential books, Thomas Szasz (1961, 1963, 1970a, b, 1976) likewise denies the existence of mental illness; Szasz argues that the mentally ill simply are nonconformists who choose to exercise human freedom in unconventional ways. He also contends that schizophrenia is the "invention" of psychiatrists: "If there is no psychiatry, there can be no schizophrenics. In other words, the identity of [the] schizophrenic depends on the existence of . . . institutional psychiatry. . . . If psychiatry is abolished, schizophrenics disappear" (Szasz 1976, 136).

While Laing and Szasz were preoccupied with denying the existence of mental illness, Erving Goffman (1961), Rosenhan (1973), and Thomas Scheff (1966, 1974) were waging warfare on mental hospitals as institutions. In his pathbreaking book *Asylums* (1961, xiii), sociologist Goffman extensively discusses mental hospitals as examples of "total institutions," or places "of residence and work where a large number of like-situated individuals, cut off from the wider society for an appreciable period of time, together lead an enclosed, formally administered round of life." Goffman sharply criticizes what he calls the "mortification of the self"—or the stripping away of one's identity—that occurs in total institutions. In mental hospitals, staff members make all the decisions for patients, so that patients gradually lose the ability of "self-determination." Goffman (1961, 13) contends that the long-term result of mortification is a devastating "deculturation," where patients at least temporarily become "incapable of managing certain features of daily life on the outside," assuming they are released. He argues that mortification within mental hospitals contributes to the emergence of informal patient subcultures and role adaptations, which by implication lead to deviance amplification. Unfortunately, Goffman does not bother to consider the possibility that mental patients may have had many more difficulties managing their daily lives *before* hospitalization. Importantly, though, he generalizes his conclusions on mental hospitals to other types of total institutions, especially to prisons. (Goffman's arguments are related to prisons later in this chapter.)

Scheff and Rosenhan are every bit as critical of mental hospitals as Goffman. As noted earlier, Scheff (1966, 1974) sees the labeling process as the most important cause of mental illness. He contends that many "normal" people engage in what he calls "residual deviance"—a catchall category of nonconforming behaviors that excludes crime, sexual perversion, alcoholism, and bad manners. An example of residual deviance is the appearance of disengagement and self-preoccupation when one is in the "public view." Powerless and socially marginal residual deviants often have the misfortune of coming under the purview of psychiatrists, who routinely place them in mental hospitals for treatment. Those who are hospitalized experience the amplification of residual deviance and go on to develop "careers" as mental patients. Echoing Schur, Scheff contends that if we "normalize" our treatment of the mentally ill by ignoring their behavior, much residual deviance will gradually disappear.

Rosenhan's classic research article "On Being Sane in Insane Places" (1973) is perhaps the most devastating of all the labeling assaults on mental hospitals. Psychologist Rosenhan recruited eight "sane" pseudopatients to feign the symptoms of schizophrenia (the pseudopatients claimed to hear voices repeating such words as "thud" and "empty") in order to gain voluntary admission into several different mental hospitals. Once admitted, the pseudopatients were instructed to act in a "normal" fashion and to claim to be "fine," in order to determine if the psychiatric staff in the hospitals could detect their "sanity." In no case did the psychiatric staff correctly diagnose the sanity of the eight pseudopatients—all were hospitalized for at least one week, and most were released from the hospitals with the diagnosis of "schizophrenia in remission." Once each pseudopatient received the label of insanity, all of their subsequent behaviors were interpreted in light of this label (à la Becker's master status and Schur's role engulfment). Furthermore, the normal personal histories of the pseudopatients were reinterpreted by hospital staff to support the diagnosis of mental illness (à la Lofland's biographical reconstruction and Schur's retrospective interpretation). Rosenhan concludes that mental hospitals do a great deal of harm to patients; psychiatrists cannot accurately diagnose the difference between "sanity" and "insanity," and yet the hospitals impose the label of insanity on patients in a definitive and highly stigmatizing manner. The result is that mental hospitals create self-fulfilling prophecies—patients who are expected to behave insanely conform to these expectations.

Rosenhan's research is often cited as a definitive study justifying policies of noninterventionism among the mentally ill (see Isaac and Armat 1990). Isaac and Armat (1990) claim that the study unquestionably dealt a tremendous blow to psychiatry in general and mental hospitals in particular. Yet Rosenhan's study in no way demonstrates either the non-existence of mental illness, or the failure of mental hospitals to help many patients who suffer from various mental diseases. On the former point, Rael Isaac and Virginia Armat (1990, 57) note that had Rosenhan sent pseudopatients "feigning symptoms of heart disease or muscular dystrophy or epilepsy to [physicians]; would he have concluded, had [the physicians] been fooled, that this proved the nonexistence of these diseases?"

While labeling theorists were mounting their misguided—yet undeniably effective—criticisms of mental hospitals, several other social forces were also at work to promote the policy of noninterventionism among the mentally ill. First, in October 1963, the U.S. Congress passed the Community Mental Health Centers (CMHC) Act, which provided for the establishment of small community-based psychiatric clinics throughout the United States (Isaac and Armat 1990; Torrey 1988). CMHCs were championed by community psychiatrists, who believed that psychosis has its roots in communitywide problems (e.g., poverty and interpersonal stress) and can be prevented through early grass-roots intervention on the local level. One of the purposes of the CMHC Act was to de-emphasize caring for the chronically mentally ill in large state hospitals and instead promote outpatient treatment.

A related development was the revolutionary introduction of various drug therapies for treating mental illness in the 1950s and 1960s. In particular, the discovery of chlorpromazine (Thorazine) in 1952 and its subsequent application in the treatment of schizophrenia fostered a belief among some psychiatrists that numerous chronically mentally ill patients could be released from state hospitals and effectively treated with drug therapies as outpatients in CMHCs.

Still another factor that contributed to the demise of state mental hospitals was several important court decisions that made it increasingly difficult to hospitalize mental patients involuntarily (see Gove 1980b; Isaac and Armat 1990). For example, in the 1971 *Wyatt v. Stickney* decision, the Federal District Court in Alabama ruled that involuntarily committed mental patients have a constitutional right to receive treatments that have a reasonable chance of improving their mental condition. While few can object to the humanitarian motives of this decision, the criteria spawned by *Wyatt* to evaluate effective treatments in hospitals were absurd; such factors as nurse-to-patient ratios and the physical amenities of hospitals became the preeminent grounds for evaluating treatment (Isaac and Armat 1990). Furthermore, the U.S. Supreme Court ruled in its *Addington v. Texas* (1979) decision that involuntary commitment to mental hospitals can occur only if there is "clear and convincing" evidence that persons "are presently both mentally ill and dangerous to either themselves or others" (Gove 1980b, 102). The standards for commitment established in *Addington* are extremely stringent, making it difficult for psychiatrists to hold patients against their will.

Finally, the costs of operating state mental hospitals skyrocketed wildly out of control during the 1960s (see Isaac and Armat 1990; Scull 1977). Andrew Scull (1977) notes three factors that contributed to these escalating costs: (1) the increased unionization of mental hospital staff, (2) the filing of numerous class action lawsuits that abolished the extensive practice of using unpaid patient labor in hospitals for custodial and maintenance services, and (3) the "right to treatment" court cases (e.g., *Wyatt v. Stickney*) that forced hospitals to refurbish and renovate buildings and to hire additional staff. In addition, the decision by the federal government in the early 1970s to provide extensive Medicaid coverage to mental patients processed as CMHC outpatients, but few funds for state hospitals, provided a monetary incentive to avoid commitment (Torrey 1988). Many conservative state politicians cynically favored the closing of mental hospitals as a means to save money and to balance state budgets (Scull 1977).

The combination of these developments led to a phenomenal nationwide implementation of noninterventionism through the "deinstitutionalization" of the mentally ill. In state after state, mental hospitals were either summarily closed down, phased out, and/or reorganized with far fewer patients. E. Fuller Torrey (1988) reports that the number of patients in state mental hospitals declined by over 430,000 (from 552,150 to 118,647) between 1955 and 1984. The most dramatic cycle of patient releases occurred from 1970 to 1975, when state hospital populations dropped at an annual rate of 11 percent (Isaac and Armat 1990). These trends offer a unique real world field experiment for examining the merits of labeling arguments and noninterventionist policy.

The appalling and disastrous social outcome of noninterventionism among the mentally ill is chronicled in two recent books: Torrey's *Nowhere to Go* (1988) and Isaac and Armat's *Madness in the Streets* (1990). Torrey (1988, 4) notes that released patients were "dumped out of mental hospitals into communities with few facilities and little aftercare." The hope was that most ex-patients would live comfortably and harmoniously with family members and voluntarily seek outpatient treatment in local CMHCs. The reality proved to be far different.

Many ex-patients at least initially moved in with family members—usually their elderly parents—who were ill-prepared to handle the immense responsibilities of caring for their chronically mentally ill relatives (Isaac and Armat 1990). Isaac and Armat (1990) note that family members were expected to assume the roles of psychiatrist, nurse, and ward attendant, without the benefit of staff shifts and without the ability to require the taking of medication. In many cases, family life became chaotic and unbearable. But gradually, "as parents died, or families broke under the stress of caring for untreated patients, or the mentally ill restlessly wandered off, rooming houses, single-room occupancy hotels (SROs), streets, and jails increasingly supplemented the family as alternatives to mental hospitals" (Isaac and Armat 1990, 287–288).

Many homeless mentally ill roamed the streets of large American cities. By the mid-1980s, Torrey (1988) estimates that over 150,000 seriously mentally ill persons were among the homeless in the United States (this is almost one-third of the estimated 500,000 homeless Americans). The homeless mentally ill experience a degrading and dangerous existence on the streets—certainly worse than anything found in modern mental hospitals. Often they become caught in the vicious cycle that Torrey (1988) calls the "criminalization of psychosis." Here ex-patients are repeatedly shuffled from the streets (where they are arrested for such bizarre behaviors as defecating in public or wandering in and out of traffic) to jails, and to the psychiatric units of general hospitals, which immediately release them back onto the streets (Belcher 1988; Wright 1992).

As a result, substantial increases have occurred in the number of mentally ill inmates found in jails (see Steadman et al. 1984; Torrey 1988): Torrey (1988) estimates that 9 percent of all incarcerated Americans—roughly 67,500 inmates—were severely mentally ill by the mid-1980s. This poses numerous management problems for correctional officials, who not only must find the additional space for the mentally ill in already overcrowded facilities but also offer special provisions—in segregation or protective custody units—for deranged inmates. The mentally ill create bedlam in correctional facilities—sometimes they threaten the staff and other inmates with violent outbursts; more often they are manipulated and exploited by more cunning and ruthless prisoners.

The jailing of the mentally ill is part of a new and disturbing trend toward the "transinstitutionalization" of mental illness (Isaac and Armat 1990;

Scull 1977). Transinstitutionalization refers to the movement of the mentally ill from hospitals, which are specifically designed, equipped, and staffed to treat mental illness, to other institutions—especially jails for the young mentally ill and nursing homes for the old—that lack the appropriate design, equipment, and staff. Scull (1977) reports dramatic increases in the number of elderly mentally ill housed in nursing homes—the number rose by 179,911 between 1963 and 1969 alone. Sadly, the mentally ill in nursing homes and correctional facilities typically receive few services and little needed treatment (Allen and Simonsen 1989; Belcher 1988; Scull 1977). It is hard to believe that even labeling theorists would consider jails and nursing homes to be preferable alternatives to mental hospitals for housing the mentally ill.

Torrey (1988) and Isaac and Armat (1990) also argue that CMHCs have failed abysmally in their mandate to treat released mental patients in the community. Following their creation in the early 1960s, CMHCs quickly carved out a new social role as counseling centers for the "worried well" (Torrey 1988). This new clientele served by the CMHCs included mostly middle-class, white, well-educated persons who had relatively minor mental problems, often relating to marital adjustment or substance abuse. Few seriously mentally ill outpatients are currently being treated by CMHCs—Isaac and Armat (1990) estimate that less than 10 percent of the severely mentally ill now residing in communities receive CMHC treatment. The discharge of mental patients into the community rarely involves any coordination of efforts between mental hospitals and CMHCs; seldom are released patients informed about the CMHC services available in the local community, and CMHC staffs aren't typically notified when mental patients return to the communities they serve. The result is that most released patients receive little or no professional treatment in the community; many of the deinstitutionalized mentally ill tragically end up seeking "self-medication" through alcohol and street drugs (Belcher 1988).

So what has been the outcome of noninterventionism/deinstitutionalization among the mentally ill? The mentally ill in the United States have gone from receiving admittedly inadequate treatment in hospitals to receiving virtually no treatment on the streets, in jails, and in nursing homes. They have gone from receiving admittedly substandard housing and meals in hospitals to living in rat-infested SRO hotels and sleeping over steam grates, standing in soup kitchen lines, and sifting through restaurant garbage bins for their next meals. They have gone from receiving admittedly inadequate and depersonalized care and attention from trained professionals in hospitals to enduring the complete public neglect and disregard they elicit from passersby as they panhandle change on the streets of large cities. Even worse, numerous studies show that the mental impairments of deinstitutionalized patients generally grow worse (Belcher 1988; Isaac and Armat 1990; James et al. 1980; Torrey 1988); diseases that were stabilized mostly through drug therapies in state hospitals now run rampant and uncontrolled among the mentally ill on the streets. Paradoxically, the withholding of labels through the implementation of a policy of noninterventionism has resulted in widespread deviance amplification among the mentally ill. As a result, mental illness in the United States has been transformed from a "mere" social problem into a national disgrace.

Although many criminologists—especially those who embrace labeling theory—strongly endorse noninterventionist arguments, the deinstitutionalization movement has made far fewer inroads into corrections than in the treatment of the mentally ill. Even during the heyday of the deinstitutionalization movement in the early 1970s, prison populations were still annually increasing in the United States (although at a far slower rate than today—Scull 1977). One area in corrections where deinstitutionalization appeared to affect policy, however, was the treatment of juvenile offenders; the number of youths throughout the United States housed in state reformatories fell from 43,447 in 1969 to 28,001 in 1974 (Vinter, Downs, and Hall 1975).

As I have noted elsewhere (see Wright 1992), though, recent evidence shows that the apparent deinstitutionalization of juvenile offenders in the 1970s was more illusory than real. Few youth were actually deinstitutionalized; rather, most were *trans*institutionalized from state-supported reformatories to private and state-supported mental health facilities, youth centers and group homes, chemical dependency clinics, and special schools (Klein 1979; Sarri 1981; Schwartz, Jackson-Beck, and Anderson 1984; Scull 1977; Wright 1992). In effect, transinstitutionalization represents an alternative form of encapsulation; juvenile offenders are simply "recycled" from the juvenile justice system into alternative facilities (Klein 1979; Sarri 1981).

The most extensive and well-publicized deinstitutionalization program for juvenile offenders to date was implemented by Jerome G. Miller in Massachusetts in the early 1970s (see Bakal 1973a; Coates, Miller, and Ohlin 1978). On 28 October 1969, Miller was appointed commissioner of the Massachusetts Department of Youth Services, the agency responsible for operating the five state reform schools and four regional detention centers for juvenile delinquents (Bakal 1973b). Miller by training is a social worker who has a strong professional commitment to the psychiatric variations of labeling theory; in the published version of a keynote address that he presented at a 1972 conference on deinstitutionalization, Miller (1973) mentions the work of Laing as the major influence on his thinking. Like Laing, Miller (1973, 6) contends that much of the "behavior of the diagnosed person is created by the person diagnosing him [sic]." He adds that juvenile justice systems create "self-defeating social roles and delinquent self-concepts" when they label youthful offenders (Miller 1973, 3). These statements reflect Miller's firm belief in the secondary deviation proposition in labeling theory.

As the new commissioner of Youth Services in Massachusetts, Miller almost immediately embarked on a policy to close all five state-operated reform schools. Miller apparently acted quickly and decisively to avoid any organized opposition from the public, politicians, and reformatory staff (Bakal 1973b; Coates, Miller, and Ohlin 1973). The Bridgewater Guidance Center was the first to be shut down in the spring of 1970, followed by the Oakdale Residential Treatment Unit and the Shirley Industrial School for Boys in 1971 (Bakal 1973b; Coates, Miller, and Ohlin 1973). In January 1972, while the legislature was in recess, Miller announced plans to close the two remaining state reformatories—the Lyman School for Boys and the Lancaster Industrial School for Girls (Bakal 1973b). By the end of 1972, Massachusetts was "officially" out of the reformatory business.

Or was it? Although there are heady enthusiasm and much self-congratulating about the demise of the reformatories in the published proceedings (see Bakal 1973a) from the 1972 conference on deinstitutionalization (a conference dominated entirely by Miller, his assistants, and his allies), some of the details offered by the presenters suggest that deinstitutionalization in Massachusetts was a matter of semantics, smoke, and mirrors. The early reformatory closings were apparently accomplished partially by transferring youth from one school to another; it appears that many offenders were not paroled outright into the community (Bakal 1973b; Coates and Miller 1973). More importantly, the reformatories were replaced by a complex system of privately operated group homes. In 1972, Miller established seven regional Department of Youth Services offices throughout the state; these offices were organized to assist private agencies in starting and operating group homes and to coordinate the placement of youth in these facilities (Coates, Miller, and Ohlin 1973).

In effect, Miller's highly publicized deinstitutionalization effort concealed much behind-the-scenes transinstitutionalization. Yitzhak Bakal (1973b) records that in the year immediately following the announcement of the last reformatory closings (1972), the Department of Youth Services received 1,200 adjudicated youth from the Massachusetts juvenile courts.

Of these offenders, 500 were placed in privately operated group homes, 190 were placed in foster homes, 150 went to various private residential institutions (psychiatric hospitals and schools), and 40 more "high-risk" offenders were incarcerated by the state under a contract arrangement with a private agency. (Ironically, the 40 high-risk youths were held in one of the old reformatories recently abandoned by the state—Scull 1977.) Note that the *majority* of juvenile offenders processed by the Department of Youth Services were still being held in at least quasi-institutional settings, away from their families. Specifically, 690 offenders—or 57.5 percent of those processed—were held in privately operated, quasi-institutional settings (e.g., group homes and psychiatric hospitals); when foster care is included in these numbers, 880 offenders—or 73.3 percent of those processed—were held apart from their families. In retrospect, it is probably more accurate to consider the so-called deinstitutionalization program in Massachusetts as the first comprehensive statewide experiment in the *privatization* of corrections.

Although Miller and his supporters may consider the replacement of large state reformatories with smaller group homes—or the transition from "big houses" to "little houses"—as deinstitutionalization, research shows the prisoners are a good deal more suspicious about these developments. Ann Cordilia's (1983) interviews of male offenders paroled from prison into halfway houses indicates that many view the latter as an extension of the prison experience. Halfway house "residents" often resent the fact that they continue to have their lives structured and their freedoms restricted; Cordilia (1983, 88) remarks that residents frequently refer to halfway house staff "as guards and wardens in disguise." Residents sometimes cynically note that the very name "halfway" house conveys the meaning that they are still halfway *in* prison. One suspects that many Massachusetts juvenile offenders over the years have experienced similar ambivalent feelings toward privately operated group homes.

If the secondary deviation proposition in labeling theory is accurate, one would predict that offender recidivism rates should have declined as a result of the implementation of Miller's program. Interestingly, a major evaluation study of deinstitutionalization in Massachusetts shows no evidence of this (see Coates, Miller, and Ohlin 1978). Coates, Miller, and Ohlin (1978) compared the recidivism rates (measured by subsequent arrests and court appearances for new charges for one year after release from Department of Youth Services custody) for two representative samples of offenders—308 boys and girls processed through the older reformatory system in 1968 and 491 boys and girls processed under the new system following "deinstitutionalization" (in a 1974 sample). The recidivism rates were actually somewhat *higher* in the 1974 sample of deinstitutionalized youth, a finding that again contradicts labeling theory but supports specific deterrence arguments.

A labeling theorist could dismiss these results by noting—as I have—that there was much pretense in the implementation of deinstitutionalization in Massachusetts. Perhaps the new community-based group homes labeled and stigmatized youth every bit as much as the older reformatories (see Klein 1979), and only total nonintervention would have averted secondary deviation. However, buried within Coates, Miller, and Ohlin's (1978) findings is evidence that recidivism rates were *highest* among juvenile offenders who were simply released to their families and received no services whatsoever under deinstitutionalization. As the authors (1978, 155 [italics added]) conclude: "It is worth noting that youths in our 'no program' category reappear in court at a very high rate and receive moderately severe [subsequent] dispositions. . . . *Thus it seems clear that leaving these youngsters alone did not result in their staying out of trouble and in fact seemed to make matters worse.*" This suggests that the youth who were least labeled and least stigmatized by the state had the highest recidivism rates, a finding that delivers an enormous blow to labeling/noninterventionist arguments.

Recent metaevaluation studies of nonintervention further corroborate the failure of this policy for juvenile offenders (see Gensheimer et al. 1986; Lab and Whitehead 1988; Whitehead and Lab 1989). Leah Gensheimer et al. (1986) reviewed forty-four studies published from 1967 to 1983 of programs that diverted young offenders from formal juvenile court processing. They found "that diversion intervention [*sic*] had no effect on [recidivism] measures" (Gensheimer et al. 1986, 50). Furthermore, Steven Lab and John Whitehead's (1988) and Whitehead and Lab's (1989) analyses of fifty studies of juvenile treatment programs published from 1975 to 1984 (see chapter 3) show that only diversion programs implemented *within* the formal juvenile justice system apparatus show *any* promise whatsoever for reducing offender recidivism. Whitehead and Lab (1989, 289–290 [italics added]) conclude that this finding "contradicts the labeling perspective that claims that system contact and intervention tend to 'label' or stigmatize youth as delinquent and cause them to commit future deviant acts. *It would appear that [formal juvenile justice] system involvement has the greatest potential for reducing recidivism.*"

To summarize, the actual practice of noninterventionism through the implementation of policies of deinstitutionalization among the mentally ill—and, to a lesser extent, juvenile offenders—offers no support for the secondary deviation proposition in labeling theory. The deinstitutionalization movement has clearly not resulted in decreased residual deviance among the mentally ill. On the contrary, the mental health and living conditions of the mentally ill deteriorated dramatically as a result of noninterventionism/deinstitutionalization. There is also no evidence to suggest that the more limited and partial implementation of deinstitutionalization among juvenile offenders lowered recidivism rates. The overwhelming empirical evidence reviewed here shows that in contemporary American society, policies of labeling deviants, of interventionism, and of institutionalization—far from contributing to deviance amplification—on balance, in fact, *reduce* deviant behavior. This conclusion is consistent with the earlier reviews of the deterrence and incapacitation literature in chapters 4 and 5.

In particular, those who endorse noninterventionism/deinstitutionalization for criminal offenders should pause to consider carefully the disastrous failure of these policies among the mentally ill. In 1985, John Talbott (1003) argued in his presidential address to the American Psychiatric Association: "[T]he presence of thousands of severely and chronically mentally ill and gravely disabled Americans wandering aimlessly across our nation's landscape attests to the failure of our state governments' policy of mental hospital depopulation." Earlier, Talbott (1979, 622) called some of the theoretical assumptions behind the deinstitutionalization movement for mental patients "the stuff of sheer fantasy." This is also an appropriate characterization of noninterventionist/deinstitutionalization proposals relating to juvenile and adult offenders.

It is quite likely that a "less is better" policy where criminals are "turned away" from traditional incarceration would result in the dangerous spectacle of released convicts "wandering aimlessly across our nation's landscape." Perhaps even worse, this policy would lower the risks associated with crime, conveying the irresponsible message to many offenders that "crime pays." Elsewhere I concluded that

noninatervention among offenders and the deinstitutionalization of prisoners [could prove disastrous]. Specifically, a substantial decrease in the number of imprisoned offenders almost certainly would result in dramatic increases in street crime and the number of persons jailed. Given the current conservative political mood [in the United States]—where the public is demanding *more* rather than less punishment—and the failed precedent of the release of mental patients from state hospitals, noninterventionism/deinstitutionalization is an unworkable policy for criminal offenders. (Wright 1992, 109)

A NOTE ON THE "OVERPRISONIZED" CONCEPTION OF INMATES

As mentioned at the beginning of this chapter, most of those who favor a noninterventionist policy for offenders believe in the "prisons as crime schools" myth (Hawkins 1976). In criminology, the idea that prisons invariably change inmates in undesirable ways traces its roots to Clemmer's classic study *The Prison Community* (1940). Clemmer (1940, 299) coined the term *prisonization* to refer to this process; he defined prisonization as "the taking on in greater or lesser degree of the folkways, mores, customs, and general culture of the penitentiary." Clemmer considers prisonization to be an extremely harmful side effect of incarceration, because it assimilates the inmate into an antisocial—and procriminal—prison subculture. He also argues that the longer that inmates are incarcerated, the more prisonized they usually become. In discussing the inadequacies of noninterventionist arguments, it is important to review the empirical evidence relating to prisonization.

Early research on prisons and other total institutions is consistent with the idea of prisonization (see Sykes 1958; Goffman 1961). This research supports the "deprivation model" of inmate social psychological adjustments to the conditions of imprisonment. The deprivation model originally was proposed by Gresham Sykes in his influential book *The Society of Captives* (1958), a study of the New Jersey State Prison in Trenton (a maximum security men's facility). Sykes argues that the "pains of imprisonment"—including the deprivations of liberty, of material goods and services, of heterosexual relationships, of autonomy, and of personal security—contribute to the formation of a distinctive inmate society with well-defined prisoner roles. Prisonization becomes the means by which inmates compensate for the harshness of prison life; such unique inmate types as the "gorilla" (tough inmates who extort scarce goods from weaker inmates), the "fag" (homosexual inmates who act and groom themselves like women to attract the attentions of other men), and the "ball buster" (extremely defiant inmates who are always harassing correctional officers) are social psychological adjustments for the losses of goods, services, friendships, and freedoms readily available in the outside world. Importantly, Sykes argues for the "indigenous origin" of inmate societies—the peculiar conditions of confinement lead to the development of a criminogenic subculture found only within prisons.

Although he collected most of his data from mental institutions, Goffman's *Asylums* (1961) is also considered by some to offer empirical support for the deprivation/indigenous origin model. Recall that Goffman argues that total institutions engage in mortification of the self—or the stripping away of the inmate's preinstitutional identity. Part of the mortification process entails the deprivation of many of the usual physical "props" that persons in the outside world use to identify who they are as individuals—street clothes, wallets, and jewelry are locked away in preference to the issuance of standard uniforms, one's hair is cut in a close-cropped, military style, and one is denied access to cars, homes, and other material possessions that are important parts of one's self-identity. Total institutions also use "privilege systems"—a set of detailed rules, with clearly specified rewards for obedience and punishments for disobedience—in an attempt to "reassemble" the inmate's identity. Finally, a sharply delimited "caste chasm" exists in total institutions between the empowered and independent staff and the powerless and dependent inmates.

Goffman contends that inmates achieve some sense of self-control in the face of these deprivations and "assaults on the self" by developing an informal inmate subculture, which includes its own counternorms and role adaptations. The most important inmate role adaptation for coping with institutional deprivation is "playing it cool"—where inmates show deference in the presence of staff but independence and defiance toward the staff and support for the counternorms of the inmate subculture when only other inmates are present. Like Sykes, Goffman believes that inmate subcultures have an indigenous origin—again, the peculiar conditions of the total institution cause the emergence of a distinctive set of counternorms and role adaptations. Prisonization can be conceptualized as the unique type of inmate subculture and socialization pattern that develops in prisons as total institutions.

Numerous criticisms of prisonization and the related deprivation/indigenous origin argument have emerged in recent years. One of the most important challenges was the proposal by Irwin and Donald Cressey (1962; see also Irwin [1970] 1987) of the "importation model" as an alternative to the deprivation/ indigenous origin explanation for prisoner societies. The importation model views preprison experiences as the most important factors shaping the development of prison subcultures. Irwin and Cressey argue that prison subcultures and prison roles for the most part aren't adjustments to the deprivations of confinement; rather, they are composites of various criminal and conventional street identities that are imported into the prison. In his 1966 study of 116 male parolees from prisons in California, Irwin ([1970] 1987) identifies eight convict types, *all* imported from the outside world: "thieves" (professional armed robbers and burglars), "hustlers" (petty con artists), "dope fiends" (opiate addicts), "heads" (marijuana, acid, and methamphetamine users), "disorganized criminals" (a catchall category of criminal "fuck-ups" who lack any discernible skills and specializations), "state-raised youth" (prisoners who spent their adolescent years in juvenile reformatories), "lower-class 'men' " (conventional lower-class persons who for some reason find themselves in prison), and "square johns" (conventional middle-class persons who end up in prison). In general, the importation model rejects the prisonization argument that inmates are corrupted by a unique, antisocial prisoner subculture; Irwin and Cressey contend that whatever "corruption" exists among inmates has its origins mostly in the outside world.

Although some debate still exists among criminologists about the relative merits of the deprivation/indigenous origin and importation models (see Hawkins and Alpert 1989), two important studies suggest that the importation argument is a more accurate explanation of prisoner subcultures in contemporary American prisons (see Carroll 1977; Jacobs 1977). Leo Carroll's (1977; see also Carroll [1974] 1988) study of 200 prisoners from the "Eastern Correctional Institution" (his pseudonym for the men's maximum security penitentiary in Rhode Island) shows that numerous recent correctional reforms (including more liberal visitation privileges, permission to wear street clothes and street hairstyles, and permission to bring television sets and radios into prisons) mean that inmates are no longer isolated from the outside world. He (1977, 45) concludes that these reforms enable "prisoners to retain their attachments to reference groups beyond the prison walls. And within the prison the freedom to dress and to decorate their cells as they please . . . permits prisoners to interact on the basis of preprison identities, rather than solely as convicts."

James Jacobs's (1977) influential study of prison gangs in Stateville Penitentiary—a notorious men's maximum security facility in Illinois—similarly supports the importation model. This research shows that four Chicago "supergangs"—the Black P Stone Nation, the Conservative Vice Lords, the Devil's Disciples, and the Latin Kings—imported from the streets of Chicago dominate the informal prisoner subculture in Stateville. Gang members bring with them into prison "intact organizational structures, highly charismatic leaders, support from the streets, and a long history of inter-gang warfare" (Jacobs 1977, 146). Stateville inmates interact with each other on the basis of these street-imported gang identities, rather than in terms of their statuses as prisoners. Like Carroll, Jacobs notes that recent correctional reforms allow prisoners to maintain close contacts with the outside world; liberal visitation and telephone privileges keep imprisoned gang members in touch with the events on the streets.

Note again that both Carroll and Jacobs emphasize that correctional reforms—which have alleviated some of the deprivations of captivity—are an important reason street identities are imported into contemporary American prisons. These prison reforms are a direct result of the abandonment by the federal courts of their traditional "hands-off" policy toward prisons. Under this policy, the federal judiciary seldom intervened in the internal operations of prisons. Since the mid-1960s, however, federal courts have pursued an "interventionist" policy, by closely monitoring the activities of correctional officials and by extending certain basic rights to inmates. An archetypical court decision that illustrates the older hands-off judicial precedent was *Ruffin v. Commonwealth* in 1871. In *Ruffin*, a lower court in Virginia legally defined prison inmates as "slaves of the state" who had no basic constitutional protections. The U.S. Supreme Court decision that best exemplifies the new spirit of judicial interventionism is *Wolff v. McDonnell* (1974). Here, Justice Byron White, speaking for the Court, offered the opinion that although prisoners had "diminished rights," they could not be "wholly stripped of [their] constitutional protections" and the due process of the law (see Jacobs 1983, 42). The important *Wolff* decision formally recognized the supervision of prison conditions and operations as the prerogative of the judiciary.

Two examples of recent court decisions relating to the protection of First Amendment rights illustrate how court-prompted correctional reforms have broken down the barriers between prisons and the outside world, enabling inmates to retain their preprison identities. First, the 1964 *Cooper v. Pate* decision by the U.S. Supreme Court cleared the way for the extension of considerable freedom of religion to prison inmates. Before this time, only the practices of the Protestant, Catholic, and Jewish faiths were permitted in most penitentiaries; the literature, sacraments, and clergy of other faiths were banned. However, the *Cooper* decision held that inmates in state prisons could file suits against prison officials pertaining to the denial of their civil rights and specifically ordered a federal district court to hear a case involving the conduct of Black Muslim religious services in Stateville Penitentiary in Illinois (see Jacobs 1977, 1983; Palmer 1991). Since *Cooper*, numerous lower court decisions have affirmed the rights of imprisoned Black Muslims, Buddhists, Native Americans, and other groups to practice their respective faiths. The historic *Cooper* case is now viewed as the pivotal Supreme Court decision that signaled an end to the hands-off judicial policy on prisons (Jacobs 1983; Palmer 1991).

Another series of court decisions in the 1970s also all but abolished the censorship of inmate mail, permitting a limited degree of freedom of speech in prisons. In *Palmigiano v. Travisono* (1970), a federal district court ruled that incoming mail could be opened by prison officials to check for contraband (primarily drugs and paper money), but in *Procunier v. Martinez* (1974), the Supreme Court ruled that incoming and outgoing mail could not be censored, unless the contents threatened the governmental interests in "security, order, and rehabilitation" (Palmer 1991). The *Procunier* decision requires prison officials to have some compelling reason for censoring mail, for example, the thwarting of specific inmate plans for escape. In the previously mentioned *Wolff v. McDonnell* (1974) decision, the Supreme Court further ruled that prison officials cannot read any correspondence between inmates and their attorneys but only search these letters for contraband (Palmer 1991). Although the Supreme Court qualified the *Procunier* and *Wolff* decisions by permitting prison officials to censor inmate-to-inmate mail (sent from one prison to another) between inmates who are not relatives (in *Turner v. Safley*, 1987) and to censor specific issues of publications from outside sources if these issues contained content that may "facilitate criminal activity" (in *Thornburgh v. Abbott*, 1989), the cumulative effect of the earlier decisions still means that prison officials routinely open all incoming mail to inmates (to check for contraband) but seldom censor either incoming or outgoing mail.

These and related court decisions mean that contemporary prisoners are far less isolated from events on the streets than were the inmates interviewed by Clemmer in the 1930s and Sykes in the 1950s. The deprivation and mortification processes that supposedly result in distinctive inmate subcultures and prisonization depend on the isolation of convicts from outside associates and influences; remember that one of Goffman's (1961, xiii) defining characteristics of total institutions is that inmates are "cut off from the wider society." Prisoners today simply are not cut off from the wider society; court-prompted correctional reforms have saturated modern prisons with outside influences. In particular, prisoners today have incredible access to mass media sources; inmates watch essentially the same television shows, listen to the same music, and read the same magazines as the proverbial man (or woman) on the street. For example, young "heavy metal" toughs still watch the latest Guns 'N Roses videos on MTV through cable television hookups in maximum security prisons and retain their subscriptions to "headbanger" magazines. Access to the mass media and related outside world influences helps to sustain and to nourish the preprison identities of contemporary convicts; as a result, mortification and prisonization exist today only in the out-of-date discussions appearing in many corrections textbooks and in the stale lecture notes of many criminology professors.

Another important challenge to the prisonization argument centers around Clemmer's (1940) debatable assertion that a direct relationship exists between the time that inmates spend in prison and their degree of prisonization. One can understand the logic behind this prediction: if prisons are crime schools with strong antisocial/procriminal subcultures, then the longer that inmates are exposed to this subculture, the worse their attitudes will become. However, numerous studies have failed to support this claim (e.g., see Atcheley and McCabe 1968; Garabedian 1963; Wheeler 1961).

Stanton Wheeler's (1961) study of inmates at Washington State Reformatory in Monroe (a men's maximum security facility) suggests that a curvilinear—U-shaped—relationship exists between inmate attitudes and the length of imprisonment (in the corrections literature today this finding is referred to as "Wheeler's U curve"). Wheeler devised a hypothetical conflict situation between prison staff and inmates to measure prostaff and antistaff inmate attitudes. He divided his inmate sample into three groups—those imprisoned less than seven months (beginning-of-sentence inmates); those imprisoned seven months or more, with at least seven months more time to serve (midsentence inmates); and those with fewer than seven months remaining to serve (end-of-sentence inmates). Wheeler's findings indicate that beginning and end-of-sentence inmates generally hold conventional, prostaff attitudes, while midsentence inmates are more antistaff in their beliefs. The conventional attitudes of the outside world exert a powerful influence over inmates at the beginning and the end of their sentences; this contradicts Clemmer's notion of progressive prisonization. Many replication studies have supported Wheeler's findings in a variety of different prison settings (see Glaser 1964; Tittle 1969b; Tittle and Tittle 1964; Wellford 1967).

Still other studies in other ways dispute the time component of Clemmer's prisonization argument. For example, Peter Garabedian's (1963) study of Washington State Penitentiary in Walla Walla (a men's maximum security facility) shows that the effects of imprisonment on inmate attitudes vary over time for different types of inmates; "square johns" and "right guys" (professional street criminals) conform to Wheeler's U curve; "politicians" (the leaders of officially recognized prisoner organizations, such as "Jay Cee" chapter presidents) hold mostly prostaff attitudes throughout their imprisonment; "dings" (eccentric, "screwball" inmates) develop stronger prostaff attitudes the longer they are imprisoned; and only "outlaws" (conspicuously antisocial, "loner" inmates) conform to Clemmer's progressive prisonization model. Furthermore, Robert Atcheley and Patrick McCabe's (1968) study of federal penitentiary inmates suggests that in treatment-oriented prisons, an *inverse* relationship exists between the length of imprisonment and the degree of inmate prisonization (directly contradicting Clemmer's claim).

Atcheley and McCabe's (1968) findings are consistent with several other studies (see Berk 1966; Grusky 1959; Street 1965) that show that the extent of inmate prisonization is related to the type of prison in which inmates are confined. These studies indicate that inmates incarcerated in treatment-oriented institutions generally hold stronger prostaff attitudes than those incarcerated in custodial/punitive institutions. Oscar Grusky (1959, 67) specifically concludes that in treatment-oriented prisons, "a pattern of co-operation between the informal [inmate] leaders and [prison] authorities may be established which promotes rather than hinders treatment. [In treatment-oriented prisons] the inmate culture [is] organized not around the most hostile, but rather the most co-operative, offenders." Bernard Berk's (1966) comparison of three minimum security men's prisons and David Street's (1965) comparison of four juvenile reformatories support Grusky's (1959) findings.

To summarize, there is little empirical evidence to back the "prisons are crime schools"/prisonization argument. In his review of the prisonization literature, Daniel Glaser (1964, 118) concludes:

Our findings from several different types of inquiry [indicate] that inmates have a predominant interest in adjusting to the demands of the institution and that they have strong noncriminal aspirations. . . . Evidence and deductive reasoning [support] the notion that inmates and others generally overestimate the extent of inmate opposition to the staff-supported standards.

Hawkins (1976, 71) even more bluntly concludes that the prisonization hypothesis "conflicts with reality." He adds (1976, 71): "If the crime school theory [of prisons is] simple nonsense, [then the] prisonization [argument is] nonsense on sociological stilts."

In his classic essay "The Oversocialized Conception of Man [*sic*] in Modern Sociology," Dennis Wrong (1961) criticizes sociologists for exaggerating the impact of social institutions on human behavior. Wrong (1961, 192) complains that sociologists tend to depict human conduct as "totally shaped by common norms or institutionalized patterns" located within the social structure. By emphasizing that humans are "completely molded by the norms and values of the culture," sociologists adopt a "one-sided [oversocialized] view of human nature" that ignores the "forces in man [*sic*] which are resistant to socialization" (Wrong 1961, 191–192).

Wrong's criticisms of sociology have particular relevance to noninterventionist, labeling, and prisonization arguments. Noninterventionists see criminals as totally shaped by the labels imposed by the state and inmates as rigidly prisonized by the total institutions in which they are confined. Once exposed to deviant subcultures in society at large and convict subcultures within prisons, criminals/inmates mechanistically respond by adopting antisocial/procriminal attitudes and by engaging in secondary deviation. Lost in this image of crime and punishment is the idea that offenders may be able to resist the forces of socialization by exercising human choice and by pursuing rationally motivated self-interests. As Hawkins (1976, 78) contends, prisonization theorists are misguided because they do not envision prisoners as "fully responsible agents but rather as 'managed' creatures moved or pushed in certain directions by extrinsic pressures." In short, noninterventionists in general are guilty of embracing an "overprisonized" conception of inmates.

Epilogue

A FEW SIMPLE TRUTHS ABOUT PRISONS

What can one generally conclude about the effectiveness of prisons in achieving positive social/individual outcomes?

—Imprisonment fails to achieve the recompense social outcome of retribution. The severity of prison sentences simply cannot be calibrated to match the seriousness of various crimes.

—Imprisonment for the most part fails to achieve the utilitarian social outcomes of the rehabilitation of offenders and the promotion of social solidarity. Prison treatment programs can be justified on humanitarian grounds but not on the benefits that they produce for society. Furthermore, there is little evidence to suggest that punishments bring law-abiding people closer together by reinforcing conventional norms and values.

—Imprisonment is *modestly effective* in achieving the utilitarian social/individual outcomes of general deterrence and specific deterrence and the utilitarian social outcome of incapacitation. For deterrence, imprisonment is most effective in preventing offenses among the more law-abiding segments of the population (i.e., noncriminals and novice offenders). For incapacitation, imprisonment is most effective in preventing offenses among the least law-abiding segments of the population (i.e., chronic offenders). Furthermore, crime is prevented among the more law-abiding segments of the population mostly through the *certainty* of arrest and detention; in contrast, crime is prevented among the least law-abiding segments of the population mostly through the *severity* of punishments (i.e., the length of incarceration). Deterrence and incapacitation research offers moderate *positive support* for the effectiveness of imprisonment in reducing the crime rate.

—The noninterventionist alternative to imprisonment holds little promise for more effectively reducing crime rates than current incarceration policies. The failure of nonintervention offers strong *negative support* for the retention of imprisonment as a social reaction to crime.

A LINEAR PROPOSAL . . .

These few simple truths about prisons suggest that a rational criminal justice policy should involve a combination of *selective deterrence* sentencing (emphasizing the certainty of brief periods of detention) for nonoffenders and initial offenders and *selective incapacitation* sentencing (emphasizing severity through long periods of incarceration) for chronic offenders (Wright 1992). The failure of retributive/presumptive sentencing schemes means that prison sentences could reasonably be streamlined into three classes—*detention sentences* (say, flat six-month terms), *incarceration sentences* (say, flat ten-year terms), and *life sentences* (without the possibility for parole). The following guidelines are proposed for assigning these three classes of sentences for those convicted of serious, FBI index offenses (murder, rape, aggravated assault, robbery, burglary, larceny-theft, motor vehicle theft, and arson):

—First-time convictees for one murder or one rape should receive incarceration sentences, given the great social repugnance for these crimes.

—All second-time (or more) convictees for murder and rape—and all multiple first-time convictees for murder and /or rape—should receive life sentences, again given the great social repugnance for these crimes.

—First-time convictees for index offenses other than murder and rape should receive detention sentences, emphasizing selective deterrence.

—Second-time convictees for index offenses other than murder and rape should receive *either* detention or incarceration sentences, again emphasizing selective deterrence. Because second-time convictees obviously were not deterred by their first detention experience, the punishment risk for these offenders must be increased. Rather than modifying the three-class sentencing system, I propose the *random assignment* of either detention or incarceration sentences for second-time convictees. These offenders could face a "punishment lottery," where they would have, say, a one-in-ten chance of randomly "drawing" a longer incarceration sentence, rather than the shorter detention sentence. The possibility of randomly drawing a far longer incarceration sentence not only is fair (because the assignment of longer sentences would not discriminate on the basis of offender characteristics) but also should be a powerful deterrent for those already convicted for one previous index offense.

—All third-time (or more) convictees for index offenses other than murder and rape should receive incarceration sentences, emphasizing selective incapacitation.

These are sharply focused sentencing guidelines for a punishment system that combines selective deterrence for nonoffenders and initial offenders with selective incapacitation for chronic offenders. Rather than blur these sentencing proposals with cognate suggestions about what to do with misdemeanants, other felons, aggravating or mitigating circumstances associated with offenses (e.g., an offender's age), or the implementation of actuarial prediction instruments for selective incapacitation purposes, I prefer to join the sentencing debate with a starkly stated, straightforward position that promises to maximize the effectiveness of prisons as vehicles of deterrence and incapacitation for serious index offenses and offenders. From my extensive review of the current empirical research in criminology and corrections, I contend that these few simple guidelines are the most rational sentencing proposals now available.

. . . FOR A NONLINEAR CRIMINAL JUSTICE SYSTEM (AND A NONLINEAR SOCIETY)

But these are rational, linear proposals for a nonlinear criminal justice system characterized by limited rationality and limited resources. As noted in chapter 2, in the hurly-burly, politicized, real world of bargaining, negotiation, trade-offs, and appeasement among the many interest groups that affect criminal justice policy, implementing an undiluted version of the best and most rational crime/correctional policy is an impossibility. For example, no matter what the empirical evidence shows, some liberals will continue to press for the use of prisons for rehabilitation, some radicals and pacifist religious groups will continue to work for the abolition of prisons, and some aficionados of retribution will continue to advocate presumptive/proportional sentencing guidelines. Judges can be expected to offer vociferous resistance to any sentencing proposals that promise to eliminate virtually all judicial discretion in sentencing (always a sore point with the judiciary). Probation and parole officers would object because my flat sentencing guidelines might suggest the abandonment of community correctional options for those convicted of index crimes.

My sentencing proposals also probably would require the construction of new prison facilities to confine additional offenders (although one possible way to reduce the need for new prison space would be to use house confinement and electronic monitoring technologies for all offenders receiving detention sentences and reserve all prison space for offenders receiving incarceration and life sentences). Prisons in the United States are already badly overcrowded; in the last few years, I've been in correctional facilities where overflow inmates are confined in congregate sleeping units in gymnasiums and dilapidated warehouses. State and federal budgets are desperately short of funds for existing programs not only in criminal justice but in every area. In an era of widespread economic decline, taxpayers can hardly be expected enthusiastically to embrace policies that would require the spending of even more money on criminals.

Given these limitations on rationality and resources, the creation of a completely rational correctional system that efficiently combats crime will never occur. A nonlinear criminal justice system in a nonlinear, democratic society simply cannot implement a wholly linear correctional policy. Prisons currently are one among many modestly successful social institutions in an imperfect, nonlinear world. Prisons are no more—*nor are they any less*—effective in achieving their objectives than schools, corporations, churches, hospitals, and families in contemporary American society. As concerned citizens, we should not waste our time dreaming about optimally effective social institutions, but rather we should work tirelessly to make our social institutions incrementally more rational. This is the goal of my defense of prisons.

References

Abbott, Jack Henry. 1982. *In the Belly of the Beast: Letters from Prison.* New York: Vintage.

Adler, Patricia A. 1985. *Wheeling and Dealing: An Ethnography of an Upper-Level Drug Dealing and Smuggling Community.* New York: Columbia University Press.

Adler, Patricia A., and Peter Adler. 1983. "Shifts and Oscillations in Deviant Careers: The Case of Upper-Level Drug Dealers and Smugglers." *Social Problems* 31(2):195–207.

Allen, Francis A. 1959. "Criminal Justice, Legal Values and the Rehabilitation Ideal." *Journal of Criminal Law, Criminology and Police Science* 50(3):226–232.

———. 1981. *The Decline of the Rehabilitative Ideal: Penal Policy and Social Purpose.* New Haven, CT: Yale University Press.

Allen, Harry E., and Clifford E. Simonsen. 1989. *Corrections in America: An Introduction.* New York: Macmillan.

Allen, John. 1978. *Assault with a Deadly Weapon: The Autobiography of a Street Criminal,* edited by Dianne Hall Kelly and Philip Heymann. New York: McGraw-Hill.

American Friends Service Committee. 1971. *Struggle for Justice.* New York: Hill and Wang.

Andenaes, Johannes. 1952. "General Prevention—Illusion or Reality?" *Journal of Criminal Law, Criminology and Police Science* 43(2):176–198.

———. 1966. "The General Preventive Effects of Punishment." *University of Pennsylvania Law Review* 114(7):949–983.

———. 1971a. "Deterrence and Specific Offenses." *University of Chicago Law Review* 38(2):537–553.

_____. 1971b. "The Moral or Educative Influence of Criminal Law." *Journal of Social Issues* 27(2):17–31.

_____. 1974. *Punishment and Deterrence.* Ann Arbor: University of Michigan Press.

Anderson, Linda S., Theodore G. Chiricos, and Gordon P. Waldo. 1977. "Formal and Informal Sanctions: A Comparison of Deterrent Effects." *Social Problems* 25(1):103–114.

Andrews, D. A., Ivan Zinger, Robert D. Hoge, James Bonta, Paul Gendreau, and Francis T. Cullen. 1990a. "Does Correctional Treatment Work? A Clinically Relevant and Psychologically Informed Meta-Analysis." *Criminology* 28(3):369–404.

_____. 1990b. "A Human Science Approach or More Punishment and Pessimism: A Rejoinder to Lab and Whitehead." *Criminology* 28(3):419–429.

Armstrong, K. G. 1971. "The Retributive Hits Back." In *Theories of Punishment,* edited by Stanley E. Grupp, 19–40. Bloomington: Indiana University Press.

Ashford, José B., and Craig Winston LeCroy. 1990. "Juvenile Recidivism: A Comparison of Three Prediction Instruments." *Adolescence* 25 (Summer):441–450.

Atcheley, Robert, and Patrick McCabe. 1968. "Socialization in Correctional Communities: A Replication." *American Sociological Review* 33(5):774–785.

Bagdikian, Ben H. 1972. *The Shame of the Prisons.* Washington, DC: *The Washington Post* National Reports.

Bailey, Walter C. 1966. "Correctional Outcome: An Evaluation of 100 Reports." *Journal of Criminal Law, Criminology and Police Science* 57(2):153–160.

Bailey, William C., and Ruth P. Lott. 1976. "Crime, Punishment and Personality: An Examination of the Deterrence Question." *Journal of Criminal Law and Criminology* 67(1):99–109.

Bailey, William C., J. David Martin, and Louis N. Gray. 1974. "Crime and Deterrence: A Correlation Analysis." *Journal of Research in Crime and Delinquency* 11(2):124–143.

Bakal, Yitzhak, ed. 1973a. *Closing Correctional Institutions: New Strategies for Youth Services.* Lexington, MA: Lexington (Heath).

_____. 1973b. "Closing Massachusetts' Institutions: A Case Study." In *Closing Correctional Institutions: New Strategies for Youth Services,* edited by Yitzhak Bakal, 151–180. Lexington, MA: Lexington (Heath).

Barnes, Harry Elmer. 1930. *The Story of Punishment.* Boston: Stratford.

Barnes, Harry Elmer, and Negley K. Teeters. 1951. *New Horizons in Criminology.* Englewood Cliffs, NJ: Prentice-Hall.

Barnett, Arnold, Alfred Blumstein, and David P. Farrington. 1987. "Probabilistic Models of Youthful Criminal Careers." *Criminology* 25(1):83–107.

_____ . 1989. "A Prospective Test of a Criminal Career Model." *Criminology* 27(2):373–388.

Barnett, Randy E. 1977. "Restitution: A New Paradigm of Criminal Justice." In *Assessing the Criminal: Restitution, Retribution, and the Legal Process*, edited by Randy E. Barnett and John Hagel III, 349–383. Cambridge, MA: Ballinger.

Barnett, Randy E., and John Hagel III, eds. 1977. *Assessing the Criminal: Restitution, Retribution, and the Legal Process*. Cambridge, MA: Ballinger.

Bartol, Curt R. 1991. *Criminal Behavior: A Psychosocial Approach*. Englewood Cliffs, NJ: Prentice-Hall.

Bartollas, Clemens. 1990. "The Prison: Disorder Personified." In *Are Prisons Any Better? Twenty Years of Correctional Reform*, edited by John W. Murphy and Jack E. Dison, 11–22. Newbury Park, CA: Sage.

Bartollas, Clemens, and Simon Dinitz. 1989. *Introduction to Criminology: Order and Disorder*. New York: Harper and Row.

Beccaria, Cesare. [1764]1963. *On Crimes and Punishments*. Indianapolis, IN: Bobbs-Merrill.

Becker, Gary S. 1968. "Crime and Punishment: An Economic Approach." *Journal of Political Economy* 76(2):169–217.

Becker, Howard S. 1963. *Outsiders: Studies in the Sociology of Deviance*. New York: Free Press.

Bedau, Hugo Adam. 1977. "Concessions to Retribution in Punishment." In *Justice and Punishment*, edited by J. B. Cederblom and William L. Blizek, 51–73. Cambridge, MA: Ballinger.

Belcher, John R. 1988. "Are Jails Replacing the Mental Health System for the Homeless Mentally Ill?" *Community Mental Health Journal* 24(3):185–195.

Bello, Steve. 1982. *Doing Life*. New York: St. Martin's Press.

Bentham, Jeremy. [1789] 1970. *An Introduction to the Principles of Morals and Legislation*. London: Methuen.

_____ . [1802] 1931. *The Theory of Legislation*. London: Kegan, Paul, Trench, and Trubner.

_____ . [1811] 1930. *The Rationale of Punishment*. London: Robert Howard.

_____ . [1843] 1962. *The Works of Jeremy Bentham, Volume 1*. New York: Russell and Russell.

Berk, Bernard B. 1966. "Organizational Goals and Inmate Organization." *American Journal of Sociology* 71(1):522–534.

Berk, Richard A., Alec Campbell, Ruth Klap, and Bruce Western. 1992. "The Deterrent Effect of Arrest in Incidents of Domestic Violence: A Bayesian Analysis of Four Field Experiments." *American Sociological Review* 57(5):698–708.

Berk, Richard A., and Phyllis J. Newton. 1985. "Does Arrest Really Deter Wife Battery? An Effort to Replicate the Findings of the Minneapolis Spouse Abuse Experiment." *American Sociological Review* 50(2):253–262.

Biles, David F. 1979. "Crime and the Use of Prisons." *Federal Probation* 43(2):39–43.

Bishop, Donna M. 1984a. "Deterrence: A Panel Analysis." *Justice Quarterly* 1(3):311–328.

_____ . 1984b. "Legal and Extralegal Barriers to Delinquency: A Panel Analysis." *Criminology* 22(3):403–419.

Blumstein, Alfred. 1983. "Selective Incapacitation as a Means of Crime Control." *American Behavioral Scientist* 27(1):87–108.

Blumstein, Alfred, and Jacqueline Cohen. 1980. "Sentencing of Convicted Offenders: An Analysis of the Public's View." *Law and Society Review* 14(2):223–261.

Blumstein, Alfred, Jacqueline Cohen, and David R. Farrington. 1988a. "Criminal Career Research: Its Value for Criminology." *Criminology* 26(1):1–35.

_____ . 1988b. "Longitudinal and Career Criminal Research: Further Clarifications." *Criminology* 26(1):57–74.

Blumstein, Alfred, Jacqueline Cohen, and Daniel Nagin, eds. 1978. *Deterrence and Incapacitation: Estimating the Effects of Criminal Sanctions on Crime Rates.* Washington, DC: National Academy of Sciences.

Blumstein, Alfred, Jacqueline Cohen, Jeffrey A. Roth, and Christy A. Visher, eds. 1986. *Criminal Careers and "Career Criminals," Volume 1.* Washington, DC: National Academy Press.

Blumstein, Alfred, David P. Farrington, and Soumyo Moitra. 1985. "Delinquency Careers: Innocents, Desisters, and Persisters." In *Crime and Justice: An Annual Review of Research, Volume 6*, edited by Michael Tonry and Norval Morris, 187—219. Chicago: University of Chicago Press.

Blumstein, Alfred, and Daniel Nagin. 1977. "The Deterrent Effect of Legal Sanctions on Draft Evasion." *Stanford Law Review* 28(2):241–275.

Bowker, Lee H. 1981. "Crime and the Use of Prisons in the United States: A Time Series Analysis." *Crime and Delinquency* 27(2):206–212.

_____ . 1982. *Corrections: The Science and the Art.* New York: Macmillan.

Braithwaite, John, and Philip Pettit. 1990. *Not Just Deserts: A Republican Theory of Criminal Justice.* Oxford, England: Clarendon.

Brennan, Patricia A., and Sarnoff A. Mednick. 1991. "A Learning Theory Approach to Criminal Deterrence." Paper presented at the American Society of Criminology meetings, San Francisco, CA, November 20–23.

Bridges, George S., and James A. Stone. 1986. "Effects of Criminal Punishment on Perceived Threat of Punishment: Toward an Understanding of Specific Deterrence." *Journal of Research in Crime and Delinquency* 23(3):207–239.

Broderick, John. 1990. "Book Review of Robert Trojanowicz and Bonnie Bucqueroux's *Community Policing: A Contemporary Perspective*." *Justice Quarterly* 7(3):619–622.

Brodt, Stephen J., and J. Steven Smith. 1988. "Public Policy and the Serious Juvenile Offender." *Criminal Justice Policy Review* 2(1):70–85.

Bureau of Justice Statistics. 1991. *National Update.* Washington, DC: U.S. Department of Justice (Office of Justice Programs).

Burgess, Edwin W. 1928. "Factors Determining Success or Failure on Parole." In *The Workings of the Indeterminate Sentence Law and the Parole System in Illinois,* edited by Andrew A. Bruce, Edwin W. Burgess, Albert J. Harno, and John Landeseo, 205–249. Springfield: Illinois State Board of Parole.

Bursik, Robert J., Jr., Harold G. Grasmick, and Mitchell B. Chamlin. 1990. "The Effect of Longitudinal Arrest Patterns on the Development of Robbery Trends at the Neighborhood Level." *Criminology* 28(3):431–450.

Cameron, Mary Owen. 1964. *The Booster and the Snitch.* Glencoe, IL: Free Press.

Capote, Truman. 1965. *In Cold Blood.* New York: New American Library.

Carroll, Leo. [1974] 1988. *Hacks, Blacks, and Cons: Race Relations in a Maximum Security Prison.* Prospect Heights, IL: Waveland.

————. 1977. "Race and Three Forms of Prisoner Power: Confrontation, Censoriousness, and the Corruption of Authority." In *Contemporary Corrections: Social Control and Conflict,* edited by C. Ronald Huff, 40–53. Beverly Hills, CA: Sage.

Chaiken, Jan M., and Marcia R. Chaiken. 1982. *Varieties of Criminal Behavior.* Santa Monica, CA: Rand Corporation.

Chaiken, Marcia R., and Jan M. Chaiken. 1984. "Offender Types and Public Policy." *Crime and Delinquency* 30(2):195–226.

Chambliss, William J. 1966. "The Deterrent Influence of Punishment." *Crime and Delinquency* 12(1):70–75.

————. 1967. "Types of Deviance and the Effectiveness of Legal Sanctions." *Wisconsin Law Review* 1967(3):703–719.

Chamlin, Mitchell B., Harold G. Grasmick, Robert Bursik, Jr., and John K. Cochran. 1992. "Time Aggregation and the Time Lag in Macro-Level Deterrence Research." *Criminology* 30(3):377–395.

Chauncey, Robert. 1975. "Deterrence: Certainty, Severity and Skyjacking." *Criminology* 12(4):447–473.

Chiricos, Theodore G., and Gordon P. Waldo. 1970. "Punishment and Crime: An Examination of Some Empirical Evidence." *Social Problems* 18(2):200–217.

Clarke, Ronald, V., and Derek B. Cornish. 1985. "Modeling Offenders' Decisions: A Framework for Research and Policy." In *Crime and Justice: An Annual Review of Research, Volume 6,* edited by Michael Tonry and Norval Morris, 147–185. Chicago: University of Chicago Press.

Clemmer, Donald. 1940. *The Prison Community.* New York: Holt, Rinehart and Winston.

Coates, Robert B., and Alden D. Miller. 1973. "Neutralization of Community Resistance to Group Homes." In *Closing Correctional Institutions: New*

Strategies for Youth Services, edited by Yitzhak Bakal, 67–84. Lexington, MA: Lexington (Heath).

Coates, Robert, Alden D. Miller, and Lloyd E. Ohlin. 1973. "A Strategic Innovation in the Process of Deinstitutionalization: The University of Massachusetts Conference." In *Closing Correctional Institutions: New Strategies for Youth Services*, edited by Yitzhak Bakal, 127–148. Lexington, MA: Lexington (Heath).

_____ . 1978. *Diversity in a Youth Correctional System: Handling Delinquents in Massachusetts*. Cambridge, MA: Ballinger.

Cohen, Jacqueline. 1978. "The Incapacitative Effect of Imprisonment: A Critical Review of the Literature." In *Deterrence and Incapacitation: Estimating the Effects of Criminal Sanctions on Crime Rates*, edited by Alfred Blumstein, Jacqueline Cohen, and Daniel Nagin, 187–243. Washington, DC: National Academy of Sciences.

_____ . 1983. "Incapacitation as a Strategy for Crime Control: Possibilities and Pitfalls." In *Crime and Justice: An Annual Review of Research, Volume 5*, edited by Michael Tonry and Norval Morris, 1–84. Chicago: University of Chicago Press.

_____ . 1986. "Research on Criminal Careers: Individual Frequency Rates and Offense Seriousness." In *Criminal Careers and "Career Criminals," Volume 1*, edited by Alfred Blumstein, Jacqueline Cohen, Jeffrey A. Roth, and Christy A. Visher, 292–418. Washington, DC: National Academy Press.

Cohen, Mark A. 1988. "Pain, Suffering and Jury Awards: A Study of the Cost of Crime to Victims." *Law and Society Review* 22(3):537–555.

Cohen, Michael D., James C. March, and Johan P. Olsen. 1972. "A Garbage Can Model of Organizational Choice." *Administrative Science Quarterly* 17(1):1–25.

Conklin, John E. 1975. *The Impact of Crime*. New York: Macmillan.

_____ . 1989. *Criminology*. New York: Macmillan

Cook, Philip J. 1980. "Research in Criminal Deterrence: Laying the Groundwork for the Second Decade." In *Crime and Justice: An Annual Review of Research, Volume 2*, edited by Norval Morris and Michael Tonry, 211–268. Chicago: University of Chicago Press.

Cordilia, Ann. 1983. *The Making of an Inmate: Prison as a Way of Life*. Cambridge, MA: Schenkman.

Cornish, Derek B., and Ronald V. Clarke, eds. 1986. *The Reasoning Criminal*. New York: Springer-Verlag.

_____ . 1987. "Understanding Crime Displacement: An Application of Rational Choice Theory." *Criminology* 25(4):933–947.

Coser, Lewis A. 1956. *The Functions of Social Conflict*. New York: Free Press.

Criminal Justice Newsletter. 1985. "Many Cities Experimenting with Police Foot Patrols." *Criminal Justice Newsletter* 16(10):1–3.

Cullen, Francis T., and Karen E. Gilbert. 1982. *Reaffirming Rehabilitation*. Cincinnati: Anderson.

Cullen, Francis T., Bruce G. Link, and Craig W. Polanzi. 1982. "The Serious-
    ness of Crime Revisited: Have Attitudes Toward White-Collar Crime
    Changed?" *Criminology* 20(1):83–102.
Cullen, Francis T., Bruce G. Link, Lawrence F. Travis III, and John F. Wozniak.
    1985. "Consensus in Crime Seriousness: Empirical Reality or Method-
    ological Artifact?" *Criminology* 23(1):99–118.
Currie, Elliott. 1985. *Confronting Crime: An American Challenge*. New York:
    Pantheon.
Dann, Robert H. 1935. "The Deterrent Effect of Capital Punishment." *Friends'
    Social Service Series* 29:1–20.
Decker, Scott H., and Carol W. Kohfeld. 1985. "Crimes, Crime Rates, and
    Arrest Ratios: Implications for Deterrence Theory." *Criminology*
    23(3):437–450.
Dunford, Franklyn W., and Delbert S. Elliott. 1984. "Identifying Career Offend-
    ers Using Self-Reported Data." *Journal of Research in Crime and
    Delinquency* 21(1):57–86.
Dunford, Franklyn W., David Huizinga, and Delbert S. Elliott. 1990. "The Role
    of Arrest in Domestic Assault: The Omaha Police Experiement." *Crim-
    inology* 28(2):183–206.
Durkheim, Émile. [1893] 1964. *The Division of Labor in Society*. New York:
    Free Press.
_____ . [1895] 1982. *The Rules of Sociological Method*. London: Macmillan.
Eaton, William W., Jr. 1974. "Mental Hospitalization as a Reinforcement Pro-
    cess." *American Sociological Review* 39(2):252–260.
Eck, John. 1984. *Solving Crimes: The Investigation of Burglary and Robbery*.
    Washington, DC: Police Executive Research Forum.
Edelman, Murray. 1988. *Constructing the Political Spectacle*. Chicago: Univer-
    sity of Chicago Press.
Ekland-Olson, Sheldon, John Lieb, and Louis Zurcher. 1984. "The Paradoxical
    Impact of Criminal Sanctions: Some Microstructural Findings." *Law
    and Society Review* 18(2):159–178.
Erickson, Maynard L., and Jack P. Gibbs. 1979. "On the Perceived Severity of
    Legal Penalties." *Journal of Criminal Law and Criminology* 70(1):102–
    116.
Erickson, Maynard L., Jack P. Gibbs, and Gary F. Jensen. 1977. "The Deter-
    rence Doctrine and the Perceived Certainty of Legal Punishments."
    American Sociological Review 42(2):305–317.
Erikson, Kai T. 1966. *Wayward Puritans: A Study in the Sociology of Deviance*.
    New York: Wiley.
Evans, Sandra S., and Joseph E. Scott. 1984. "The Seriousness of Crime Cross-
    Culturally: The Impact of Religiosity." *Criminology* 22(1):39–59.
Ewing, Charles Patrick. 1991. "Preventive Detention and Execution: The Con-
    stitutionality of Punishing Future Crimes." *Law and Human Behavior*
    15(2):139–163.

Farber, M. A. 1981. "A Killing at Dawn Beclouds Ex-Convict Writer's New Life." *New York Times* July 26: A1, A26.

Farrington, David P. 1977. "The Effects of Public Labelling." *British Journal of Criminology* 17(2):112–125.

_____. 1987. "Predicting Individual Crime Rates." In *Crime and Justice: An Annual Review of Research, Volume 9*, edited by Don M. Gottfredson and Michael Tonry, 53–101. Chicago: University of Chicago Press.

Ferri, Enrico. [1901] 1971. "The Positive School of Criminology." In *Theories of Punishment*, edited by Stanley E. Grupp, 229–242. Bloomington: Indiana University Press.

Figlio, Robert M. 1975. "The Seriousness of Offenses: An Evaluation by Offenders and Nonoffenders." *Journal of Criminal Law and Criminology* 66(2):189–200.

Fisher, Gene A., and Maynard L. Erickson. 1973. "On Assessing the Effects of Official Reactions to Juvenile Delinquency." *Journal of Research in Crime and Delinquency* 10(2):177–194.

Fishman, Robert. 1977. "An Evaluation of Criminal Recidivism in Projects Providing Rehabilitation and Diversion Services in New York City." *Journal of Criminal Law and Criminology* 68(2):283–305.

Fogel, David. 1975. *"...We Are the Living Proof . . ." The Justice Model for Corrections.* Cincinnati: Anderson.

Forst, Brian. 1984. "Selective Incapacitation: A Sheep in Wolf's Clothing?" *Judicature* 68(4 and 5):153–160.

Forst, Brian, William Rhodes, James Dimm, Arthur Gelman, and Barbara Mullin. 1983. "Targeting Federal Resources on Recidivists: An Empirical View." *Federal Probation* 47(2):10–20.

Friedberg, Ardy. 1980. *America Afraid.* New York: New American Library.

Gallup, George H., Sr. 1981. "Americans See Surge of Crime." *The Gallup Report* 187(April):4–19.

Garabedian, Peter G. 1963. "Social Roles and Processes of Socialization in the Prison Community." *Social Problems* 11(2):139–152.

Garfinkel, Harold. 1956. "Conditions of Successful Degradation Ceremonies." *American Journal of Sociology* 61(5):420–424.

Garland, David. 1990. *Punishment and Modern Society: A Study in Social Theory.* Chicago: University of Chicago Press.

Garrett, Carol J. 1985. "Effects of Residential Treatment on Adjudicated Delinquents: A Meta-Analysis." *Journal of Research in Crime and Delinquency* 22(4):287–308.

Geerken, Michael, and Walter R. Gove. 1975. "Deterrence: Some Theoretical Considerations." *Law and Society Review* 9(3):497–514.

_____. 1977. "Deterrence, Overload, and Incapacitation: An Empirical Evaluation." *Social Forces* 56(2):424–447.

Geis, Gilbert. 1972. "Jeremy Bentham." In *Pioneers in Criminology*, edited by Hermann Mannheim, 51–68. Montclair, NJ: Patterson Smith.

Gendreau, Paul, and Robert R. Ross. 1979. "Effective Correctional Treatment: Bibliotherapy for Cynics." *Crime and Delinquency* 25(4):463–489.

―――――. 1987. "Revivification of Rehabilitation: Evidence for the 1980s." *Justice Quarterly* 4(3):349–407.

Gensheimer, Leah K., Jeffrey P. Mayer, Rand Gottschalk, and William S. Davidson. 1986. "Diverting Youth from the Juvenile Justice System: A Meta-Analysis of Intervention Efficacy." In *Youth Violence: Programs and Prospects*, edited by Steven J. Apter and Arnold P. Goldstein, 39–57. New York: Pergamon.

Gibbs, Jack P. 1968. "Crime, Punishment, and Deterrence." *Southwestern Social Science Quarterly* 48(4):515–530.

―――――. 1975. *Crime, Punishment, and Deterrence*. New York: Elsevier.

―――――. 1986. "Deterrence Theory and Research." In *The Law as a Behavioral Instrument: Nebraska Symposium on Motivation*, edited by Gary B. Melton, 87–130. Lincoln: University of Nebraska Press.

Gibbs, Jack P., and Glenn Firebaugh. 1990. "The Artifact Issue in Deterrence Research." *Criminology* 28(2):347–367.

Glaser, Daniel. 1955. "The Efficacy of Alternative Approaches to Parole Prediction." *American Sociological Review* 20(3):283–287.

―――――. 1962. "Prediction Tables as Accounting Devices for Judges and Parole Boards." *Crime and Delinquency* 8(3):239–258.

―――――. 1964. *The Effectiveness of a Prison and Parole System*. Indianapolis: Bobbs-Merrill.

―――――. 1975. "Achieving Better Questions: A Half Century's Progress in Correctional Research." *Federal Probation* 39(3):3–9.

Glassner, Barry, Margret Ksander, Bruce Berg, and Bruce D. Johnson. 1983. "A Note on the Deterrent Effect of Juvenile Versus Adult Jurisdiction." *Social Problems* 31(2):219–221.

Glueck, Sheldon, and Eleanor T. Glueck. 1930. *Five Hundred Criminal Careers*. New York: Knopf.

Goffman, Erving. 1961. *Asylums: Essays on the Social Situation of Mental Patients and Other Inmates*. Garden City, NY: Anchor (Doubleday).

Golding, Martin P. 1977. "Criminal Sentencing: Some Philosophical Considerations." In *Justice and Punishment*, edited by J. B. Cederblom and William L. Blizek, 89–105. Cambridge, MA: Ballinger.

Gottfredson, Stephen D., and Don M. Gottfredson. 1986. "Accuracy of Prediction Models." In *Criminal Careers and "Career Criminals," Volume 2*, edited by Alfred Blumstein, Jacqueline Cohen, Jeffrey A. Roth, and Christy A. Visher, 212–290. Washington, DC: National Academy Press.

Gove, Walter R. 1970. "Who Is Hospitalized? A Critical View of Some Sociological Studies of Mental Illness." *Journal of Health and Social Behavior* 11(4):294–303.

―――――. 1980a. "Labelling and Mental Illness: A Critique." In *The Labelling of Deviance: Evaluating a Perspective*, edited by Walter R. Gove, 53–99. Beverly Hills, CA: Sage.

_____. 1980b. "Labelling and Mental Illness: Postscript." In *The Labelling of Deviance: Evaluating a Perspective*, edited by Walter R. Gove, 99–109. Beverly Hills, CA: Sage.

Gove, Walter R., and Terry Fain. 1973. "The Stigma of Mental Hospitalization: An Attempt to Evaluate Its Consequences." *Archives of General Psychiatry* 28(April):494–500.

Gove, Walter, R., and Patrick Howell. 1974. "Individual Resources and Mental Hospitalization: A Comparison and Evaluation of the Societal Reaction and Psychiatric Perspectives." *American Sociological Review* 39(1):86–100.

Grasmick, Harold G., and Lynn Appleton. 1977. "Legal Punishment and Social Stigma: A Comparison of Two Deterrence Models." *Social Science Quarterly* 58(1):15–28.

Grasmick, Harold G., and George J. Bryjak. 1980. "The Deterrent Effect of Perceived Severity of Punishment." *Social Forces* 59(2):471–491.

Grasmick, Harold G., and Robert J. Bursik, Jr. 1990. "Conscience, Significant Others, and Rational Choice: Extending the Deterrence Model." *Law and Society Review* 24(3):837–861.

Grasmick, Harold G., and Donald E. Green. 1980. "Legal Punishment, Social Disapproval and Internalization as Inhibitors of Illegal Behavior." *Journal of Criminal Law and Criminology* 71(3):325–335.

_____. 1981. "Deterrence and the Morally Committed." *Sociological Quarterly* 22(1):1–14.

Grasmick, Harold G., Darlene Jacobs, and Carol B. McCollom. 1983. "Social Class and Social Control: An Application of Deterrence Theory." *Social Forces* 62(2):359–374.

Grasmick, Harold G., and Herman Milligan, Jr. 1976. "Deterrence Theory Approach to Socioeconomic/Demographic Correlates of Crime." *Social Science Quarterly* 57(3):608–617.

Green, Gary S. 1985. "General Deterrence and Television Cable Crime: A Field Experiment in Social Control." *Criminology* 23(4):629–645.

Greenberg, David F. 1975. "The Incapacitative Effect of Imprisonment: Some Estimates." *Law and Society Review* 9(4):541–580.

_____. 1977. "The Correctional Effects of Corrections: A Survey of Evaluations." In *Corrections and Punishment*, edited by David R. Greenberg, 111–148. Beverly Hills, CA: Sage.

Greenberg, David F., and Ronald C. Kessler. 1982. "The Effect of Arrests on Crime: A Multivariate Panel Analysis." *Social Forces* 60(3):771–790.

Greenberg, David F., Ronald C. Kessler, and Colin Loftin. 1983. "The Effect of Police Employment on Crime." *Criminology* 21(3):375–394.

Greenberg, David F., Ronald C. Kessler, and Charles H. Logan. 1979. "A Panel Model of Crime Rates and Arrest Rates." *American Sociological Review* 44(5):843–850.

Greenwood, Peter W. 1982. *Selective Incapacitation*. Santa Monica CA: Rand Corporation.

Greenwood, Peter W., and Joan Petersilia. 1975. *The Criminal Investigation Process, Volume 1: Summary and Policy Implications*. Santa Monica, CA: Rand Corporation.

Greenwood, Peter W., and Susan Turner. 1987. *Selective Incapacitation Revisited: Why the High-Rate Offenders Are Hard to Predict*. Santa Monica, CA: Rand Corporation.

Grusky, Oscar. 1959. "Organizational Goals and the Behavior of Informal Leaders." *American Journal of Sociology* 65(1):59–67.

Haan, Willem de. 1990. *The Politics of Redress: Crime, Punishment, and Penal Abolition*. London: Unwin Hyman.

Hagan, John. 1974. "Extra-Legal Attributes and Criminal Sentencing: An Assessment of a Sociological Viewpoint." *Law and Society Review* 8(3):357–383.

———. 1989. "Why Is There So Little Criminal Justice Theory? Neglected Macro- and Micro-Level Links Between Organization and Power." *Journal of Research in Crime and Delinquency* 26(2):116–135.

Hamparian, Donna Martin, Richard Schuster, Simon Dinitz, and John P. Conrad. 1978. *The Violent Few: A Study of Dangerous Juvenile Offenders*. Lexington, MA: Lexington (Heath).

Hart, H.L.A. 1968. *Punishment and Responsibility: Essays in the Philosophy of Law*. New York: Oxford University Press.

Hartjen, Clayton A. 1974. *Crime and Criminalization*. New York: Praeger.

Hawkins, Gordon. 1971. "Punishment and Deterrence: The Educative, Moralizing, and Habituative Effects." In *Theories of Punishment*, edited by Stanley E. Grupp, 163–180. Bloomington: Indiana University Press.

———. 1976. *The Prison: Policy and Practice*. Chicago: University of Chicago Press.

Hawkins, Richard, and Geoffrey P. Alpert. 1989. *American Prison Systems: Punishment and Justice*. Englewood Cliffs, NJ: Prentice-Hall.

Hegel, Georg W. F. [1821] 1967. *Philosophy of Right*. London: Oxford University Press.

Henry, Lewis C. 1965. *Best Quotations for All Occasions*. Greenwich, CT: Fawcett.

Hoffman, Peter B. 1983. "Screening for Risk: A Revised Salient Factor Score (SFS 81)." *Journal of Criminal Justice* 11(6):539–547.

Hood, Roger, and Richard Sparks. 1970. *Key Issues in Criminology*. New York: McGraw-Hill.

Horney, Julie, and Ineke Haen Marshall. 1991. "Measuring Lambda Through Self-Reports." *Criminology* 29(3):471–495.

———. 1992. "Risk Perceptions Among Serious Offenders: The Role of Crime and Punishment." *Criminology* 30(4):575–594.

Horwitz, Allan, and Michael Wasserman. 1979. "The Effect of Social Control on Delinquent Behavior: A Longitudinal Test." *Sociological Focus* 12(1):53–70.

Hospers, John. 1977a. "Punishment, Protection, and Retaliation." In *Justice and Punishment*, edited by J. B. Cederblom and William L. Blizek, 21–50. Cambridge, MA: Ballinger.

————. 1977b. "Retribution: The Ethics of Punishment." In *Assessing the Criminal: Restitution, Retribution, and the Legal Process*, edited by Randy E. Barnett and John Hagel III, 181–209. Cambridge, MA: Ballinger.

Howard, John. [1777] 1929. *The State of the Prisons*. London: J. M. Dent.

Irwin, John. [1970] 1987. *The Felon*. Berkeley: University of California Press.

————. 1980. *Prisons in Turmoil*. Boston: Little, Brown.

————. 1985. *The Jail: Managing the Underclass in American Society*. Berkeley: University of California Press.

Irwin, John, and Donald R. Cressey. 1962. "Thieves, Convicts and the Inmate Culture." *Social Problems* 10(2):142–155.

Isaac, Rael Jean, and Virginia C. Armat. 1990. *Madness in the Streets: How Psychiatry and the Law Abandoned the Mentally Ill*. New York: Free Press.

Ives, George. [1914] 1970. *A History of Penal Methods*. Montclair, NJ: Patterson Smith.

Jackson, George. 1970. *Soledad Brother*. New York: Bantam.

————. 1972. *Blood in My Eye*. New York: Random House.

Jacobs, James B. 1977. *Stateville: The Penitentiary in Mass Society*. Chicago: University of Chicago Press.

————. 1983. *New Perspectives on Prisons and Imprisonment*. Ithaca, NY: Cornell University Press.

James, J. Frank, Dick Gregory, Renee K. Jones, and O. H. Rundell. 1980. "Psychiatric Morbidity in Prisons." *Hospital and Community Psychiatry* 31(10):674–677.

Janus, Michael G. 1985. "Selective Incapacitation: Have We Tried It? Does It Work?" *Journal of Criminal Justice* 13(2):117–129.

Jensen, Gary F. 1969. " 'Crime Doesn't Pay': Correlates of a Shared Misunderstanding." *Social Problems* 17(2):189–201.

Jensen, Gary F., Maynard L. Erickson, and Jack P. Gibbs. 1978. "Perceived Risk of Punishment and Self-Reported Delinquency." *Social Forces* 57(1):57–78.

Johnson, Lester Douglas. 1970. *The Devil's Front Porch*. Lawrence: University Press of Kansas.

Jolin, Annette. 1983. "Domestic Violence Legislation: An Impact Assessment." *Journal of Police Science and Administration* 11(4):451–454.

Kant, Immanuel. [1787] 1933. *Critique of Pure Reason*. London: Macmillan.

————. [1797] 1964. *The Metaphysical Principles of Virtue*. Indianapolis, IN: Bobbs-Merrill.

————. [1797] 1965. *The Metaphysical Elements of Justice*. Indianapolis, IN: Bobbs-Merrill.

Kassebaum, Gene, David Ward, and Daniel Wilner. 1971. *Prison Treatment and Parole Survival: An Empirical Assessment.* New York: Wiley.

Kaufmann, Walter. 1977. "Retribution and the Ethics of Punishment." In *Assessing the Criminal: Restitution, Retribution, and the Legal Process*, edited by Randy E. Barnett and John Hagel III, 211–230. Cambridge, MA: Ballinger.

Kelling, George L. 1978. "Police Field Services and Crime: The Presumed Effects of a Capacity." *Crime and Delinquency* 24(2):173–184.

Kelling, George L., Tony Pate, Duane Dieckman, and Charles E. Brown. 1974. *The Kansas City Preventive Patrol Experiment: A Summary Report.* Washington, DC: Police Foundation.

Klein, Malcolm W. 1974. "Labeling, Deterrence and Recidivism: A Study of Police Dispositions of Juvenile Offenders." *Social Problems* 22(2):292–303.

———. 1979. "Deinstitutionalization and Diversion of Juvenile Offenders: A Litany of Impediments." In *Crime and Justice: An Annual Review of Research, Volume 1*, edited by Norval Morris and Michael Tonry, 145–201. Chicago: University of Chicago Press.

Klein, S., and M. Caggiano. 1986. *The Prevalence, Predictability, and Policy Implication of Recidivism.* Santa Monica, CA: Rand Corporation.

Kleinig, John. 1973. *Punishment and Desert.* The Hague: Martin Nijhoff.

Klemke, Lloyd W. 1978. "Does Apprehension for Shoplifting Amplify or Terminate Shoplifting Activity?" *Law and Society Review* 12(3):391–403.

Klepper, Steven, and Daniel Nagin. 1989. "The Deterrent Effect of Perceived Certainty and Severity of Punishment Revisited." *Criminology* 27(4):721–746.

Kobrin, Solomon. 1980. "Outcome Variables in Program Evaluaton: Crime Control, Social Control, and Justice." In *Handbook of Criminal Justice Evaluation*, edited by Malcolm W. Klein and Katherine S. Teilmann, 447–458. Beverly Hills, CA: Sage.

Kohfeld, Carol W., and John Sprague. 1990. "Demography, Police Behavior, and Deterrence." *Criminology* 28(1):111–136.

Kraut, Robert E. 1976. "Deterrent and Definitional Influences on Shoplifting." *Social Problems* 23(3):358–368.

Lab, Steven P., and John T. Whitehead. 1988. "An Analysis of Juvenile Correctional Treatment." *Crime and Delinquency* 34(1):60–83.

———. 1990. "From 'Nothing Works' to 'The Appropriate Works': The Latest Stop on the Search for the Secular Grail." *Criminology* 28(3):405–417.

Laing, R. D. 1965. *The Divided Self.* Baltimore: Penguin.

———. 1967. *The Politics of Experience.* New York: Ballantine.

Langworthy, Robert H. 1989. "Do Stings Control Crime? An Evaluation of a Police Fencing Operation." *Justice Quarterly* 6(1):27–45.

Lemert, Edwin M. 1951. *Social Pathology.* New York: McGraw-Hill.

_____. 1967. *Human Deviance, Social Problems, and Social Control.* Englewood Cliffs, NJ: Prentice-Hall.

Lempert, Richard. 1981–1982. "Organizing for Deterrence: Lessons from a Study of Child Support." *Law and Society Review* 16(4):513–568.

Lerman, Paul. 1975. *Community Treatment and Social Control: A Critical Analysis of Juvenile Correctional Policy.* Chicago: University of Chicago Press.

Lewis, C. S. [1948] 1971. "The Humanitarian Theory of Punishment." In *Theories of Punishment*, edited by Stanley E. Grupp, 301–308. Bloomington: Indiana University Press.

Lewis, Dan A., and Greta Salem. 1986. *Fear of Crime: Incivility and the Production of a Social Problem.* New Brusnwick, NJ: Transaction.

Lipton, Douglas, Robert Martinson, and Judith Wilks. 1975. *The Effectiveness of Correctional Treatment: A Survey of Treatment Evaluation Studies.* New York: Praeger.

Loeber, Rolf, and Thomas Dishion. 1983. "Early Predictors of Male Delinquency: A Review." *Psychological Bulletin* 94(1):68–99.

Lofland, John. 1966. *Deviance and Identity.* Englewood Cliffs, NJ: Prentice-Hall.

Loftin, Colin, and David McDowall. 1982. "The Police, Crime, and Economics Theory: An Assessment." *American Sociological Review* 47(3):393–401.

Logan, Charles H. 1972. "General Deterrent Effects of Imprisonment." *Social Forces* 51(1):64–73.

Lotz, Roy, Eric D. Poole, and Robert M. Regoli. 1985. *Juvenile Delinquency and Juvenile Justice.* New York: Random House.

Lundman, Richard J. 1986. "One-Wave Perceptual Deterrence Research: Some Grounds for the Renewed Examination of Cross-Sectional Methods." *Journal of Research in Crime and Delinquency* 23(4):370–388.

Mabbott, J. D. 1971. "Punishment." In *Theories of Punishment*, edited by Stanley E. Grupp, 41–57. Bloomington: Indiana University Press.

MacDonald, John M. 1975. *Armed Robbery: Offenders and Their Victims.* Springfield, IL: Charles C. Thomas.

McGuire, William J., and Richard G. Sheehan. 1983. "Relationships Between Crime Rates and Incarceration Rates." *Journal of Research in Crime and Delinquency* 20(1):73–85.

McNulty, Faith. 1989. *The Burning Bed: The True Story of an Abused Wife.* New York: Avon.

Mailer, Norman. 1980. *The Executioner's Song.* New York: Warner.

Martinson, Robert. 1974. "What Works?—Questions and Answers About Prison Reform." *The Public Interest* 35(Spring):22–54.

Mathiesen, Thomas. 1974. *The Politics of Abolition.* New York: Wiley.

_____. 1990. *Prison on Trial: A Critical Assessment.* Newbury Park, CA: Sage.

Meier, Robert F., Steven R. Burkett, and Carol A. Hickman. 1984. "Sanctions, Peers, and Deviance: Preliminary Models of a Social Control Process." *Sociological Quarterly* 25(1):67–82.

Meier, Robert F., and Weldon T. Johnson. 1977. "Deterrence as Social Control: The Legal and Extralegal Production of Conformity." *American Sociological Review* 42(2):292–304.

Menninger, Karl. 1968. *The Crime of Punishment*. New York: Viking.

Miethe, Terance D. 1982. "Public Consensus on Crime Seriousness: Normative Structure or Methodological Artifact?" *Criminology* 20(3–4):515–526.

Miller, Jerome G. 1973. "The Politics of Change: Correctional Reform." In *Closing Correctional Institutions: New Strategies for Youth Services*, edited by Yitzhak Bakal, 3–8. Lexington, MA: Lexington (Heath).

Minor, W. William, and Joseph Harry. 1982. "Deterrent and Experiential Effects in Perceptual Deterrence Research: A Replication and Extension." *Journal of Research in Crime and Delinquency* 19(2):190–203.

Miranne, Alfred C., and Michael R. Geerken. 1991. "The New Orleans Inmate Survey: A Test of Greenwood's Predictive Scale." *Criminology* 29(3):497–518.

Monachesi, Elio. 1972. "Cesare Beccaria." In *Pioneers in Criminology*, edited by Hermann Mannheim, 36–50. Montclair, NJ: Patterson Smith.

Monk, Richard C. 1991. "Introduction: The Study of Crime and Criminology." In *Taking Sides: Clashing Views on Controversial Issues in Crime and Criminology*, edited by Richard C. Monk, xii–xvii. Guilford, CT: Dushkin.

Montgomery, Paul L. 1982. "Abbott Convicted of Manslaughter in Stabbing of East Village Waiter." *New York Times* 22 January: A1, B5.

Mundle, C.W.K. 1971. "Punishment and Desert." In *Theories of Punishment*, edited by Stanley E. Grupp, 58–75. Bloomington: Indiana University Press.

Murphy, Jeffrie G. 1970. *Kant: The Philosophy of Right*. London: Macmillan.

Murray, Charles A., and Louis A. Cox, Jr. 1979. *Beyond Probation: Juvenile Corrections and the Chronic Delinquent*. Beverly Hills, CA: Sage.

Murton, Tom. 1989. "Back to the Future: An Alternative to the Prison Dilemma." In *Taking Sides: Clashing Views on Controversial Issues in Crime and Criminology*, edited by Richard C. Monk, 274–281. Guilford, CT: Dushkin.

Murton, Tom, and Joe Hyams. 1969. *Accomplices to the Crime*. New York: Grove.

Nagel, William G. 1973. *The New Red Barn: A Critical Look at the Modern American Prison*. New York: Walker.

Nagin, Daniel. 1978b. "Crime Rates, Sanction Levels, and Constraints on Prison Population." *Law and Society Review* 12(3):341–366.

_____. 1978b. "General Deterrence: A Review of the Empirical Evidence." In *Deterrence and Incapacitation: Estimating the Effects of Criminal Sanctions on Crime Rates*, edited by Alfred Blumstein, Jacqueline

Cohen, and Daniel Nagin, 95–139. Washington, DC: National Academy of Sciences.

Nagin, Daniel, and Raymond Paternoster. 1991. "The Preventive Effects of the Perceived Risk of Arrest: Testing an Expanded Conception of Deterrence." *Criminology* 29(4):561–587.

Nettler, Gwynn. 1984. *Explaining Crime*. New York: McGraw-Hill.

Newman, Graeme. 1978. *The Punishment Response*. Philadelphia: Lippincott.

Packer, Herbert L. 1968. *The Limits of the Criminal Sanction*. Stanford, CA: Stanford University Press.

Palmer, John W. 1991. *Constitutional Rights of Prisoners*. Cincinnati: Anderson.

Palmer, Ted. 1975. "Martinson Revisited." *Journal of Research in Crime and Delinquency* 12(2):133–152.

Parker, Jerry, and Harold G. Grasmick. 1979. "Linking Actual and Perceived Certainty of Punishment: An Exploratory Study of an Untested Proposition in Deterrence Theory." *Criminology* 17(3):366–379.

Pate, Antony M., and Edwin E. Hamilton. 1992. "Formal and Informal Deterrents to Domestic Violence: The Dade County Spouse Assault Experiment." *American Sociological Review* 57(5):691–697.

Paternoster, Raymond. 1987. "The Deterrent Effect of Perceived Certainty and Severity of Punishment: A Review of the Evidence and Issues." *Justice Quarterly* 4(2):173–217.

Paternoster, Raymond, and Leeann Iovanni. 1989. "The Labeling Perspective and Delinquency: An Elaboration of the Theory and an Assessment of the Evidence." *Justice Quarterly* 6(3):359–394.

Paternoster, Raymond, Linda E. Saltzman, Gordon P. Waldo, and Theodore G. Chiricos. 1983. "Perceived Risk and Social Control: Do Sanctions Really Deter?" *Law and Society Review* 17(3):457–479.

———. 1985. "Assessments of Risk and Behavioral Experience: An Explanatory Study of Change." *Criminology* 23(3):417–436.

Pepinsky, Harold E. 1992. "Abolishing Prisons." In *Corrections: An Issues Approach*, edited by Lawrence F. Travis III, Martin D. Schwartz, and Todd R. Clear, 131–139. Cincinnati: Anderson.

Perrow, Charles. 1986. *Complex Organizations: A Critical Essay*. New York: Random House.

Petersilia, Joan, Peter W. Greenwood, and Marvin Lavin. 1977. *Criminal Careers of Habitual Felons*. Santa Monica, CA: Rand Corporation.

Peterson, Mark A., and Harriet B. Braiker. 1980. *Doing Crime: A Survey of California Prison Inmates*. Santa Monica, CA: Rand Corporation.

Peterson, Mark A., Harriet B. Braiker, and Suzanne M. Polich. 1981. *Who Commits Crime: A Survey of Prison Inmates*. Cambridge, MA: Oelgeschlager, Gunn, and Hain.

Pfuhl, Erdwin H., Jr. 1983. "Police Strikes and Conventional Crime: A Look at the Data." *Criminology* 21(4):489–503.

Phillips, Llad. 1980. "Cost Analysis." In *Handbook of Criminal Justice Evaluation*, edited by Malcolm W. Klein and Katherine S. Teilmann, 459–472. Beverly Hills, CA: Sage.

Piliavin, Irving, Rosemary Gartner, Craig Thornton, and Ross L. Matsueda. 1986. "Crime, Deterrence, and Rational Choice." *American Sociological Review* 51(1):101–119.

Pincoffs, Edmund L. 1977. "Are Questions of Desert Decidable? In *Justice and Punishment*, edited by J. B. Cederblom and William L. Blizek, 75–88. Cambridge, MA: Ballinger.

Police Foundation. 1981. *The Newark Foot Patrol Experiment*. Washington, DC: Police Foundation.

Pung, Orville B. 1983. "A Defense of Prisons." In *Corrections: An Issues Approach*, edited by Lawrence F. Travis III, Martin D. Schwartz, and Todd R. Clear, 73–80. Cincinnati: Anderson.

Quay, Herbert C. 1977. "The Three Faces of Evaluation: What Can Be Expected to Work." *Criminal Justice and Behavior* 4(4):341–354.

Quinney, Richard. 1974. *Critique of Legal Order: Crime Control in Capitalist Society*. Boston: Little, Brown.

Raub, Richard A. 1984. "Effect of Antifencing Operations on Encouraging Crime." *Criminal Justice Review* 9(2):78–83.

Rausch, Sharla. 1983. "Court Processing Versus Diversion of Status Offenders: A Test of Deterrence and Labeling Theories." *Journal of Research in Crime and Delinquency* 20(1):39–54.

Rawls, John. 1971. *A Theory of Justice*. Cambridge: Harvard University Press.

Reckless, Walter C. 1967. *The Crime Problem*. New York: Appleton-Century-Crofts.

Reynolds, Morgan O. 1990. "Crime Pays, But So Does Punishment." *Journal of Social, Political, and Economic Studies* 15(3):259–300.

Richards, Pamela, and Charles R. Tittle. 1981. "Gender and Perceived Chances of Arrest." *Social Forces* 59(4):1182–1199.

_____. 1982. "Socioeconomic Status and Perceptions of Personal Arrest Probabilities." *Criminology* 20(3–4):329–346.

Robison, James, and Gerald Smith. 1971. "The Effectiveness of Correctional Programs." *Crime and Delinquency* 17(1):67–80.

Rose, G.N.G. 1966. "Concerning the Measurement of Delinquency." *British Journal of Criminology* 6(4):414–421.

Rosenhan, D. L. 1973. "On Being Sane in Insane Places." *Science* 179(January 19):250–258.

Ross, H. Laurence. 1973. "Law, Science and Accidents: The British Road Safety Act of 1967." *Journal of Legal Studies* 2(1):1–78.

_____. 1984. *Deterring the Drinking Driver: Legal Policy and Social Control*. Lexington, MA: Lexington (Heath).

Ross, H. Laurence, Donald T. Campbell, and Gene V. Glass. 1970. "Determining the Social Effects of a Legal Reform: The British 'Breathalyser' Crackdown of 1967." *American Behavioral Scientist* 13(4):493–509.

Rossi, Peter, and Howard E. Freeman. 1985. *Evaluation: A Systematic Approach.* Beverly Hills, CA: Sage.

Rossi, Peter H., Emily Waite, Christine E. Bose, and Richard E. Berk. 1974. "The Seriousness of Crimes: Normative Structure and Individual Differences." *American Sociological Review* 39(2):224–237.

Rothbard, Murray N. 1977. "Punishment and Proportionality." In *Assessing the Criminal: Restitution, Retribution, and the Legal Process*, edited by Randy E. Barnett and John Hagel III, 259–270. Cambridge, MA: Ballinger.

Rothman, David J. 1971. *The Discovery of the Asylum: Social Order and Disorder in the New Republic.* Boston: Little, Brown.

———. 1980. *Conscience and Convenience: The Asylum and Its Alternatives in Progressive America.* Boston: Little, Brown.

Saltzman, Linda, Raymond Paternoster, Gordon P. Waldo, and Theodore G. Chiricos. 1982. "Deterrent and Experiential Effects: The Problem of Causal Order in Perceptual Deterrence Research." *Journal of Research in Crime and Delinquency* 19(2):172–189.

Sampson, Robert J., and Jacqueline Cohen. 1988. "Deterrent Effects of the Police on Crime: A Replication and Theoretical Extension." *Law and Society Review* 22(1):163–189.

Sarri, Rosemary. 1981. "The Effectiveness Paradox: Institutional Versus Community Placement of Offenders." *Journal of Social Issues* 37(3):34–50.

Savitz, Leonard D. 1958. "A Study in Capital Punishment." *Journal of Criminal Law, Criminology and Police Science* 49(4):338–341.

Scheff, Thomas J. 1966. *Being Mentally Ill: A Sociological Theory.* Chicago: Aldine.

———. 1974. "The Labelling Theory of Mental Illness." *American Sociological Review* 39(3):444–452.

Schuessler, Karl F. 1952. "The Deterrent Influence of the Death Penalty." *The Annals of the American Academy of Political and Social Science* 284(November):54–62.

Schur, Edwin M. 1965. *Crimes Without Victims: Deviant Behavior and Public Policy.* Englewood Cliffs, NJ: Spectrum (Prentice-Hall).

———. 1971. *Labeling Deviant Behavior: Its Sociological Implications.* New York: Harper and Row.

———. 1973. *Radical Nonintervention: Rethinking the Delinquency Problem.* Englewood Cliffs, NJ: Spectrum (Prentice-Hall).

———. 1979. *Interpreting Deviance: A Sociological Introduction.* New York: Harper and Row.

Schwartz, I. M., Marilyn Jackson-Beck, and Roger Anderson. 1984. "The 'Hidden System' of Juvenile Control." *Crime and Delinquency* 30(3):371–385.

Schwartz, Richard D., and Sonya Orleans. 1967. "On Legal Sanctions." *University of Chicago Law Review* 34(2):274–300.

Scott, Joseph E., and Fahad Al-Thakeb. 1977. "The Public's Perceptions of Crime: A Comparative Analysis of Scandinavia, Western Europe, the Middle East, and the United States." In *Contemporary Corrections: Social Control and Conflict*, edited by Ronald Huff, 78–88. Beverly Hills, CA: Sage.

Scull, Andrew T. 1977. *Decarceration: Community Treatment and the Deviant—A Radical View*. Englewood Cliffs, NJ: Spectrum (Prentice-Hall).

Sechrest, Lee, Susan O. White, and Elizabeth D. Brown, eds. 1979. *The Rehabilitation of Criminal Offenders: Problems and Prospects*. Washington, DC: National Academy of Sciences.

Selke, William L. 1983. "Celerity: The Ignored Variable in Deterrence Research." *Journal of Police Science and Administration* 11(1):31–37.

Sellin, Thorsten. 1967. *Capital Punishment*. New York: Harper and Row.

———. 1976. *Slavery and the Penal System*. New York: Elsevier.

Sellin, Thorsten, and Marvin E. Wolfgang. 1964. *The Measurement of Delinquency*. New York: Wiley.

Shannon, Lyle W. 1982. *Assessing the Relationship of Adult Criminal Careers to Juvenile Careers: A Summary*. Washington, DC: U.S. Department of Justice (Office of Juvenile Justice and Delinquency Prevention).

———. 1988. *Criminal Career Continuity: Its Social Context*. New York: Human Sciences Press.

Shapiro, Perry, and Harold L. Votey, Jr. 1984. "Deterrence and Subjective Probabilities of Arrest: Modeling Individual Decisions to Drink and Drive in Sweden." *Law and Society Review* 18(4):583–604.

Shaw, Clifford R., and Henry D. McKay. 1942. *Juvenile Delinquency and Urban Areas*. Chicago: University of Chicago Press.

Shaw, Clifford R., Frederick Zorbaugh, Henry D. McKay, and Leonard S. Cottrell. 1929. *Delinquency Areas: A Study of the Geographic Distribution of School Truants, Juvenile Delinquents, and Adult Offenders in Chicago*. Chicago: University of Chicago Press.

Shaw, George Bernard. 1946. *The Crime of Imprisonment*. New York: Philosophical Library.

Sherman, Lawrence W. 1990. "Police Crackdowns: Initial and Residual Deterrence." In *Crime and Justice: A Review of Research, Volume 12*, edited by Michael Tonry and Norval Morris, 1–48. Chicago: University of Chicago Press.

Sherman, Lawrence W., and Richard A. Berk. 1984. "The Specific Deterrent Effects of Arrest for Domestic Assault." *American Sociological Review* 49(2):261–272.

Sherman, Lawrence W., Janell D. Schmidt, Dennis P. Rogan, Patrick R. Gartin, Ellen G. Cohn, Dean J. Collins, and Anthony R. Bacich. 1991. "From Initial Deterrence to Long-Term Escalation: Short-Custody Arrest for Poverty Ghetto Domestic Violence." *Criminology* 29(4):821–850.

Sherman, Lawrence W., and Douglas A. Smith. 1992. "Crime, Punishment, and Stake in Conformity: Legal and Informal Control of Domestic Violence." *American Sociological Review* 57(5):680–690.

Shinnar, Shlomo, and Reuel Shinnar. 1975. "The Effects of the Criminal Justice System on the Control of Crime: A Quantitative Approach." *Law and Society Review* 9(4):581–612.

Shover, Neal. 1983. "The Later Stages of Ordinary Property Offender Careers." *Social Problems* 31(2):208–218.

Silberman, Matthew. 1976. "Toward a Theory of Criminal Deterrence." *American Sociological Review* 41(3):442–461.

Skolnick, Jerome H., and David H. Bayley. 1986. *The New Blue Line: Police Innovation in Six American Cities.* New York: Free Press.

Smith, Douglas A., and Patrick R. Gartin. 1989. "Specifying Specific Deterrence: The Influence of Arrest on Future Criminal Activity." *American Sociological Review* 54(1):94–106.

Sommer, Robert. 1976. *The End of Imprisonment.* New York: Oxford University Press.

Steadman, Henry J., John Monahan, Barbara Duffee, Eliot Hartstone, and Pamela Clark Robbins. 1984. "The Impact of State Mental Hospital Deinstitutionalization on United States Prison Populations, 1968–1978." *Journal of Criminal Law and Criminology* 75(2):474–490.

Steinman, Michael. 1991. "Arrest and Recidivism Among Woman Batterers." *Criminal Justice Review* 16(2):183–197.

Stender, Fay. 1973. "Violence and Lawlessness at Soledad Prison." In *The Politics of Punishment: A Critical Analysis of Prisons in America*, edited by Erik Olin Wright, 222–233. New York: Harper Torchbooks.

Street, David. 1965. "The Inmate Group in Custodial and Treatment Settings." *American Sociological Review* 30(1):40–55.

Sutherland, Edwin H., and Donald R. Cressey. 1966. *Principles of Criminology.* Philadelphia: Lippincott.

Sykes, Gresham M. 1958. *The Society of Captives: A Study of a Maximum Security Prison.* Princeton, NJ: Princeton University Press.

Szasz, Thomas S. 1961. *The Myth of Mental Illness.* New York: Harper and Row.

———. 1963. *Law, Liberty and Psychiatry.* New York: Macmillan.

———. 1970a. *Ideology and Insanity.* Garden City, NY: Anchor (Doubleday).

———. 1970b. *The Manufacture of Madness: A Comparative Study of the Inquisition and the Mental Health Movement.* New York: Harper and Row.

———. 1976. *Schizophrenia: The Sacred Symbol of Psychiatry.* New York: Basic.

Talbott, John A. 1979. "Deinstitutionalization: Avoiding the Disasters of the Past." *Hospital and Community Psychiatry* 30(9):621–624.

———. 1985. "Presidential Address—Our Patients' Future in a Changing World: The Imperative of Psychiatric Involvement in Public Policy." *American Journal of Psychiatry* 142(9):1003–1008.

Thomas, Charles W., and Donna M. Bishop. 1984. "The Effect of Formal and Informal Sanctions on Delinquency: A Longitudinal Comparison of Labeling and Deterrence Theories." *Journal of Criminal Law and Criminology* 75(4):1222–1245.

Thomas, Charles W., Robin J. Cage, and Samuel C. Foster. 1976. "Public Opinion on Criminal Law and Legal Sanctions: An Examination of Two Conceptual Models." *Journal of Criminal Law and Criminology* 67(1):110–116.

Thorsell, Bernard A., and Lloyd W. Klemke. 1972. "The Labeling Process: Reinforcement and Deterrent?" *Law and Society Review* 6(3):393–403.

Tittle, Charles R. 1969a. "Crime Rates and Legal Sanctions." *Social Problems* 16(4):309–423.

_____. 1969b. "Inmate Organization: Sex Differentiation and the Influence of Criminal Subcultures." *American Sociological Review* 34(4):492–505.

_____. 1975. "Deterrents or Labeling?" *Social Forces* 53(3):399–410.

_____. 1980a. "Labelling and Crime: An Empirical Evaluation." In *The Labelling of Deviance: Evaluating a Perspective*, edited by Walter R. Gove, 241–263. Beverly Hills, CA: Sage.

_____. 1980b. *Sanctions and Social Deviance: The Question of Deterrence.* New York: Praeger.

Tittle, Charles R., and Debra Curran. 1988. "Contingencies for Dispositional Disparities in Juvenile Justice." *Social Forces* 67(1):23–58.

Tittle, Charles R., and Charles H. Logan. 1973. "Sanctions and Deviance: Evidence and Remaining Questions." *Law and Society Review* 7(3):371–392.

Tittle, Charles R., and Alan R. Rowe. 1974. "Certainty of Arrest and Crime Rates: A Further Test of the Deterrence Hypothesis." *Social Forces* 52(4):455–462.

Tittle, Charles R., and Drollen P. Tittle. 1964. "Social Organization of Prisoners: An Empirical Test." *Social Forces* 43(2):216–221.

Torrey, E. Fuller. 1988. *Nowhere to Go: The Tragic Odyssey of the Homeless Mentally Ill.* New York: Harper and Row.

Tracy, Paul E., Marvin E. Wolfgang, and Robert M. Figlio. 1990. *Delinquency Careers in Two Birth Cohorts.* New York: Plenum.

Tullock, Gordon. 1974. "Does Punishment Deter Crime?" *The Public Interest* 36(Summer):103–111.

Tunnell, Kenneth D. 1990. "Choosing Crime: Close Your Eyes and Take Your Chances." *Justice Quarterly* 7(4):673–690.

Uchida, Craig, and Robert Goldberg. 1986. *Police Employment and Expenditure Trends.* Washington, DC: Bureau of Justice Statistics.

van den Haag, Ernest. 1975. *Punishing Criminals: Concerning a Very Old and Painful Question.* New York: Basic Books.

van Dine, Stephan, Simon Dinitz, and John P. Conrad. 1977. "The Incapacitation of the Dangerous Offender: A Statistical Experiment." *Journal of Research in Crime and Delinquency* 14(1):22–35.

Vinter, Robert D., George Downs, and John Hall. 1975. *Juvenile Corrections in the States: Residential Programs and Deinstitutionalization: A Preliminary Report*. Ann Arbor: University of Michigan School of Social Work.

Visher, Christy A. 1986. "The Rand Inmate Survey: A Reanalysis." In *Criminal Careers and "Career Criminals," Volume 2*, edited by Alfred Blumstein, Jacqueline Cohen, Jeffrey A. Roth, and Christy A. Visher, 161–211. Washington, DC: National Academy Press.

———. 1987. "Incapacitation and Crime Control: Does a 'Lock 'Em Up' Strategy Reduce Crime?" *Justice Quarterly* 4(4):513–543.

Visher, Christy A., Pamela K. Lattimore, and Richard L. Linster. 1991. "Predicting the Recidivism of Serious Youthful Offenders Using Survival Models." *Criminology* 29(3):329–366.

Vold, George B. 1952. "Extent and Trend of Capital Crimes in the United States." *The Annals of the American Academy of Political and Social Science* 284(November):1–7.

von Hirsch, Andrew. 1976. *Doing Justice: The Choice of Punishments*. New York: Hill and Wang.

———. 1985. *Past or Future Crimes: Deservedness and Dangerousness in the Sentencing of Criminals*. New Brunswick, NJ: Rutgers University Press.

———. 1988. "Selective Incapacitation Reexamined: The National Academy of Sciences' Report on *Criminal Careers and 'Career Criminals.'*" *Criminal Justice Ethics* 7(1):19–35.

Waldo, Gordon P., and Theodore G. Chiricos. 1972. "Perceived Penal Sanction and Self-Reported Criminality: A Neglected Approach to Deterrence Research." *Social Problems* 19(4):522–540.

Walker, Nigel. 1965. *Crime and Punishment in Britain*. Edinburgh, Scotland: Edinburgh University Press.

Ward, David A. 1973. "Evaluative Research for Corrections." In *Prisoners in America*, edited by Lloyd E. Ohlin, 184–206. Englewood Cliffs, NJ: Spectrum (Prentice-Hall).

Warr, Mark. 1989. "What Is the Perceived Seriousness of Crimes?" *Criminology* 27(4):795–821.

Weihofen, Henry. 1971. "Punishment and Treatment: Rehabilitation." In *Theories of Punishment*, edited by Stanley E. Grupp, 255–263. Bloomington: Indiana University Press.

Wellford, Charles. 1967. "Factors Associated with Adoption of the Inmate Code: A Study of Normative Socialization." *Journal of Criminal Law, Criminology and Police Science* 58(2):197–203.

West, Donald J. 1969. *Present Conduct and Future Delinquency*. London: Heinemann.

———. 1982. *Delinquency: Its Roots, Careers, and Prospects*. London: Heinemann.

West, Donald J., and David P. Farrington. 1973. *Who Becomes Delinquent?* London: Heinemann.

————. 1977. *The Delinquent Way of Life*. London: Heinemann.

Wheeler, Gerald R., and Rodney V. Hissong. 1988. "Effects of Criminal Sanctions on Drunk Drivers: Beyond Incarceration." *Crime and Delinquency* 34(1):29–42.

Wheeler, Stanton. 1961. "Socialization in Correctional Communities." *American Sociological Review* 26(2):697–712.

Whitehead, John T., and Steven P. Lab. 1989. "A Meta-Analysis of Juvenile Correctional Treatment." *Journal of Research in Crime and Delinquency* 26(3):276–295.

Wicker, Tom. 1975. *A Time to Die*. New York: Ballantine.

Wilde, Oscar. [1898] 1973. "The Ballad of Reading Gaol." In *De Profundis and Other Writings*, 229–252. Middlesex, England: Penguin.

Wilkins, Leslie. 1964. *Social Deviance*. Englewood Cliffs, NJ: Prentice-Hall.

————. 1969. *Evaluation of Penal Measures*. New York: Random House.

Williams, Kirk R., and Richard Hawkins. 1986. "Perceptual Research on General Deterrence: A Critical Review." *Law and Society Review* 20(4):545–572.

Williams, Robin. 1970. *American Society*. New York: Knopf.

Willman, Mark T., and John R. Snortum. 1984. "Detective Work: The Criminal Investigative Process in a Medium-Size Police Department." *Criminal Justice Review* 9(1):33–39.

Wilson, James Q. 1977. "Thinking Practically About Crime." In *Assessing the Criminal: Restitution, Retribution, and the Legal Process*, edited by Randy E. Barnett and John Hagel III, xiii–xxv. Cambridge, MA: Ballinger.

————. 1985. *Thinking About Crime*. New York: Vintage.

Wilson, James Q., and Barbara Boland. 1978. "The Effect of the Police on Crime." *Law and Society Review* 12(3):367–390.

Wilson, James Q., and Richard J. Herrnstein. 1985. *Crime and Human Nature*. New York: Simon and Schuster.

Wolff, Kurt H., ed. 1950. *The Sociology of Georg Simmel*. New York: Free Press.

Wolfgang, Marvin E. 1958. *Patterns in Criminal Homicide*. Philadelphia: University of Pennsylvania Press.

Wolfgang, Marvin E., Robert M. Figlio, and Thorsten Sellin. 1972. *Delinquency in a Birth Cohort*. Chicago: University of Chicago Press.

Wolfgang, Marvin E., Robert M. Figlio, Paul E. Tracy, and Simon I. Singer. 1985. *The National Survey of Crime Severity*. Washington, DC: Department of Justice (Bureau of Justice Statistics).

Wolfgang, Marvin E., Terence P. Thornberry, and Robert M. Figlio. 1987. *From Boy to Man, from Delinquency to Crime*. Chicago: University of Chicago Press.

Wright, Erik Olin, ed. 1973. *The Politics of Punishment: A Critical Analysis of Prisons in America*. New York: Harper Torchbooks.

Wright, Richard A. 1990. "Ten Recent Criminology Textbooks: Diversity Without Currency or Quality." *Teaching Sociology* 18(4):550–561.

————. 1992. "In Support of Prisons." In *Corrections: An Issues Approach*, edited by Lawrence F. Travis III, Martin D. Schwartz, and Todd R. Clear, 99–114. Cincinnati: Anderson.

————. 1993. "A Socially Sensitive Criminal Justice System." In *Open Institutions: The Hope for Democracy*, edited by John W. Murphy and Dennis L. Peck, 141–160. Westport, CT: Praeger.

Wright, William E., and Michael C. Dixon. 1977. "Community Prevention and Treatment of Juvenile Delinquency." *Journal of Research in Crime and Delinquency* 14(1):35–67.

Wrong, Dennis H. 1961. "The Oversocialized Conception of Man in Modern Sociology." *American Sociological Review* 26(2):183–193.

Zedlewski, Edwin W. 1987. *Making Confinement Decisions*. Washington, DC: National Institute of Justice.

————. 1989. "New Mathematics of Imprisonment: A Reply to Zimring and Hawkins." *Crime and Delinquency* 35(1):169–173.

Zimring, Franklin E. 1978. "Policy Experiments in General Deterrence: 1970–1975." In *Deterrence and Incapacitation: Estimating the Effects of Criminal Sanctions on Crime Rates*, edited by Alfred Blumstein, Jacqueline Cohen, and Daniel Nagin, 140–186. Washington, DC: National Academy of Sciences.

Zimring, Franklin E., and Gordon Hawkins. 1971. "The Legal Threat as an Instrument of Social Change." *Journal of Social Issues* 27(2):33–48.

————. 1973. *Deterrence: The Legal Threat in Crime Control*. Chicago: University of Chicago Press.

————. 1986. *Capital Punishment and the American Agenda*. New York: Cambridge University Press.

————. 1988. "The New Mathematics of Imprisonment." *Crime and Delinquency* 34(4):425–436.

Cases

Addington v. Texas 441 U.S. 418 (1979).
Barefoot v. Estelle 463 U.S. 880 (1983).
Cooper v. Pate 378 U.S. 546 (1964).
Jurek v. Texas 428 U.S. 262 (1976).
Palmigiano v. Travisono 317 F.Supp. 776 (D.R.I. 1970).
Procunier v. Martinez 416 U.S. 396 (1974).
Ruffin v. Commonwealth 62 Va. 790 (1871).
Schall v. Martin 467 U.S. 253 (1984).
Thornburgh v. Abbott 109 U.S. 1874 (1989).
Turner v. Safley 482 U.S. 78 (1987).
United States v. Salerno 481 U.S. 739 (1987).
Wolff v. McDonnell 418 U.S. 539 (1974).
Wyatt v. Stickney 325 F.Supp. 781 (M.D.Ala. 1971).

Index

About the Author

RICHARD A. WRIGHT, Associate Professor of Sociology, University of Scranton, is the author of many publications dealing with the sociology of punishment, and his recent books include *Crime and Control: Syllabi and Instructional Materials for Criminology and Criminal Justice* (1989). His current research interests deal with deterrence, women and crime, and teaching criminal justice.

DATE DUE

OCT 2 5 1994			
APR 2 1 1995			
MAR 2 2 1996			
SEP 28 96			
MAY 0 8 1997			
APR 2 8 1998			
NOV 2 2 1998			
MAR 3 0 2000			
MAY 0 6 2000			
APR 2 2 2001			
			Printed in USA